The Schizophrenic Reactions:

A Critique of
The Concept, Hospital Treatment, and
Current Research

The Proceedings of The Menninger Foundation
Conference on the Schizophrenic Syndrome

ROBERT CANCRO, M.D., Editor

BRUNNER/MAZEL Publishers • New York • 1970

TO G.M.C.

Table of Contents

Preface

"A clash of doctrines is not a disaster—it is an opportunity. . . ."

A. N. WHITEHEAD

THIS VOLUME PRESENTS THE PROCEEDINGS of The Menninger Foundation Conference on the Schizophrenic Syndrome held in April, 1969. The conviction behind the organization of the Conference was that scientific understanding could be advanced by means of a dialogue representing the confrontation of different scientific viewpoints. It is only when scientists can present and debate their differences that there is an opportunity for these differences either to be resolved or better defined.

The basic technique used in the Conference was to bring together each day a small, highly selected group of participants who represented different points of view on an important aspect of the schizophrenic syndrome. The aspect under consideration on the first day was the validity of the concept; on the second day it was the role of hospital treatment; and on the final day it was the current status of selected research areas. The speakers presented their ideas and defined their positions in the morning session. Under the leadership of the session chairman, the afternoon was used by the panel members to enter into the kind of dialogue that we, at The Menninger Foundation, believed would produce a clearer identification of the issues and, hopefully, even resolve some differences.

The organization of the Conference along the lines of an adversary system was unique. It was our intention for the Conference to create a number of conversations, some of which we realized would go on in parallel without having any perceptible effect on each other, while others would interact, cross-fertilize, and produce something new. We did not expect to resolve the critical issues concerning the schizophrenic syndrome. We fully expected that the audience as well as the participants would

v

leave the Conference with less, rather than greater, certainty. Perhaps this very diminution in certainty is an essential prerequisite for examining the broad issues with a more open and receptive mind. If the Conference perturbed our certainty in our favorite answers, it might force us to rephrase the questions in more meaningful and thereby more productive terms. This perturbation of dogma was the method for achieving the scientific goal.

Behind every highly abstract goal of the sort just described there always lurks at least one other which is more affectively charged. The Conference on the Schizophrenic Syndrome was no exception. Part of our intention in organizing the Conference was to acknowledge the many contributions of and to do honor to Dr. Karl Augustus Menninger. While we recognized the immodesty of The Menninger Foundation honoring Doctor Karl, we also recognized its appropriateness. The appropriateness outweighed the immodesty. At the age of seventy-five many men, looking back to a far less illustrious career, would be satisfied to reminisce and live in their memories. Kansas breeds a different stock which we can admire and attempt to emulate. When they have exhausted one solar system, they look for new worlds to conquer.

One brief but revealing vignette is worth recording in this context. When Doctor Karl initially agreed to participate in the Conference, I failed to inform him of this more personal motivation. When he subsequently saw a preliminary draft of the program he quickly noticed that he was the lead speaker and questioned the appropriateness of this. He felt that he should not be given this honor but rather should be "buried" somewhere in the rest of the group. While it would be difficult to come up with a more illustrious group in which to be "buried," it tells us a great deal about the man. I felt quite uncertain as to what to do with this request. Those readers who know Doctor Karl are aware that requests and suggestions are not things that he makes casually and then forgets. He is rather persistent in these matters. I finally decided to opt for an administrative solution which is an equivalent statement to throwing it into the lap of Fate. For each Conference day the major speakers were listed alphabetically!

There is a problem in translating a Conference into a book. To the extent that this volume is successful, the credit belongs to the individual participants who were kind enough to rewrite their papers from the point of view of a written rather than a verbal presentation. My editorial vigor was kept in check so that the chapters reflect not only the thought but the style of the individual author. In the cases of Chapters 8, 14, and 21, the panel discussion has been condensed down to what I believe to be the most salient and interesting points. I assume the responsibility for the selection and apologize in advance to those readers who heard the unedited panel discussions and disagree with my choices.

The Menninger Foundation would like to acknowledge the financial assistance of the following organizations whose generous grants-in-aid helped to make the Conference on the Schizophrenic Syndrome possible: Hoffman-La Roche, Inc.; Topeka Veterans Administration Hospital; Merck Sharp & Dohme Post-Graduate Program; Schering Corporation; Smith Kline & French Laboratories; Sandoz Pharmaceuticals; Wyeth Laboratories; Knoll Pharmaceutical Company; and Lakeside Laboratories. Various members of the Research Department of The Menninger Foundation contributed to the recording, transcription, and preparation of this volume. Their efforts—particularly those of Mrs. Jean Hahn, Mr. Marc Hillmer, and Mrs. Mary Patton—are gratefully acknowledged. Neither the Conference nor the publication of its proceedings would have been possible without the yeoman efforts of Mrs. Jean Abernathy and Mrs. Hazel Bruce whom I again must list alphabetically. Their hard work, dedication, patience, and never failing good humor were a source of continuous support. My list of acknowledgments would be totally inadequate if I did not mention my perpetual debt to my wife, without whose constancy none of this would have been possible.

ROBERT CANCRO, M.D.

Topeka, Kansas
June, 1969

PARTICIPANTS

MARK D. ALTSCHULE, M.D. is Consultant Clinical Physiologist at McLean Hospital, an Associate Member in Medicine at Beth Israel Hospital, Consultant at Boston City Hospital, an Assistant Clinical Professor of Medicine at Harvard University and Lecturer in Medicine at Yale University.

SILVANO ARIETI, M.D. is Professor of Clinical Psychiatry at New York Medical College as well as training and supervising analyst at the William Alanson White Institute and a practicing psychoanalyst in New York.

LEOPOLD BELLAK, M.D. is Visiting Professor of Psychiatry in the Postdoctoral Program at New York University as well as being the Principal Investigator for the Schizophrenia Research Project at Roosevelt Hospital and in the private practice of psychoanalysis.

DONALD L. BURNHAM, M.D. is a Research Psychiatrist with the National Institute of Mental Health as well as being a training analyst at the Washington Psychoanalytic Institute and a Trustee for the William Alanson White Psychiatric Foundation.

ROBERT CANCRO, M.D. is on leave of absence from The Menninger Foundation where he was Director of the Research Training Program. He currently holds a joint appointment at the University of Illinois as Visiting Professor of Computer Science and Visiting Associate in the Center for Advanced Study.

ROBERT W. GIBSON, M.D. is a training and supervising analyst in the Washington Psychoanalytic Institute as well as being the Medical Director of the Sheppard and Enoch Pratt Hospital.

ROY R. GRINKER, SR., M.D. is Director of the Institute for Psychosomatic and Psychiatric Research and Training as well as Chairman of the Department of Psychiatry at Michael Reese Hospital and a training and supervising analyst at the Chicago Institute for Psychoanalysis.

ix

ERNEST M. GRUENBERG, M.D. is Professor of Psychiatry at Columbia University, Director of the Psychiatric Epidemiology Research Unit of the New York State Department of Mental Hygiene, and Visiting Lecturer in Epidemiology at Harvard University.

PHILIP S. HOLZMAN, PH.D. is Professor of Psychoanalysis and Professor of Psychology in the Departments of Psychiatry and Psychology at the University of Chicago and a training analyst at the Chicago Institute for Psychoanalysis.

SEYMOUR S. KETY, M.D. is Professor of Psychiatry at Harvard Medical School and Director of the Psychiatric Research Laboratories at The Massachusetts General Hospital.

KARL MENNINGER, M.D. is Dean of The Menninger School of Psychiatry, Chairman of the Board at The Menninger Foundation, Senior Consultant of the Stone-Brandel Center and Professor of Psychiatry at the University of Chicago, Chicago Medical School and Loyola University.

HERBERT C. MODLIN, M.D. is the Director of the Department of Preventive Psychiatry and Director of the Community Psychiatry Training Program of The Menninger Foundation.

PAUL W. PRUYSER, PH.D. is Director of the Department of Education at The Menninger Foundation as well as Lecturer in Psychology at the McCormick Theological Seminary in Chicago.

DAVID ROSENTHAL, PH.D. is the Chief of the National Institute of Mental Health Laboratory of Psychology and has done extensive genetic research in schizophrenia.

DAVID SHAKOW, PH.D. is Senior Research Psychologist at the National Institute of Mental Health.

HERBERT E. SPOHN, PH.D. is Senior Research Psychologist of The Menninger Foundation.

ALFRED H. STANTON, M.D. is Associate Professor of Psychiatry at Harvard Medical School and Psychiatrist-in-Chief at McLean Hospital.

PAUL THETFORD, PH.D. is a Senior Research Psychologist at The Menninger Foundation and Co-Principal Investigator on "Attention and Psychological Deficit in Schizophrenia."

OTTO A. WILL, JR., M.D. is Clinical Professor in the Department of Psychiatry at Cornell University, serves on the faculty of the William Alanson White Institute and is the Medical Director of the Austen Riggs Center.

Section I

THE VALIDITY OF THE CONCEPT

1

A Historical Review
of the Development of
the Concept of Schizophrenia

ROBERT CANCRO, M.D. and PAUL W. PRUYSER, Ph.D.

ACCORDING TO GREEK MYTHOLOGY, the goddess Athena sprang from Zeus' brow perfect, complete, and fully formed. What may be true for gods is manifestly untrue for men: they grow with various spurts and plateaux and with occasional regressions. And after much faltering, they wither away and die. And so it is with the products of human thinking: the concepts which man has derived from his encounters with reality are often imprecise, vague, fragmentary, and sometimes just outright poor and mistaken. And unfortunately, some of these concepts will not die, no matter how much they falter. It is only because of the marvel of words that some concepts keep circulating despite their inadequacy, or still lead a kind of mock life long after the bell has tolled for them.

Words are gorgeous indeed. Suppose the mighty roll of the Latin phrase *Dementia Praecox* had never been intoned; or assume that the Greek of *Schizophrenie*, manufactured in Switzerland, and later duly Latinized for English-speaking consumers into *schizophrenia*, had never been heard. Would such a linguistic loss have thwarted our ability to see madness when it occurs, or curbed our attempts at understanding it? We think not.

Because words are so important, it is good for psychiatrists to listen from time to time to literary masters who use words sensitively for the portrayal of much that goes on in the human mind or heart. Three months before his death at the age of 72, one such master wrote the following: "Who in the rainbow can draw the line where the violet tint ends and the

3

orange tint begins? Distinctly we see the difference of the color, but where exactly does the first one visibly enter into the other? So with sanity and insanity. In pronounced cases there is no question about them. But in some cases, in various degrees supposedly less pronounced, to draw the line of demarcation few will undertake, though for a fee some professional experts will. There is nothing nameable but that some men will undertake to do for pay. In other words, there are instances where it is next to impossible to determine whether a man is sane or beginning to be otherwise."

This quote from Herman Melville's *Billy Budd* (23), written in 1891, which so aptly and succinctly describes one major problem in psychiatry, also leads us back to the point we need to clarify. There is hardly a better way of showing the fallacies and limitations of psychiatric naming than by asking you to consider what is happening at this very time to another word, born only yesterday, and already caught up in serious misunderstandings of its own making. It is the word *Borderline*, whatever merit the underlying concept may have. According to any dictionary, a borderline is a boundary line or line of demarcation; that is, something that is drawn between something and something else, both of which need to be spelled out if sense is to be found in using the word. Mind you, it is a line, i.e., a series of points, and therefore by definition without substance. Few people bother any more to spell out between what things exactly *Borderline* is a borderline. No, *Borderline* is now generally approached as an entity with a certain thickness and substance, and all sorts of subsidiary reasoning is marshalled in substantiating its presumed substance. Thus we hear of the Borderline Case, Borderline Syndrome, and even of Borderline Personality or Borderline Character. What for heaven's sake could a Borderline Personality be? Another literary giant, Wordsworth (31), reminds us that:

> "Science appears but what in truth she is
> Not as our glory and our absolute boast
> But as a succedaneum, and a prop
> To our infirmity. . . .
> 　　　　　　That false secondary power
> By which we multiply distinctions, then
> Deem that our puny boundaries are things
> That we perceive, and not that we have made."

While it may be countered that the imaginations and words of novelists and poets are printed and sold like things, there is nevertheless not much danger that they will ever become reified, as scientific concepts often are. The poet's words are only a stimulus for the aesthetic moment; the scientist's words tend to carry a heavy baggage of materiality. And if not materiality, then grave consequentialness, for despite their avowed nominalism, many scientists are realists at heart. The medium becomes the message. On a visit to mental hospitals in Germany one of us has observed that the message conveyed to certain patients by the staff was: "Oh, poor soul, you are so terribly ill; stay here and have your illness!" The pity is that such diagnostic and prognostic attitudes can be conveyed with all the trappings of humane concern and even with considerable aesthetic thrill over such a fascinating illness.

Much in psychiatry is a struggle with language, or, as psychoanalysts would have it, a struggle in combining the right idea with the proper word and the appropriate affect. Long before the concept of dementia praecox began to be formed, Pinel (28) complained about the paucity of words to describe the prevailing psychiatric disorders he saw. He admired the new ideas of the "modern psychologists," i.e., Locke and Condillac, and hoped that psychiatrists could make use of their dissertations on perception, imagination, judgment, emotion and action, or what we should now call the part processes of mental functioning. He himself, however, described certain disorders as *démence,* many of which would now be considered as schizophrenic syndromes, while continuing to use, in the title of his book of 1801, the generic term *la manie,* for all or most forms of mental aberration. No such concern with language is apparent in the various nosological synopses assembled by Cullen (6) in 1780, which abound in Latinisms and hierarchical ordering systems with classes, orders, and genera. Pinel's search for appropriate words was thus new enough, and one may well hold the humanitarian thrust of the French revolution with its belief in *liberté, égalité* and *fraternité* responsible for it.

A similar concern for language comes through in the work of Haslam (11) of Bethlehem Hospital. The whole first chapter of his book on Madness and Melancholy is a linguistic exercise. Haslam's work is also of relevance to this section of the volume because of his observation that between "the furious and melancholic paroxysms . . . there is an intermediate state which cannot be termed maniacal nor melancholic: a state of complete insanity, yet unaccompanied by furious or depressing Passions." And to show Haslam's interest in words again, the word "Passion" in the last sentence leads to a footnote in which he exclaims: "Why should the most active characteristics of our nature be termed Passions?" Like

Pinel, he described cases which would now undoubtedly be seen as schizophrenic. Doctor Altschule (1) is certainly for historical justice in having proposed that the word schizophrenia be replaced by the eponym Pinel-Haslam Syndrome. Guislain (10), in 1826, also used the term *démence* rather lavishly in his descriptions of psychiatric syndromes. It is of interest that he recognized both physical and psychological causes of *démence,* and included in the latter group eight cases in which politics was the cause of the outbreak, i.e., when revolutionary events caused a person to lose self-esteem and forced him to alter his habits of living!

In 1835 the concern with language goes on unabated. In Prichard's *Treatise on Insanity* (29) we find the following passage: "There are many reasons which render it advisable to adopt English rather than Latin technical expressions, as far as the former are available. For example, if a physician informs a jury summoned in an inquiry 'de lunatico,' that the person who is the subject of examination is in a state of dementia, he will probably convey no information, and must be prepared with a definition of the term, which involves a discussion. By using the term incoherence he will convey a correct idea, if not a complete one, of his meaning."

When we heard recently the news reports of psychiatric testimony in the Sirhan trial, the reporters' attempts to translate schizophrenic as "split personality" brought the acumen of Prichard's warning to mind.

The French term *démence précoce* was first used by the Belgian psychiatrist Morel (27) not as a distinct entity, but as an unassuming description of a process of *démence* in a patient whose symptoms started at the age of 14. Like others in his time, Morel assumed genetic determination, and saw his case as a variant of moral, i.e., psychological, degeneracy.

In Falret's textbook of 1864 (7) we find an example of the increasing preoccupation during the second half of the nineteenth century with the ideas of the "march of symptoms" and the "course of illness," which were to play such a large role in the diagnostic formulations of Kraepelin. The era was also dominated by Griesinger's textbook (9), which went through several editions in 1845, 1861, and 1871, and which fostered the doctrinaire belief that all mental disease is brain disease.

Unlike some of the wiser English and French writers, German authors continued to display their learning by a heavy use of Latin and Greek terms, many of them of their own invention, and with the ever-present implication that classical languages say something about the really real which ordinary language is unable to capture. An excellent example of this propensity is von Krafft-Ebing's textbook (22). In the same linguistic vein, Hecker (12) described *hebephrenia* in 1871, and Kahlbaum (16,17) called attention to *catatonia* in 1874. Note that both terms are nouns, not adjectives; not modest descriptions of symptoms of mood and action, but postulations about specific diseases; not disorders and even less dysfunctions, but entities!

The rest of the story has often been told. Kraepelin's fascination with the course of illness is already apparent in his short *Compendium* (18) published in 1883; in the fifth edition (1896) of his famous *Psychiatrie* (19) he groups dementia praecox, catatonia, and dementia paranoides under *Verbloedungsprocesse* (processes of dementing) and finally, in the sixth edition of 1899 (20) we see dementia praecox arise as one of the two great groups of endogenous psychoses which have permeated all psychiatric classifications ever since. It is to Kraepelin's credit that he was able to modify his thought during his very productive life, and in his later writings he recognized that even typical cases of his dementia praecox did not always eventuate in deterioration, nor did they always begin in youth.

Bleuler's monograph (4) on the group of schizophrenias appeared in 1911. He himself saw his influential book as an "attempt to apply the ideas of Freud to dementia praecox." He objected to the term dementia praecox, taking as his points of departure the clinically observable facts that typical patients did not always go on to deterioration and did not always have the onset of their disease in early youth. It is often emphasized that Bleuler considered these diseases at least partially incurable because they do "not permit a full *restitutio ad integrum*." However, another portion of the same Germanically long sentence says that they "can stop or retrograde at any stage." Later in this same volume he stated that the illness "may take a course which is both qualitatively and temporally rather irregular. Constant advances, halts, recrudescences, or remissions are possible at any time." Bleuler suggested the term *Schizophrenie*, or rather the plural *Schizophrenien*, because he saw the essential feature of these disorders to be a splitting or loss of harmony between various groups of mental functions. Bleuler occupied, in a sense, a midposition between the Meyerian and Kraepelinian schools in that he included personality and psychogenic factors as determinants of symptom content and form, but still believed the primary cause of these disorders to be an organic one, probably toxic-metabolic factors. He also made a division of schizophrenic symptomatology into *fundamental or essential symptoms* and *accessory symptoms*. The value of this division will be discussed later in this chapter. Bleuler's most significant contribution was to reject dementia praecox as a single disease and to see it as a group which "includes several diseases." He insisted that dementia praecox was a group of disorders "in the same sense as the organic psychoses," but distinct in sharing the feature of splitting.

In the eighth edition of his textbook of psychiatry (1909-1915) Kraepelin (21) made a division between the endogenous and exogenous etiology of mental disease, while crediting this distinction to Möbius. Karl Jaspers (15) commented in 1913 on this distinction, but did not feel it applied particularly well to schizophrenia. In the fourth edition of his *Textbook* Bleuler (5) also commented on the distinction between *reactive* and *process* schizophrenia but was not particularly enthusiastic and said, "no division can be based on these classes because the two symptomatologies intermingle." Bleuler tended to see the terms *process* and *reactive* as synonymous with organic and psychogenic etiology respectively. In 1932 Frank (8) returned to this distinction when he spoke of the *nuclear* group of schizophrenics. He was following the same model of classification which has proved to be helpful in epilepsy, hypertension, and alcoholism. It is the same approach as was taken by Bleuler in classifying the symptoms of the disorder. In other words, it is assumed that the population includes a group of true or essential cases which can be distinguished from cases which share a similar symptomatology but differ in origin. This approach has been extensively utilized by Langfeldt who prefers the terms *true schizophrenia* and *schizophreniform psychoses*. While the reactive cases present similar symptoms to the process cases, they tend to have a different premorbid history, different course, and a different outcome. All of these more recent approaches stress outcome although they do not rely on it exclusively. Part of the misunderstanding surrounding the process-reactive distinction has been the tendency on the part of those who misunderstand to de-emphasize the concept of statistical tendency. The *nuclear* or *process*, or *endogenous*, or *true* subgroup demonstrates statistically a different premorbid adjustment, a different clinical course, and a poorer prognosis than the *reactive*, or *exogenous*, or *schizophreniform* subgroup.

It was this sort of consideration that led Sullivan (30) and others who followed him, to make a distinction between dementia praecox and schizophrenia. The very attempt to parcel out a particular subgroup as the essential or true variety of the disorder means that the larger group is seen only as a syndrome, and not as a disease entity. On the other hand, this approach also implies the idea that the essential subgroup represents a true disease entity, whereas in fact it may only represent a somewhat more homogeneous syndrome. A fundamental misconception which frequently appears in the literature is that process cases do not recover. This is not what is meant by the process-reactive distinction. Recovery alone is neither a sufficient nor a necessary criterion for classifying as complex a group of disorders as the so-called schizophrenias.

This chapter can not restrict itself solely to the validity of a particular classification but must extend to the more general question as well. It may be useful to draw a distinction between diagnosis *per se* and classification. A diagnosis is an attempt to unite general knowledge concerning illness with particular knowledge concerning a patient as a means to help that patient. Contemporary diagnosis tries to remove the host-parasite, object-subject distinction which is the heritage of the infectious disease model. Instead, it focuses on a new biopsychosocial model which could be put briefly as the patient-environment interaction, with the special understanding of an outer as well as an inner environment, and with special interactions maintained in the doctor-patient relation (25).

It is of some importance here to mention the special merit of Adolf Meyer (26) in regard to both diagnosis and classification. In his idea of the life chart, Meyer laid the groundwork for a precise recording of forms of patient-environment interaction, and thus worked implicitly with the concepts of stress and tension. In the uncommon "common sense" of this psychiatrist all mental illness was, among other things, a form of adaptation. Though Meyer too had his unfortunate bouts with language and took recourse to some very odd Greek nouns of his own making, the salubrious effect of his thought came through in the various diagnostic and statistical manuals of mental disorders, experimentally used by the Veterans Administration since 1951, then formalized by the American Psychiatric Association in 1952 (2), which—until recently—demanded that major psychiatric syndromes be described in the first place as *Disorders,* and then, to boot, as *Reactions.* Thus, for some years, the official language was *Schizophrenic Reaction,* such and such type. In the light of our argument one needs no special sensitivity to realize what a serious loss for American psychiatry was occasioned by last year's adoption of the new *Statistical Manual* (3) which copies the international guidelines with heavy Kraepelinian influence and sacrifices the hard-won gains of Meyer's heritage.

In the field of psychiatry a diagnosis is, or should be, a statement of what is troubling the patient at a given time, in a given context, in a particular manner. Classifying is quite different from diagnosing. It is an essential method of science. Classification intends to bring order out of disorder by arranging a mass of data in a logical manner. In this way it may act as an adjunct or assist to our conceptual abilities. The history of classificatory methods in psychiatry reflects the persistence of a need to organize the data (24). The purposes of classifying vary with the age. Unfortunately, in an era of therapeutic nihilism taxonomy and diagnosis are held to be the same. But in a therapeutic age we must sharply distinguish between the two. The means and purposes of organization vary; only the need for organization remains constant. In a way, any classification, including one of mental illness, is artificial, as Wordsworth noted with such poetic perspicacity. Classification is an imposition on the data of a view of the data. In other words, we are organizing data in a manner that matches the bandwidth of *our* perceptual and cognitive apparatus. A Martian who perceives with different sense organs foreign to ours, and who organizes the input according to cognitive modes alien to ours, would conceive of a totally different classificatory schema. There is no reason why our classifications must be Platonic in nature, except for a persistent ontological trend even among scientists. They need not be The Truth. All we should ask from classifications is that they be useful. Classifications, as all other scientific instruments, must be evaluated in terms of what they do in the here and now, or enable us to discover in the future. If they are helpful, in the sense of being productive of testable hypotheses and generating new insights into the mass of data, then they are of value. If they become a sterile collection of pigeonholes in which observations can be filed without new knowledge being derived, they are worthless. John Hughlings Jackson (13, 14) suggested two classifications, one for scientific and one for practical purposes. But that is only a temporary expedient. If clinical work is to be not only an art, but also a science, the question is how one will be able to combine both the uniqueness of each patient and the multiplicities of illness in one classification. In general, the tendency is for the therapeutically zealous clinician to focus on the patient and go easy on the illness; whereas the student of psychopathology and the statistician will go strong on the illness with the risk of losing sight of the patient.

In either case, the "multiplying of distinctions" of which Wordsworth spoke is an ever-present danger. For it may be said that each of the two realities which classification must combine is both singular and multiple. For people are both unique and share a common humanity, as Hippocrates knew; and disorders are both one and many, as Plato knew. And thus we wish to remind you once more, but now on a double front, of the poet's acumen in spotting that "false secondary power by which we multiply distinctions, then deem that our puny boundaries are things that we perceive, and not that we have made."

REFERENCES

1. Altschule, M.D.: Whichophrenia, or the Confused Past, Ambiguous Present, and Dubious Future of the Schizophrenia Concept. *Journal of Schizophrenia*, 1:8-17, 1967.
2. American Psychiatric Association: *Diagnostic and Statistical Manual: Mental Disorders*. Washington, D.C.: American Psychiatric Association, 1952.
3. American Psychiatric Association: *Diagnostic and Statistical Manual of Mental Disorders*. 2d ed. Washington, D.C.: American Psychiatric Association, 1968.
4. Bleuler, E.: Dementia Praecox oder die Gruppe der Schizophrenien. In Aschaffenburg, G. (Ed.), *Handbuch der Psychiatrie*. Leipzig: Deuticke, 1911.
5. Bleuler, E.: *Lehrbuch der Psychiatrie*. 4th ed. Berlin: Jul. Springer, 1923.
6. Cullen, G. (Ed.): *Synopsis Nosologiae Methodicae*. 3d ed. Edinburgh: Creech, 1780.
7. Falret, J. P.: *Des Maladies Mentales et des Asiles d'Aliénés*. Paris: Baillière, 1864.
8. Frank, J.: Psychoanalyse und Psychiatrie. *Sammlung psychoanalytischer Aufsätze*, 99-102, 1932.
9. Griesinger, W.: *Die Pathologie und Therapie der Psychischen Krankheiten*. Braunschweig: Wreden, 1871.
10. Guislain, J.: *Traité sur l'Aliénation Mentale et sur les Hospices des Aliénés*. Amsterdam: van der Hey, 1826.
11. Haslam, J.: *Observations on Madness and Melancholy*. 2d ed. London: Hayden, 1809.
12. Hecker, E.: Die Hebephrenie. *Archiv für pathologische Anatomie und Physiologie und klinische Medizin*, 52:394-429, 1871.
13. Jackson, J. H.: On the Scientific and Empirical Investigation of Epilepsies. In Taylor, J. (Ed.) *Selected Writings of John Hughlings Jackson*, Vol. I. New York: Basic Books, 1958.
14. Jackson, J. H.: On Syphilitic Afflictions of the Nervous System. In Taylor, J. (Ed.) *Selected Writings of John Hughlings Jackson*, Vol. II. New York: Basic Books, 1958.
15. Jaspers, K.: *Allgemeine Psychopathologie*. Berlin: Springer, 1913.
16. Kahlbaum, K. L.: *Die Katatonie oder das Spannungsirresein*. Berlin: Hirschwald, 1874.
17. Kahlbaum, K. L.: *Die Gruppierung der psychischen Krankheiten*. Danzig: Kafemann, 1863.
18. Kraepelin, E.: *Compendium der Psychiatrie*. Leipzig: Abel, 1883.
19. Kraepelin, E.: *Psychiatrie. Ein Lehrbuch für Studierende und Arzte*. 5th ed. Leipzig: Barth, 1896.

20. Kraepelin, E.: *Psychiatrie. Ein Lehrbuch für Studierende und Arzte.* 6th ed. Leipzig: Barth, 1899.

21. Kraepelin, E.: *Psychiatrie. Ein Lehrbuch für Studierende und Arzte.* 8th ed. Leipzig: Barth, 1909-1915.

22. Krafft-Ebing, R. von: *Lehrbuch der Psychiatrie.* 3d ed. Stuttgart: Enke, 1888.

23. Melville, H.: *Billy Budd, Sailor.* (1891) Chicago: University of Chicago Press, 1962.

24. Menninger, K., Mayman, M., and Pruyser, P. W.: *The Vital Balance.* New York: Viking Press, 1963.

25. Menninger, K., Mayman, M., and Pruyser, P. W.: *A Manual for Psychiatric Case Study.* 2d ed. New York: Grune and Stratton, 1962.

26. Meyer, A.: The Life Chart and the Obligation of Specifying Positive Data in Psychopathological Diagnosis. In Winters, E. E. (Ed.), *The Collected Papers of Adolf Meyer.* Vol. III, Medical Teaching. Baltimore: Johns Hopkins Press, 1951.

27. Morel, B. A.: *Etudes Cliniques: Traité Théorique et Pratique des Maladies Mentales.* Paris: Masson, 1852-1853.

28. Pinel, P.: *Traité Médico-Philosophique sur l'Aliénation Mentale, ou la Manie.* Paris: Richard, Caille et Ravier, 1801.

29. Prichard, J. C.: *A Treatise on Insanity and Other Disorders Affecting the Mind.* London: Sherwood, Gilbert & Pipes, 1835.

30. Sullivan, H. S.: Conceptions of Modern Psychiatry. *Psychiatry,* 3:1-117, 1940.

31. Wordsworth, W.: *The Prelude.* Book II. Boston: D. C. Heath and Co., 1899.

2

Disease Entity, Syndrome, State of Mind, or Figment?

MARK D. ALTSCHULE, M.D.

"HOW IS IT THAT, one fine morning, Duchenne discovered a disease that probably existed in the time of Hippocrates?" asked Charcot (5). Charcot answered the question himself, saying: "Disease is ancient and nothing about it has changed. It is we who change, as we learn what was formerly imperceptible." Charcot should have added that what we learn about diseases more often makes us modify or even discard a diagnostic entity than it leads us to discover new ones. We must consider whether the schizophrenia concept, now somewhat over half a century old, is worth preserving.

Complete agreement between people is so uncommon that Matthew (18:19) was led to declare: "Again I say unto you, That if two of you shall agree on earth as touching any thing that they shall ask, it shall be done for them of my Father which is in heaven." It appears that Matthew considered agreement next to godliness. However the fact that the contributors to this volume express more disagreement than agreement should not by itself be taken as an indication of their ungodliness. The disagreements are owing largely to vagueness of definition and scarcity of data. These two phenomena are often related and in fact potentiate each other. Diminishing one may ultimately lead to diminution of the other. Thus an increase in data must lead to improved definitions. Improved definitions on the other hand may direct inquiry to promising directions and help to evaluate new data.

Certain diagnostic definitions should be abandoned automatically. This is true because treatment depends on diagnosis in large measure. It is evident that a diagnosis that negates any active treatment in favor of custodial care, or that encourages wrong treatment (that is, treatment based on a misconception) is best abandoned.

Psychiatrists differ today about what the word schizophrenia means. Many nonpsychiatrists doubt that the word has any universally acceptable meaning. This skepticism concerning the schizophrenia concept should not be destructive. Skepticism should be stimulating and constructive. As Josiah Royce (10) stated in his *Spirit of Modern Philosophy,* "Doubt is never the proper end of thinking, but it is a good beginning." He was merely rephrasing the remarks of many previous philosophers, notably Abelard (1), who remarked (around 1100 A.D.), "By doubting we come to enquiry, by enquiring we perceive the truth." It is to be hoped that the enquiries made by the various contributors to this volume will produce this effect. In general we must judge the value of a diagnostic term on the basis of the help it gives in understanding and treating illnesses. Before we can do this for schizophrenia we should consider certain basic propositions.

From time to time observation at the bedside calls attention to the inadequacy of current views about some clinical disorders. This is owing to the accumulation of new data. It is important to remember that although medicine contains a huge and rapidly growing multitude of bits of data, it contains few if any facts. The clinical and laboratory data on which medicine is based are accumulated and then interpreted to yield conclusions; however the conclusions are continually changing. This situation exists because the data themselves cannot be separated from or interpreted independently of the methods used to obtain them. The context largely determines the conclusions. When the context changes, the conclusion usually does likewise, although there may not have been any changes in the data under consideration themselves. Most physicians have grown accustomed to the instability of their current clinical knowledge and, at least when this knowledge does not permit satisfactory treatment, are willing to change it. However few physicians are willing to change their ideas about the basic nature of disease, or are even aware of the need to do so. Accordingly this matter will be discussed first.

Clinical medicine became firmly based on clinical observation in the eighteenth century. At that time definitions and their related classifications were based entirely on signs and symptoms. Physicians of that period were firmly convinced of the possibility of gaining a complete understanding of any condition from an analysis of the symptoms and a few superficially detectable physical signs. It should be noted that some of those who today believe that schizophrenia is a disease entity subscribe to the notion that it is proper to diagnose a disease from the symptoms alone.

The application of biological sciences to the study of diseases in the nineteenth century soon showed the futility of classifying diseases, adducing etiologies, and devising therapeutic approaches from symptoms alone. In the nineteenth century the successive rises of pathology and bacteriology led to the conception that a disease was an entity with a known etiology, or, if the etiology was still unknown, it would soon be revealed by research. In any case, the known etiologic factor was believed to cause a few readily recognizable anatomical changes, recognizable at least by a well trained pathologist. Knowledge of these changes led to conclusions about functional derangements and thence to the interpretation of the signs and symptoms that could be used diagnostically. The subsequent development of pathologic physiology in the late nineteenth and early twentieth centuries, if anything, established more firmly this concept of disease. To this way of thinking, a syndrome differed from a disease entity because it was a group of signs and symptoms that were caused by different etiologic factors, and perhaps had varying anatomical lesions. Another group of disorders was believed to be owing to the action of the brain via the autonomic nervous system; these disorders were called "functional" or sometimes "merely functional" and suitable to women, children and unstable men. However these seemingly clear distinctions often proved far from clear. For example, the classification of angina pectoris (and the associated but then as yet unrecognized myocardial infarction) required the invention of ingenious but far from demonstrable functional mechanisms. Similarly, diabetes mellitus created difficulties, because postmortem study revealed no gross anatomic lesions. The case of myxedema was even more interesting. This condition was considered a form of mental disease, and many of those who had it in severe degree were kept in mental institutions. Not until the late nineteenth century was the condition recognized as owing to a lack of thyroid.

Actually the recognition of the nature of metabolic disorders seemed to strengthen the triple classification here discussed, because it explained some of the ambiguities involved in classifying these disorders as diseases despite the absence of grossly visible lesions.

This apparently stable situation had two defects. One was that there was still some uncertainty about which of the three main categories should include such disorders as ulcerative colitis, rheumatoid arthritis, peptic ulcer, and bronchial asthma. The spread of allegorical thinking in medicine, owing largely to acceptance of psychoanalytic concepts, led a few physicians to conclude that one or more of these clearly organic illnesses either were symbolic representations of a state of mind or else were organic changes produced by the functional factors activated by some state of mind. For example one ingenious author declared peptic ulcer to be a wound inflicted by the bite of the introjected mother.

The second defect of the apparently stable system of categories was much more serious—so serious that it has in fact destroyed the system. This has happened in the last ten or fifteen years owing to the development of methods of measuring simply and accurately a large number of biochemical functions. One result has been to show that what we believed to be a simple disease is not; for example, uncomplicated diabetes mellitus now proves to be a group of more than thirty diseases. Hence the concept of a disease as an entity caused by a single etiologic factor cannot be maintained, at least with respect to metabolic diseases. The same thing has happened with respect to some nonmetabolic diseases, e.g., lymphoma; this is now recognized to be a heterogeneous group of disorders of different known or unknown etiology and responding to different forms of treatment. In short, many conditions that were formerly considered to be disease entities now have to be considered syndromes. How far this process will go is not clear, but it is possible that the only disease entities recognized at some future time will be those caused by simple trauma or by some infections.

A second effect of the current revolution in clinical biochemical testing has been the demonstration that states of mind may be accompanied by physiologic or biochemical changes indistinguishable from those of some so-called organic diseases. For example the high plasma corticoid levels seen in depressed patients resemble those seen in primary hyperadrenocorticism. Accordingly physiologic distinctions between diseases or syndromes on the one hand and functional states, i.e., states of mind, on the other hand, have lost their sharpness.

A third effect of the current revolution in clinical biochemical testing is the finding that far more people have biochemical abnormalities than have clinical disorders. When studies are made on the close relatives of patients with metabolic disorders many of them are found to have the same biochemical disorders but to have no clinically recognizable illness. This has been known with respect to gout for over a half a century and is now coming to be appreciated for other disorders, e.g., phenylketonuria.

A fourth effect of the revolution here discussed has been to establish the fact that single biochemical disorders are rare, if they occur at all, and that such disorders occur in somewhat variable clusters, not all the components of which have any evident logical connection with the others.

The net result of all these changes in clinical biochemistry is to reinforce what many clinicians have known for many years, i.e., that there is never a one-to-one relation between biochemical and clinical disorders. Attempts to use biochemical measurements to distinguish with certainty diseases from syndromes and from states of mind have no basis, with the possible exceptions, as noted previously, of the effects of simple trauma and certain infections. Any decision about whether what is presently called schizophrenia is a disease, a syndrome or a state of mind cannot be made on the basis of any criteria currently acceptable to medicine. Moreover any attempt to find a biochemical test specific for what is called schizophrenia is not likely to succeed. (This is not to say that there are no biochemical changes in this disorder. There are several but they are not specific.)

The problem created by these conclusions is obvious. What is the nature of illness?

Claude Bernard (4) wrote a century ago: "There always comes under consideration the organism in which the phenomenon takes place and the outward circumstance or the environment which determines or invites the organism to exhibit its properties. The conjunction of these conditions is essential to the appearance of the phenomenon. If we suppress the environment the phenomenon disappears, just as if the body had been taken away."

The idea that man is a biologic organism in equilibrium with his environment is one of the most persistent—and useful—ideas in medicine. However, despite the fact that physicians of every era have studied the role of environmental influences in health and disease, the concept of health and disease as different equilibriums naturally could not play a definite role in medical thinking until the existence of these equilibriums was demonstrated.

The idea that man (like all other living organisms) takes from and gives up to his environment is obviously both ancient and prevalent. The quantitative nature of these relations began to be evident when Sanctorius (11) published his observations on insensible perspiration and other matters in the early seventeenth century. In the late eighteenth century the observations of Lavoisier, de Laplace, and Crawford on heat exchange stimulated a brilliant group of nineteenth-century biochemists —Leibig, von Voit, von Pettenkoffer, and Rubner—to study bodily chemical processes in terms of energy balances. Their epoch constituted one of the most glorious in the history of science. Twentieth-century extension and elaboration of their work have enormously increased knowledge of the physiology of health and disease. Claude Bernard's development of the idea that the internal environment is relatively constant in health extended the concept of life as an equilibrium by giving it a purpose, i.e., the maintenance of a normal internal state. This concept was elaborated by Cannon, who coined the term *homeostasis* to denote the overall mechanism.

In the meantime several clinicians, among them Jacob Bigelow (Professor of Materia Medica at Harvard) and Oliver Wendell Holmes (Professor of Anatomy at Dartmouth), had begun to emphasize the importance in medicine of the idea of equilibriums between man and his environment. They wrote (6) in 1839: "The observation of phenomena occurring in the living body, whether in health or disease, is attended with peculiar difficulties. These phenomena are the results of the mutual action of external influences and of living organs upon each other. The influences are extremely numerous, they are constantly changing, and many of them imperfectly appreciable. The living system on which they act itself presents an assemblage of powers and susceptibilities, the extent and balance of which vary at every moment of life. A perfect history of any given case would require a complete exposition of all these external influences and all these internal changes. . . ." (Bigelow and Holmes then provided a form for history-taking that compares favorably with that used today.)

Virchow (2) epitomized this view of the importance of equilibriums when he strongly reiterated Boerhaave's idea that disease is nothing but life under altered circumstances. The idea that life is a state of equilibrium (not absolute physicochemical fixity) leads to a corollary: that diseases are equilibriums set at different levels with respect to a variety of physiologic factors. Death occurs when equilibriums within certain limits cannot be obtained. (A state of disequilibrium may, of course, exist with respect to nutritional or electrolyte balance until stores of accumulated reserves are exhausted; in the case of substances or phenomena of which there are no reserves, disequilibrium cannot long exist.) The internal adjustments that lead to new equilibriums in various abnormal states permit life but do not permit normal function. The new equilibriums, though initially helpful, may sometimes become harmful and create new disequilibriums. This concept applies not only to the patient but also to the factors that caused this illness. They too change. This is most clearly seen with respect to infecting organisms; these also have their equilibriums and they are influenced by the changing status of the host. In chronic infections the host and the infecting organisms may both be in a state of complete equilibrium; where this does not occur, either the host or the organisms must die. Similarly social and other environmental factors may also be changed by the illness and made to participate in a new equilibrium.

Appreciation of the general principle here discussed leads to increased understanding of disease. Wide application of this principle to social and emotional aspects of medicine would be extremely fruitful. In fact understanding the effects on the social and emotional environment of the interposition of different diseases depends on some such concept. Similarly, the mechanisms by which reaction patterns—normal or neurotic—develop in the patient and in his environment can be understood only in terms of the concept. However the successful use of the concept in this respect presupposes a less hypothetic and superficial knowledge of psychology and sociology than is currently found in most medical writings.

In short, it is impossible for me to consider any illness except as a reaction pattern brought about by bodily and environmental changes —the two are inseparable—and producing a new state of equilibrium consistent with life under the altered circumstances. The new state, although life-saving, does not necessarily produce comfort, and in fact it may produce serious discomforts, but it permits the individual to function well enough to continue living. The new equilibrium requires physico-chemical, physiologic, psychologic and sociologic adjustments, sometimes more of one than of another, but always involving all aspects of the organism's function. This scheme does not admit the existence of an illness that is purely physicochemical, or physiologic, or psychologic, or sociologic. However it does allow the disequilibrium that initiates an illness—a search for a new equilibrium—to *originate* in any one of the four spheres mentioned. Moreover it does not rule out the possibility that a given illness may be initiated by one type of disequilibrium in one person and by another type in another. This is not to say that all these aspects of all disease can be treated with equal effectiveness or in fact that they all need to be treated with equal intensity. However they should all be recognized.

It is evident that according to the concepts discussed here schizophrenia, if it exists at all, must be a reaction pattern. Although it may be precipitated by a state of mind in some or many patients, it cannot be solely a state of mind in any of them. It must be—if it exists—a disorder in which physicochemical, physiologic, psychologic and sociologic components participate. If this is true—and it must be if schizophrenia exists—

then those who attempt to prove that what they call schizophrenia is one but not any of the other of the types of disequilibrium listed here must be wrong. The ideas of proponents of the unitary nature of schizophrenia call to mind the story of the four blind men and the elephant. This raises the question, which cannot and probably need not be answered here, how many blind men will be needed to define schizophrenia?

I am convinced that there are at least as many reaction patterns in medicine as there are patients. Experienced physicians constantly see in their patients evidence of the great diversity of human nature and recognize its importance. This diversity manifests itself in the severity and even in the occurrence of symptoms, and in the nature and speed of reactions, both favorable and unfavorable, to treatment. Experienced physicians are fully aware of these phenomena and take them into account in their practice; only the inexperienced are surprised (and often chagrined) by man's variability under basal conditions and to a greater extent under stress.

For example, there are 10,000,000,000,000,000,000 possible combinations of blood groups alone. (This number is made smaller by the fact that some blood factors occur in groups; on the other hand, the number is probably larger, since there still must be unrecognized blood groups.) This great possible diversity of individuals is multiplied almost to infinity by combinations with other genetic factors. Indeed, the finding of two completely identical persons must be extremely rare: although uniovular twins are presumably identical for a time after conception, their growth histories probably differ in utero and certainly differ after birth. In addition, their respective exposures to infection and trauma and hence the effects of these factors must also be different during life.

Great as is this human physical diversity, it is probably exceeded by mankind's mental diversity. This is owing to the fact that the nervous systems and life experiences of different people are all different. In addition, as Ernst Mach (8) said in his *Contributions to the Analysis of the Sensations*, "There can hardly be greater differences in the egos of different people, than occur in the course of years in one person." The psychological variation (and variability) of men has brought about many attempts to classify men. It is not possible to criticize classifications now currently in use with finality (although all seem manifestly absurd). It is enough to note that no classification of past eras, however firmly and permanently it seemed to be established, is now regarded with anything but amusement.

On the other hand, physicians are required to use definitions and classifications no matter how ephemeral these prove to be. Nosology can have no absolutes; it must be developed so as to provide useful concepts and terms. Accordingly no matter what modifications may be required in order to understand and treat an individual patient some broad concepts must be developed so that physicians may communicate with each other intelligibly. The schizophrenia concept should be considered in this connection. One might conclude, with Plato, that if anything has a name that fact is valid proof of its existence. Or, as a famous eighteenth century English jurist stated, there must have been a great number of witches in England at one time because there were so many laws against them. On either such basis—the existence of the name or the fact that much has been written about it—schizophrenia exists. These two criteria are, however, inadequate to make a concept acceptable to physicians. Such acceptance depends on demonstrable clinical utility. In fact there is currently a need for a concept like the schizophrenia concept, and if it did not exist it would have had to be discovered—or at least invented. The concept of an illness that manifests itself by diminished verbal or facial expression of affect, by looseness of associations (together with the related difficulty in forming abstractions), by dissociation of mood and content in thinking, and by inattention or withdrawal, can be attested by any experienced clinician. Pinel (3) first formulated the concept and its existence was widely acknowledged by nineteenth-century physicians. Pinel's contributions require some comment. For one thing he emphasized that many patients with this illness recovered whereas others did not. However he did not conclude, as Bleuler later did, that this proved the existence of two different but related diseases. In the second place he used the word "inattention" more often than "withdrawal," and I consider this wise; "withdrawal" implies a voluntary act, and there is certainly no evidence for this. In the third place, Pinel implied no specific etiology for his syndrome. In the fourth place, Pinel did not accept the dubious conclusions of eighteenth-century pathologists about mental disease, e.g., Meckel's notion that the brain was unusually firm (he won the prize of the Prussian Academy in 1745 for his studies on brain specific gravity), and Bonet's ideas on pineal calcification. Both these superstitions were accepted by many of Pinel's leading contemporaries. However, Pinel's concept was defective in minimizing the importance of delusions, a defect that Bleuler perpetuated.

In passing we should note that Pinel was a creature of his time. He introduced the item about looseness of associations into clinical medicine after reading Hartley's *Observations on Man* (7), a book that had enormous popularity at the time. Similarly contemporary concern with the *rights of man* led Pinel to unchain his patients. We today are also creatures of our time and add items from psychology, from sociology (including family dynamics), and from biochemistry to the concept that Pinel first described and Haslam developed (3).

Although the Pinel-Haslam Syndrome was, and still remains, a valid conception, useful in clinical practice, it should not be concluded that the *schizophrenia* concept is equally valuable. In fact the word *schizophrenia* should be abandoned, for several reasons: 1. it has no priority; 2. it misleadingly implies an understanding of a supposed basic disorder; 3. its two main subdivisions are defined by responses to treatment, which is absurd; and 4. it is difficult to use in clinical practice. As regards the first point it is clear that Bleuler added nothing of value to the concept formulated by Pinel over a century previously. As regards the second point, that the *basic* disorder is dissociation, there is absolutely no evidence for it, and the word schizophrenia is therefore misleading. Moreover, it connotes a purely psychologic etiology and pathogenesis, a concept which is clinically invalid. The fact that schizophrenic symptoms may occur in association with a variety of so-called "organic diseases" has been shown by a number of physicians, among the earliest of whom was Menninger (9). An early paper by Wolff and Curran (12) is noteworthy in this respect because it showed that the symptoms of delirium and those of endogenous (i.e., psychologically-initiated) psychoses overlapped to a marked degree; indeed in some of their cases what seemed to be a delirium proved to be—or perhaps later became—an endogenous psychosis. Today internists and some others recognize that the Pinel-Haslam Syndrome may be produced not only by brain diseases, e.g., encephalitis and tumors, but also in more or less transient forms by hypothyroidism, by Cushing's syndrome, by hypoparathyroidism, by a variety of electrolyte disturbances, and by a host of acute intoxications caused by such diverse substances as metallic mercury and atropine. As clinicians we can talk about Pinel-Haslam Syndrome caused by myxedema, or by atropine poisoning, or by encephalitis, or by extreme sociologic deprivation, or by psychologic upset, or by genetic factors. We cannot do this with the term schizophrenia. As regards the third point, the belief in two distinct types of a single disease recognized largely on the basis of the response to current treatment, the history of medicine has repeatedly shown that this approach is absurd. As regards the fourth point, that the schizophrenia concept is difficult to use, the psychiatric literature strongly supports the view that a diagnosis of schizophrenia is often controversial. Even more support has been provided by organizations that sponsor research on mental disease. Some of them insist that when patients labeled schizophrenic are to be the subjects of research the diagnosis will not be acceptable unless unanimously agreed upon by a group. In medicine in general it is universally acknowledged that a single physician of sufficient competence can make any diagnosis in the field of his competence. Are we to conclude that there are no competent psychiatrists anywhere? Or are we to conclude that the condition cannot be diagnosed accurately? The latter is clearly true. Whereas a disease entity has relatively sharp diagnostic criteria, a syndrome does not. The implication that what is now called schizophrenia is anything but a syndrome—a reaction pattern of varied etiology and variable manifestations and different degrees of curability—that what is called schizophrenia is in fact anything but an unfortunately distorted version of the Pinel-Haslam Syndrome, receives no support from clinical observation. Since the word schizophrenia has many different meanings in medical writings—in fact it appears to have at least two in Bleuler's own description—it should be abandoned and the clinical disorder it presumedly is intended to describe should be designated the Pinel-Haslam Syndrome. In any case the disorder is not a disease entity on the one hand, or a figment on the other.

REFERENCES

1. Abelard, P.: Introductio ad Theologiam Prologue. In Taylor, H. O. *The Medieval Mind.* Fourth Edition. London: Macmillan, 1938.
2. Ackerknecht, E. H.: *Rudolf Virchow. Doctor, Statesman, Anthropologist.* Madison: Wisconsin University Press, 1953.
3. Altschule, M. D.: Whichophrenia, or the Confused Past, Ambiguous Present and Dubious Future of the Schizophrenia Concept. *Journal of Schizophrenia,* 1:8-17, 1967.
4. Bernard, C.: *An Introduction to the Study of Experimental Medicine.* (Trans. Greene, H. C.) New York: Macmillan, 1927.
5. Charcot, J. M.: De l'Expectation en Médecine. In *Oeuvres Complètes.* Paris: Bureaux du Progrès Med., 1888-1891.
6. Hall, M.: *Principles of the Theory and Practice of Medicine.* American Edition Revised and Enlarged by Bigelow, J. and Holmes, O. W. Boston: Little and Brown, 1839.
7. Hartley, J.: *Observations on Man.* London: Leake and Frederick, 1749.
8. Mach, E.: *Contributions to the Analysis of the Sensations.* (Trans. Williams, C. M.) Chicago: The Open Court Publishing Co., 1897.
9. Menninger, K. A.: Influenza and Schizophrenia: An Analysis of Post-Influenzal "Dementia Praecox" as of 1918 and 5 Years Later. *American Journal of Psychiatry,* 5:469-529, 1926.

10. Royce, J.: *Spirit of Modern Philosophy.* New York: Norton, 1967.
11. Sanctorious: *Medica Statica.* (Trans. Quincy, J.) Fourth Edition. London: Osborn and Longman, 1728.
12. Wolff, H. G. and Curran, D.: Nature of Delirium and Allied States. The Dysergastic Reaction. *Archives of Neurology and Psychiatry,* 33:1175-1215, 1935.

3

The Concept of Schizophrenia

SILVANO ARIETI, M.D.

AS A BACKGROUND to my own views I shall discuss three attacks commonly made in the last two decades on the concept of schizophrenia. I shall examine the three of them, one by one, to show why in my opinion they are not valid.

The first attack is the result of many psychoanalytic and psychodynamic studies. Psychodynamic research went much further than the psychobiologic (23) in demonstrating that the psychopathology of the schizophrenic patient did not start with the onset of the manifest symptomatology, but was subsequent to such factors as the unhappy marriage of the parents, the particular constitution of the family, the personality of the mother and father, a childhood characterized by exposures to early and excessive manifestations of anxiety and hostility, and so on. Additional studies revealed that, although a particular cluster of these factors is to be found much more frequently among schizophrenics than among other people, actually, no psychodynamic mechanisms exist which are found exclusively in schizophrenia.

When we emphasize the similarity of psychodynamics in many psychiatric syndromes, we then tend either to expand the concept of schizophrenia to include all these conditions or to abolish it completely and reach the conclusion that Szasz (27) is right in calling schizophrenia a *panchreston,* a term coined by Hardin to denote dangerous words which are purported to explain everything, but which actually obscure matters.

Now it seems to me that a basic error is made in this procedure. It consists of the assumption that it is in the psychodynamic mechanisms that we must find the specificity of schizophrenia. I do not want to be misunderstood on this point. The psychodynamic factors, including parental attitudes, childhood situations, and development of particular personality traits, are extremely important. Nevertheless, although I believe it to be true that without them there would be no schizophrenia, I also believe that in themselves they do not constitute schizophrenia. It is my belief, to be corroborated later, that we have a schizophrenic syndrome only when the psychodynamic conflict or content is translated or channeled into a *schizophrenic form*. For instance, an irrational feeling of self-depreciation and guilt, with special reference to the sexual area, may be evaluated in its great dynamic import and traced back to abnormal relations with the patient's mother. However, only when this conflict assumes some special forms, like that of an hallucinated voice which tells the patient that she is a prostitute, can we talk of the presence of schizophrenia. The psychodynamic conflict of guilt could have, for example, been channeled into phobic or obsessive-compulsive symptoms.

The second attack is implicitly or indirectly made by all those authors who see the patient exclusively as a part of a schizophrenic milieu—familial or sociocultural. In my opinion, these authors, not the patients, have demolished the ego-boundaries between the patient and his environment. Authors like Lidz, Wynne, Jackson, Bateson, Laing and others have greatly enlarged our understanding of schizophrenia by showing the ways in which the family affects the patient. Some of them have vividly portrayed the family drama or the social drama, involving the patient and his milieu. Let us remember, however, that as long as the drama remains a social or an interpersonal one and is not internalized in abnormal ways, we do not have schizophrenia. In order to lead to schizophrenia, the drama must injure the self very much and become a drama of the self, by virtue of high symbolic processes.

Most of these authors have clarified the psychodynamics of schizophrenia, but not schizophrenia itself. By adopting a naive environmentalistic approach, they weaken the concept of the disorder. According to some of these authors the schizophrenic patient learns his typically schizophrenic ways from his parents or his environment; the patient's irrationality is transmitted or learned from the parents, just as is language.

In my opinion this is again tantamount to confusing psychodynamics with psychopathology or content with form. A comparison between dream and schizophrenia may help us to remove this confusion. Certainly, the content of a dream has a great deal to do with the conflicts originating in dealing with other people, in most cases with the members of the family. However, the mechanisms of the dream-work, that is, such phenomena as the translation of thought into visual imagery, the bizarre way of thinking with condensation and displacement, and the loss of rules of time and space, do not originate from the environment. They are particular structures of the dream. The mind reverts to a special state where the primary process prevails. Similar phenomena occur in schizophrenia. When the psychosis takes place, special forms of cognition become available which confer the typical schizophrenic aspect to a psychodynamically loaded content. If we could accept the validity of the theory according to which schizophrenic irrationality is transmitted directly from the parents, we should more easily succeed in equating psychopathology to psychodynamics. We should have been able to make a superior synthesis and we should be pleased with the aesthetic elegance that unification theories have. But, unfortunately, at the present state of our knowledge this theory has all the aspects of being a reductionistic and invalid one.

Perhaps we can make an effort to understand how some authors can believe that schizophrenics who, let us say, hear hallucinatory voices, or believe that they are Jesus Christ, or receive communications from other planets, have learned from their parents to think in these ways. Some of these authors have correctly observed that there is a great deal of irrationality in the families of schizophrenics; they have also correctly inferred that there is a relation of causality between the irrationality of the family and the irrationality of the schizophrenic. Where they have made an error is in assuming that such irrationality, or abnormal ways of thinking, called by these authors diffused, fragmented or double-bind, are directly absorbed and duplicated. It would be like studying the intake of food but not the function of the digestive system and the metabolic processes of the body.

As an illustration of this type of thinking, I want to take an example from one of the last writings of Don Jackson (22). A young paranoid patient, while being examined in connection with the Veterans Administration, made very few statements; however, he repeatedly said, "It's all a matter of chemistry and physics." The examiner then asked the parents what they thought about their son's illness. There was a long silence and finally the mother said, "Well, we don't know anything about it. It's just a matter of chemistry and physics to us." The father and the patient joined in a mild chuckle, both repeating in a low tone, "Yeah, just a matter of chemistry and physics."

According to Jackson this is an example of schizophrenic irrationality: a learned adaptive behavior with consequent reinforcements. It is difficult to understand how Don Jackson, an author who in his short life did so much to illuminate the psychodynamics of schizophrenia, made such a basic error in relation to schizophrenic cognition. The reported example is one of psychologic habituation, even if we call it adaptive behavior with consequent reinforcements. It occurs in both schizophrenic and non-schizophrenic families. It does not constitute schizophrenia. In reference to that specific example from Jackson, I must reluctantly say that not only schizophrenics and their families but some of our fellow colleagues in the psychiatric profession believe it is all a matter of chemistry and physics.

What I want to say is that there are several ways by which the social environment may adversely affect the individual: a group of them consists of phenomena called psychological habituation, indoctrination, imitation, acceptance on faith, etc., by which a great deal of irrationality is transmitted from one generation to another. But cultural or social irrationality is not schizophrenic or delusional in a technical sense. For instance, staunch Nazis may believe that Jews are evil and must be eliminated. The acceptance of this belief is not a delusion; morally and in its practical effects it is infinitely worse than a delusion. It is cultural in origin and because of special techniques devised by society, like coercion, falsification of truths, impossibility of ventilation, etc., is transformed into an introject. The reverse is also true. If some members of a minority which has suffered from persecution for many centuries feel persecuted when they are not, their thinking is obviously not valid; their misinterpretation, however, is not necessarily or technically delusional. It may be a state of habituation which may be overcome much more easily than a delusion, and with different methods.

Similarly, when we hear or read that in some islands in the Pacific or in some remote Indian or African tribes all the members of the tribe have a paranoid and delusional attitude toward other people or groups of people, we cannot conclude that these people are schizophrenic. It would be also a misnomer to call the culture itself schizophrenic. Myths, ceremonials, rituals, and ideas transmitted from generation to generation and taken for granted as true may seem to us delusional, although we have our own examples which are no less irrational. They are learned from society. As long as they are accepted by the individual from the external world, they become part of his psychological content; they are not the product of his own alleged schizophrenic process.

When we come specifically to study the family and not the general culture, we find that in addition to the cultural irrationality there is some irrationality transmitted in every family from parents to children and between siblings. In disturbed families, like those of schizophrenic patients, the amount of irrationality is greater.

Let us remember, however, that the parents of the schizophrenics do not speak a schizophrenic language, nor do they think in a typical schizophrenic way, unless they themselves are schizophrenic; and they are so only in a small minority. They may talk in diffuse or occasionally even fragmented speech, but these characteristics are not typically schizophrenic. Schizophrenia is *not* a learned special mode of communication between family members, although it is true that some peculiar modes of communication are much more pronounced in families of schizophrenics. It is also true that in many disturbed families, and especially in schizophrenic families, the child learns that logical reality-oriented thought processes in relation to some particular matter are not accepted by his parents. He must thus accept some illogical thoughts or take their validity for granted, in order to survive; just as, in some authoritarian or medieval cultures the individual, in order to survive, had to accept some political or religious ideas.

The third type of attack on the concept of schizophrenia is explicitly or implicitly made by those authors who emphasize the fact that there is only a quantitative difference between the schizophrenic, the neurotic and the normal. This statement has at least a great deal of pragmatic therapeutic value. I believe it was in the spirit of this pragmatic value that my teacher, Frieda Fromm-Reichmann, often repeated this point of view. Her genuine identification with the patient, as well as her feelings of moral equality with and respect for every member of the human community, made her give this new formulation to Sullivan's statement (26) that what is common to the therapist and the patient is more important than what is dissimilar. Many are the authors who believe only in a quantitative difference between schizophrenia and other disorders. When such a prominent psychiatrist as Karl Menninger (24) formulates this point of view, so strongly and clearly, we must give all our attention and respect to it. This point of view has recently been reinforced by the interpretation given to some clinical observations.

In recent years I have seen an increasing number of schizophrenics with such mild symptomatology as to make the traditional diagnosis quite difficult. The point is no longer made as to whether we are dealing with latent schizophrenia, as Bleuler did (20), but whether the distinctions between diagnostic categories should be retained. Whether the increase in mild cases is more apparent than real and connected with the availability of a large number of psychiatric facilities, or whether it is real and engendered by sociocultural or other factors, is not a question for this chapter. I want to stress, however, a point that I have learned in my early studies in neuropathology. Although I know that this argument has only the value of an analogy, the possibility is not excluded that it can be applied to any kind of pathology.

In neuropathology we learn to recognize histologically such entities as general paresis, senile psychosis, or Wernicke's encephalopathy by studying the most pronounced specimens of these conditions. When the complete and full-fledged picture is well established in the mind of the neuropathologist he learns to accept as belonging to the same nosological category those mild, incomplete, or arrested forms which actually form the largest number of cases. Even a case of general paresis, which is supposed to be such a typical condition histologically, could be confused by a pathologist if he does not take as a paradigm the most pronounced cases. A case could be made that all these conditions, when not pronounced and not typical, have many histologic features in common and belong to only one entity. The history of medicine teaches us that as long as pathologists stressed what pathological conditions had in common, no substantial progress was made. It was when the unique in a given condition was recognized that a breakthrough was made. When we see pure culture cases, like a patient who states that he is Jesus Christ because he drank "Carnation milk" and therefore has been reincarnated, or uses peculiar neologisms or metonymic distortions or a typical word-salad, or sees everyone as an FBI agent spying on him, or hallucinates all the time, or is in catatonic postures, or complete withdrawal, we have a constellation or gestalt which cannot be confused.

The normal or would-be normal young bride may be a little suspicious toward the mother-in-law and misinterpret some of her remarks in a paranoid-like fashion; the tired and irritated worker may give a special meaning to the attitude of his boss and assume what may seem to be a referential point of view; in slips of the tongue all of us may create neologisms or make unpredicted puns. All these things occur, it is true; but equally true is that they do not make a schizophrenic gestalt.

However, even if we adhere to the continuous hypothesis and believe that psychiatric pictures may change by infinitesimal increments, i.e., by steps too small to be noticeable, we must be aware of the qualitative differences which may result according to when and where the change occurs. The difference in temperature between 34 and 33 degrees does not have the same effect on water as the difference between 33 and 32 degrees. There may be only a quantitative difference between a 39% and a 41% solution of a substance, but if the solute precipitates when the concentration is 40%, the two solutions will no longer be only quantitatively different. They will also be qualitatively different because one has a precipitate and the other does not. The situation is more complicated in the field of biology, and especially in the field of psychology where the element of subjectivity enters.

The psychiatric patient may have many symptoms that the nonschizophrenic patient does not have, but it is only when he accepts them as part of reality, integrates them in the context of his whole life, consequently experiences the world and himself in a different way, and alters his relationship with others, that the total quality changes and the psychosis occurs.

Similar remarks can be made in relation to homosexuality and heterosexuality. We may find some homosexual conflicts in many heterosexual patients, but it is only when the individual integrates his own sexuality along a homosexual orientation that we consider him homosexual. There is no doubt that in by far the majority of cases it is possible to decide whether a given individual is homosexual or heterosexual.

In reference again to schizophrenia, we must take another look and make another attempt—in Hegelian terms—to lay bare the core and significance of the schizophrenic event, to free it from the adventitious contingencies which—although not irrelevant accessories—are only partially causally related and of merely secondary importance. I shall make such an attempt now to show as clearly as possible what seems to me to be the essence of the schizophrenic phenomenon.

We know how the great innovators in the field of psychiatry saw the schizophrenic phenomenon in its totality. Kraepelin saw it as an almost ineluctable course toward deterioration of mental functions, and we know that he was wrong. Bleuler saw it predominantly as a loosening of associations, and we know that although he may have hit upon one of the fundamental characteristics, his formulation as a whole remains vague and unworkable. Freud saw the psychosis as an altered relation with the world, caused by a withdrawal of cathexis. Thus Freud came to interpret the psychosis more and more in the frame of reference of the libido theory, energetics, and economics. The classic Freudian school has pursued this track. Actually Freud had already made a revolutionary hypothesis that had brought more light on the schizophrenic phenomenon than any other theory. I am referring to the individualization and description of the primary process, as reported in Chapter 7 of *The Interpretation of Dreams* (21).

I think that at the present stage of our knowledge we can state that the schizophrenic syndrome is that condition in which the primary process prevails and is adopted as a way of experiencing life and dealing with it. We must qualify that always in incipient schizophrenia, and usually in chronic schizophrenia, the primary process is not adopted for most aspects of the life experience, but only for the conflictual areas.

After the remarkable breakthrough reported in Chapter 7 of *The Interpretation of Dreams,* Freud did not make other significant discoveries about the structure of the primary process. He became particularly interested in the primary process as a carrier of unconscious motivation. Moreover, inasmuch as he interpreted motivation more and more as a function of the libido theory, the primary process came to be studied by him and his disciples predominantly as a consumer of energy or a special way of binding energy.

It has been one of my main foci of interest to study the primary process, predominantly as a kind of cognitive organization. It was always difficult for me to understand how the followers of the orthodox Freudian school could conceive of the id and the primary process as an amorphous reservoir of energy and as a way of dealing with energy. I am glad to see that now, after having ignored the work done by others for several decades, some of the classical psychoanalysts like Schur and Holt have started to study the primary process from a cognitive point of view.

In my studies on the cognition of the primary process, especially in reference to schizophrenia, I have adopted a comparative developmental approach, which is a derivation of the one proposed by Heinz Werner (30). I see primary process cognition as a less differentiated, premature, microgenetic or intermediary process in the complicated hierarchy of mechanisms which eventually lead to the secondary process. Although it is true that primary process cognition is not as elaborate as that of the secondary process, it is by no means a random conglomeration of psychic functions. The primary process presents immature forms which occur also in the three types of development—phylogeny, ontogeny and microgeny. The concept of microgeny as formulated by Werner (29) is less known and requires some explanation.

As I expressed elsewhere (6, 11, 14), microgeny is the immediate unfolding of a phenomenon, i.e., the sequence of the necessary steps inherent in the occurrence of a psychological process. For instance, to the question, "Who is the author of Hamlet?" a person answers "Shakespeare." He is aware only of the question (stimulus) and of his answer (conscious response), but not of the numerous steps which in a remarkably short time led him to give the correct answer. Why did he not reply "Sophocles" or "George Bernard Shaw?" How did he reach the correct answer? There are numerous proofs that the answer was not necessarily an established and purely physical or neuronic association between Hamlet and Shakespeare, but that an actual unconscious search went on. In fact, if the same question is asked of a mental patient or of a person who is very sleepy or drunk or paying little attention, he may reply "Sophocles" or "George Bernard Shaw." These are wrong but not haphazard answers, inasmuch as they refer to playwrights. The mental search required by the answer had at least reached the category of playwrights. The numerous steps through which a mental process goes constitute its microgenetic development.

These three developments—phylogeny, ontogeny and microgeny—unfold in time, although with great variation in the quantity of time: from periods as long as geological eras in phylogeny to periods as short as fractions of a second in microgeny. What is of fundamental importance is that the three types of development tend to use the same structural plans. I do not mean literally that microgeny recapitulates ontogeny and phylogeny, but that there are certain formal similarities in the three fields of development and that we are able to individualize schemes of highest forms of generality which involve all levels of the psyche in its three types of development. Here we may find a beginning of a General System Theory of cognition.

When the primary process takes over, the whole psychological picture undergoes a transformation. The relation to the external world changes. Not only does inner reality become much more important than external reality, but it is confused with external reality. The patient becomes adualistic. He is unable to distinguish the two worlds, that of his own mind and the external. Consensual validation as well as intrapsychic feedback mechanisms become defective. The patient is less and less in contact with the external world, and like people during sensory deprivation experiments, becomes more and more dependent on primary processes. In other words, whereas secondary processes need contact with reality or feedback mechanisms to maintain such contact with reality, primary process mechanisms feed more and more on themselves (25).

In my research I have studied some mechanisms of the primary process not fully studied by Freud from the point of view of cognition. Such phenomena as the mechanism of active concretization, the principle of von Domarus, the unbalance between the connotative, denotative and verbal values of language, altered causality, perceptualization of the concepts, and related processes have been illustrated elsewhere (1, 2, 3, 6, 13, 14). I have also tried to trace back the biological origin of primary process cognition. These studies (5, 10, 14) of mine do not purport to reveal what goes on in the interplay of neurons, but they may be viewed as heuristic psychological formulations which help us to understand how primary process cognition works, at least in schizophrenia.

If we view schizophrenia as a pathological resurgence of a mechanism, which in normal conditions is controlled by higher structures, we find this phenomenon similar to many others described in general medicine. For instance, in some pathological conditions of the heart, when the sino-auricular node is injured, the more ancient auriculoventricular bundle takes over its functions. Like the auriculoventricular bundle, the primary process has normal functions in various activities of the mind, for instance in dreams.

Inasmuch as the normal adult in a state of wakefulness is organized in accordance with the predominance of the secondary process, the organization in accordance with the prevailing of the primary process must be considered pathological. To use Karl Menninger's expressive term, the vital balance is endangered.

Alas! This conclusion does not remove all the problems looming around the concept of schizophrenia. How is the reemergence of the primary process to be reconciled with the psychodynamic formulations of schizophrenia to which we strictly adhere? On one side we deal with psychodynamic factors which eventually lead to the defeat of the self. On the other side, we deal with such phenomena as archaic mechanisms, dedifferentiated structures, paleologic thinking, concretization of the abstract. It seems almost as if we embrace two logical universes, two irreconcilable views of man and nature.

I shall attempt at this point to recapitulate my views on the psychodynamics of schizophrenia. I shall then show how this psychodynamic development is, in my opinion, connected with the reemergence of the primary process.

In schizophrenia as well as in the vast majority of human psychological states the most important psychodynamic factors are those which affect the individual self and self-image. In early childhood the future schizophrenic finds himself in a family that for various reasons cannot offer him a modicum of security or basic trust. Early interpersonal relations are characterized by intense anxiety, hostility or false detachment.

The self, and self-image at this stage are already abnormal. The self-esteem is not low just because it reproduces a negative appraisal from others. The young child does not meet all appraisals and roles attributed to him in the same way. Those elements which hurt him more, and, in some cases, which please him more, stand out and are integrated disproportionately. Thus the self, although related to the external appraisals, is not a simple reproduction of them but a *grotesque* representation of them. Moreover, the self is constituted of all the defenses that are built to cope with these appraisals and their distortions. The more disturbed the environment, the more prominent is the role and lingering of that type of cognition which I have described elsewhere (12) and called primary cognition.

The grotesque representation of the self which the future schizophrenic retains in early childhood would stupefy the parents, if they were aware of it. According to my own observations, it would stupefy a large number of them, who never, consciously or unconsciously, wanted to inflict it on their children. This grotesque self-image is very painful, and would become even more painful, if the patient would continue to be aware of it and would continue to connect it with an increasing number of ramifications and implications. Fortunately, to a large extent, this image is repressed from awareness. The individual would not be able to bear it otherwise.

In various writings (2, 14, 15, 16) I have described how this inadequate self and self-image bring about a series of events; defenses, unsuccessful dealings with the world, and other complications. The time comes when the patient—adolescent, young adult or adult—will believe that his future has no hope and the promise of life will not be fulfilled. More than that he feels threatened from all sides, as if he were in a jungle. It is not a jungle where lions, tigers, snakes and spiders are to be found, but a jungle of concepts, where the threat is not to survival, but to the self-image. The dangers are concept-feelings such as that of being unwanted, unloved, unlovable, inadequate, unacceptable, inferior, awkward, clumsy, not belonging, peculiar, different, rejected, humiliated, guilty, unable to find his own way among the different paths of life, disgraced, discriminated, kept at a distance, suspected, etc. Is this a man-made jungle created by civilization in place of the jungle to which primitive tribes are exposed? The answer is in the understanding of a circular process. To a large extent the collectivity of man, in its historical heritage and present conditions has made this jungle; but to a large extent the patient too has created it. Sensitized as he is, because of his past experiences and crippling defenses, he distorts the environment. At this point, his distortion is not yet a paranoid projection or a delusion in a technical sense. It is predominantly experienced as anguish, as increased vulnerability, fear, anxiety, mental pain. In other writings (14, 15, 16) I have described in detail what happens to the patient at this stage, which I have called prepsychotic panic: prepsychotic because full-fledged psychotic symptoms are not yet manifest.

The ineluctable conceptual conclusions reached recently by the patient and their emotional accompaniment reactivate the early inner experiences of childhood, not just because of their strength but also because of their fundamental similarity. These resurging experiences reinforce the recent ones as they are in agreement with them, and the result is of dire proportions and consequences. It is this concordance, or unification of early and late experiences which first reawakens the early experiences and secondly completes and magnifies in terrifying ways the horrendous vision of the self. In the totality of his human existence, and through the depth of all his feelings, the individual now sees himself as totally defeated, without any worth or possibility of redemption. Although in the past he had undergone similar experiences which were faint, now these experiences are vivid. They are vivid, even though they are not verbalized, and occur in a nonrepresentational, almost abstract form.

The patient cannot accept this vision of himself. He must undergo a drastic metamorphosis and adopt new ways which will represent the world and his own self-image in less frightening ways. It is at this point that the primary process is summoned and acquires supremacy. It is at this point that the patient acquires not-learned, not-imitated habits, which will constitute his schizophrenic ways of seeing the world and himself. They are archaic and to a large extent unpredictable ways. They have the flavor of myths and primitivity. They finally do change the unbearable concepts into hallucinated lions and tigers; and mother and father into persecutors or kings and fairies. In other words, the individual now meets some aspects of the external world and reevaluates his past experiences in accordance with the modes of the primary process. But how do we explain the passage from a psychodynamic to a psychostructural or formal frame of reference represented by the prevailing of the primary process? We may build a bridge between determinism and psychodynamics if we view the schizophrenic patient as channeling his conflicts through a form of teleologic regression. We may formulate the phenomenon in the form of a principle. *If in a situation of severe anxiety, such as that provoked by deep injury to the self-image and to the self, the psyche cannot function at a certain level of integration and cannot attain the desired results, a strong tendency exists toward functioning at lower levels of integration in order to effect those results* (2, 14). In schizophrenia, functioning at a lower level means functioning with the mechanisms of the primary process. It means fitting a higher content into a lower form, changing the abstract into the concrete, a general threat into a specific one, something which originates from the inner self into something which comes from the external world. For instance, the feeling of self-accusation is changed into an accusation which comes from other persons, the persecutors. The regression can thus be interpreted as purposeful or teleologic. This point of view is not irreconcilable with the point of view that a biological factor —constitutional or biochemical—predisposes some individuals to this type of regression, when the mentioned circumstances occur.

The concept of progressive teleologic regression is not necessarily vitalistic or animistic; it is an additional application of concepts developed in general medicine by Claude Bernard and in psychiatry by Sigmund Freud. It is not a denial that psychological and psychopathological phenomena follow physical determinism (according to which causes have effects), but an additional affirmation that the living organism, in health or disease, seems to be subject to both mechanical and teleologic causalities. An example from physical medicine may clarify the matter. An infective disease produces an invasion of foreign proteins in an organism, and foreign proteins bring about a temperature rise, i.e., fever. All this follows mechanical causality. We know, however, that fever has a purpose: to combat the invasion of the foreign proteins. Here the organism seems to follow purposeful causality. Obviously, in the course of evolution only those organisms survived which had such inherited biochemical properties that enabled them to respond with fever to bacterial invasion. To us, who are interested in survival, the mechanisms seem teleological. It is teleological at our level of human values. In the same way we may admit that when the evolution of the nervous system reached the human level, the psyche, in order to survive, had to develop the capacity of readjusting at least at some psychopathological levels. In Freudian language, we could say that the symptoms could not be just regressive but also restitutional. A psychological defense is a pathological readjustment and purposeful, although determined by previous causes.

Schizophrenic regression, contrary to other types, is progressive because—although to some extent purposeful—with few exceptions it fails of its purpose and tends to repeat itself. A human being who is deprived of the highest levels of integration can in a very rough way be compared to an animal experimentally deprived of the neopallic cortex. This animal will not be in a physiological condition comparable to that of an organism of a lower species which does not possess that cortex. Rather, it remains in an abnormal condition, because its whole organism is attuned to the neopallic cortex, or integrated with the functions of the cerebral cortex (28).

In a similar way the schizophrenic patient will *regress to,* but will not successfully *integrate at,* a lower level: he will remain to a considerable extent disorganized. What I am trying to say is that the schizophrenic organization remains a disorganization. Unless treatment is instituted or unforeseeable fortunate events occur, the organism then defends itself from the disorganization with further regression to an even lower level. The process repeats itself in a vicious circle that can lead to complete dilapidation. The situation is thus different from that occurring in other psychopathologic conditions. For instance, the phobic patient also undergoes a regression. His phobia is a regressive form through which his higher level problems are expressed. However, the phobic patient as a rule remains arrested at a phobic level, without progression toward lower mechanisms.

This description of the schizophrenic process should not be misinterpreted as acceptance of an ineluctable pathological course. Nothing could be further from the truth. In my modest contributions to the psychotherapy of schizophrenia I have tried to show that when interpersonal relatedness is established in the treatment of the patient, he can become more aware of the active role he plays in his illness. At first he becomes aware of how he translates his conflicts into psychotic mechanisms, in which the primary process prevails. Then he learns that at times he can actually choose between the realm of psychosis and the realm of reality. He finds out how even in such apparently immutable processes as hallucinations and delusions, he can recognize that it is up to him to resist the seduction of the abnormal mechanisms and to accept the anxiety and suffering of a meaning that is not masked by psychotic media. The patient will be able to do so if he feels that the therapist is there to share the anxiety and suffering of his conflict. In other words, the patient is not expected to passively absorb interpretation, freely offered to him. By resorting to special techniques that I have described in various publications (4, 7, 8, 9, 11), the therapist gives the patient tools with which he himself must fight his own illness; that is, the prevailing of his primary process.

Perhaps, in an additional attempt to find a more accurate definition of the concept, I can reformulate part of what I have said in the frame of reference of von Bertalanffy's General System Theory (17, 18, 19).

Prior to becoming schizophrenic the patient can be seen as an open system in a steady state. His final state, or any state, is not unequivocally determined by the initial conditions. Thus the psychiatrists who stress only early childhood experiences and overlook the fact that the individual is always open to new possibilities which may alter the cycle of life ignore the principle of equifinality. Any individual may increase negative entropy, and develop towards states of increased order and organization, even if he has to cope with a great deal of psychodynamic pathology, inside and outside himself. But when he becomes schizophrenic, that is when his way of living will be in accordance with the prevailing of the primary process, he tends to become a closed system, to follow the second principle of thermodynamics and to move toward progressive simplification and homogeneity. The aim of therapy is to reopen the system. By reestablishing relatedness with the patient, we shall feed him again with negative entropy. By learning special techniques, the patient will become much more able to choose to be less homogenous, less passive, more complex, and to accept more and more his autonomous meeting with the world.

REFERENCES

1. Arieti, S.: Special Logic of Schizophrenia and Other Types of Autistic Thought. *Psychiatry*, 11:325-338, 1948.
2. Arieti, S.: *Interpretation of Schizophrenia*. New York: Brunner, 1955.
3. Arieti, S.: Schizophrenia. In Arieti, S. (Ed.), *American Handbook of Psychiatry*. New York: Basic Books, 1959.
4. Arieti, S.: Introductory Notes on the Psychoanalytic Therapy of Schizophrenia. In Burton, A. (Ed.), *Psychotherapy of the Psychoses*. New York: Basic Books, 1961.
5. Arieti, S.: The Loss of Reality. *Psychoanalysis and Psychoanalytic Review*, 48:3-24, 1961.
6. Arieti, S.: The Microgeny of Thought and Perception. *Archives of General Psychiatry*, 6:454-468, 1962.
7. Arieti, S.: Psychotherapy of Schizophrenia. *Archives of General Psychiatry*, 6:112-122, 1962.
8. Arieti, S.: Hallucinations, Delusions and Ideas of Reference Treated with Psychotherapy. *American Journal of Psychotherapy*, 16:52-60, 1962.
9. Arieti, S.: The Psychotherapy of Schizophrenia in Theory and Practice. In Azima, H. and Glueck, B. C. (Eds.), *Psychotherapy of Schizophrenic and Manic Depressive States* (Psychiatric Research Report 17). Washington, D.C.: American Psychiatric Association, 1963.
10. Arieti, S.: Studies of Thought Processes in Contemporary Psychiatry. *American Journal of Psychiatry*, 120:58-64, 1963.

11. Arieti, S.: The Schizophrenic Patient in Office Treatment. In Muller, C. and Benedetti, G. (Eds.), *Psychotherapy of Schizophrenia*. Basel: Karger, 1965.
12. Arieti, S.: Contributions to Cognition from Psychoanalytic Theory. In Masserman, J. (Ed.), *Science and Psychoanalysis*, Vol. VIII. New York: Grune and Stratton, 1965.
13. Arieti, S.: Conceptual and Cognitive Psychiatry. *American Journal of Psychiatry*, 122:361-366, 1965.
14. Arieti, S.: *The Intrapsychic Self: Feeling, Cognition and Creativity in Health and Mental Illness*. New York: Basic Books, 1967.
15. Arieti, S.: New Views on the Psychodynamics of Schizophrenia. *American Journal of Psychiatry*, 124:453-458, 1967.
16. Arieti, S.: The Psychodynamics of Schizophrenia. *American Journal of Psychotherapy*, 22:366-381, 1968.
17. Bertalanffy, L. von: General System Theory. In Bertalanffy, L. and Rapaport, A. (Eds.), *General Systems Yearbook of the Society for the Advancement of General System Theory*. Ann Arbor: University of Michigan Press, 1956.
18. Bertalanffy, L. von: General System Theory and Psychiatry. In Arieti, S. (Ed.), *American Handbook of Psychiatry*. New York: Basic Books, 1966.
19. Bertalanffy, L. von: *General System Theory: Foundations, Development, Applications*. New York: Braziller, 1968.
20. Bleuler, E.: *Dementia Praecox or the Group of Schizophrenias*. New York: International Universities Press, 1950.
21. Freud, S.: *The Interpretation of Dreams*. New York: Basic Books, 1955.
22. Jackson, D. D.: The Transactional Viewpoint. *International Journal of Psychiatry*, 4:543-544, 1967.
23. Lief, A. (Ed.): *The Commonsense Psychiatry of Dr. Adolf Meyer: Fifty-Two Selected Papers*. New York: McGraw-Hill, 1948.
24. Menninger, K., Mayman, M. and Pruyser, P. W.: *The Vital Balance*. New York: Viking Press, 1963.
25. Noy, P.: Personal Communication, 1968.
26. Sullivan, H. S.: *Conceptions of Modern Psychiatry*. Washington: W. A. White Psychiatric Foundation, 1947.
27. Szasz, T.: The Problem of Psychiatric Nosology: A Contribution to a Situational Analysis of Psychiatric Operations. *American Journal of Psychiatry*, 114:405-413, 1957.
28. Taylor, J. (Ed.): *Selected Writings of John Hughlings Jackson*. London: Hodder and Stoughton, 1932.
29. Werner, H.: Microgenesis and Aphasia. *Journal of Abnormal and Social Psychology*, 52:347-353, 1956.
30. Werner, H.: *Comparative Psychology of Mental Development*. New York: International Universities Press, 1957.

4

The Validity and Usefulness
of the Concept of the
Schizophrenic Syndrome

LEOPOLD BELLAK, M.D.

A DIAGNOSTIC CONCEPT is a heuristic hypothesis. It involves propositions concerning the etiology, treatment and prognosis of the disease or syndrome under consideration. In that sense, the diagnostic hypothesis must be measured by the traditional scientific criteria of validity and reliability. In the broadest sense, the usefulness of a diagnostic hypothesis is indicated by its ability to help one understand, predict and control: to understand means to see the particular set of conditions involved in the diagnosis in the matrix of a sequence of causal events. Prediction in the medical sense means prognosis, and I hasten to add right here—*long-range* and *short-range* prognoses, if the statements are really to be useful. Control in a medical setting means therapeutic control, changing the sequence of events by clearly formulated steps of intervention.

Regrettably, clinicians are not usually explicitly aware of all the propositions involved in their work. The series of diagnostic procedures a clinician employs in the attempt to arrive at a diagnosis are informal attempts to insure the validity and coherence of the diagnostic hypothesis. In that sense, his initial diagnosis is a hypothesis of lower validity than his final diagnosis. In clinical medicine and surgery, the pathologist of a given hospital is often a much dreaded figure as the final judge of the validity of the diagnostic hypothesis. Psychiatric concepts have had a measure of difficulties because of the absence of that particular checking device.

An important aspect of the usefulness of a concept in a hypothesis is also the range of its applicability, the width of phenomena it encompasses. While much is to be said for the idiographic approach, for the progress of science, nomothetic statements, permitting a broad level of generalization, are necessary. I do not believe that this implies abdication to the computer: every nomothetic diagnosis has room for a specific, personalized, idiographic statement, as I propose to show for the concept of schizophrenia.

The concept of schizophrenia has had some problems concerning validity and reliability. Diagnostic fashions vary from country to country, from state to state, from hospital to hospital, and from clinician to clinician. One might call this problem of diagnosis one of inter-rater reliability. Another problem, as Aaron Beck (1) points out, is what one might call "temporal reliability"; that is, once several "judges" agree that a patient is to be considered schizophrenic, what are the chances that he will remain usefully described as schizophrenic, rather than as manic depressive, sociopathic, neurotic or normal? We shall return to both these problems, but I believe that they are more related to artifacts and misconceptions than to an intrinsic lack of validity of the concept.

Doctors Cancro and Pruyser (12) have traced the history of the concept. Also, in *The Vital Balance,* Doctor Menninger (17) has eruditely discussed the history and fate of psychiatric nosology generally and of schizophrenia specifically. He points out that the diagnostic disease concept leads to a proliferation of diagnostic terms and eventual fragmentation. He seems to suggest a unitary disease concept but makes quite clear that he does not mean to discard terminology or syndrome applications, including the schizophrenic syndrome.

What he militates against, apparently, is a *reification* of a disease concept, "Schizophrenia"—or saying a patient with *a* schizophrenia. Such a position is not only easy to agree with, but is the only one that seems to make sense. Whether one refers to a patient as "being schizophrenic," however, is merely a semantic nicety to which one might or might not be able to pay consistent attention in the usual clinical shorthand talk. The important proof of one's broad conception lies in the implications for therapy and prognosis.

In the age of field theory and, specifically, Selye's stress and field theory, there is hardly any place anywhere in medicine for a reified concept, be it of kidney dysfunction or schizophrenia. The psychodynamic basis for our thinking, which must be part of the biosociopsychic dynamics, is the only one that makes sense. It permits us to see an interplay of forces on a continuum. It permits us to see a person suffering from the schizophrenic syndrome as possibly moving to a neurotic or depressed one. I formulated these thoughts graphically as a diagnostic continuum with mobility in both directions (5).

To what extent any dynamic constellation may become a structural one is a problem to return to later in this chapter. It relates, however, to a difference in viewpoint often raised. There are those who feel that there is only a quantitative difference between neurotic and schizophrenic syndromes, and those who feel there are qualitative ones—that schizophrenics are "different." My continuum of ego functions obviously is one of quantitative difference but there need not be any quarrel about it. From Hegel's concept of *"Umschlag von Quantität zu Qualität"* to gestalt psychology and the processes in chemistry it is quite clear that quantitative changes may result in newly emergent qualitative ones. Frequently, a quantitative change in the opposite direction may again reverse the qualitative changes.

With this understanding of diagnosis, I want to reaffirm my own belief in the usefulness of the concept of the schizophrenic syndrome. It is valid and useful both clinically and for research if one defines it appropriately. For over two decades, I have spoken of the schizophrenic syndrome as the final common path of a number of etiologic and pathogenic factors. These are effective sometimes, possibly, alone, but most often, probably, in combination, and are primarily genogenic, chemogenic, psychogenic, and neurogenic factors. I have called my theory the *multiple-factor, psychosomatic, ego-psychological theory* because I believe that psychic and somatic factors play a role, and that they all lead to a severe impairment of ego functions. For the sake of convenience, one can speak of the sum total of ego functions as "ego strength" with about as much, or as little, justification as one can subsume Wechsler's ten subcategories on the WAIS under intelligence. There is as much need to pay heed to the pattern of subscores on ratings of ego functions as on intelligence tests. Schizophrenia is seen then as a range at one end of a continuum of ego strength, falling somewhere within the 23% that the Midtown Study found to be severely disturbed. On the other end of the range of the continuum would be the 18% which the Midtown Study found without significant emotional pathology. In between ranges the average "community representative," shading into more and more neurosis and eventually borderline states as the schizophrenic end is approached. I want to make quite clear that we are speaking of a *range* of ego disturbances on *both* ends of the continuum. For our purposes that means that there are clearly more and less ill schizophrenics and well and less well adjusted normals. *In principle,* every person can move in either direction over the whole continuum. Also, different people, as well as different schizophrenics definitely have different ego function patterns, e.g., some have poor Object Relations and others have primarily poor Thought Processes, etc.

All these statements are meaningful only if they can be made operationally, and be verified quantitatively by independent raters, and that is precisely what we have attempted. Over the last four years we have carried on a study of ego function patterns of schizophrenic, neurotic, and normal subjects, approximately equated for sex, age, education, I.Q., and socioeconomic status. These were rated for twelve ego functions by independent judges from interview material, psychological tests and psychological laboratory procedures. The twelve ego functions are Reality Testing, Judgment, Sense of Reality, Regulation and Control of Drives, Object Relations, Thought Processes, Adaptive Regression in the Service of the Ego (ARISE), Defensive Functions, Stimulus Barrier, Autonomous Functions, Synthetic Functions, and Mastery-Competence. Our work thus far has shown that independent raters correlate very highly and significantly with each other in their appraisal of these ego functions and with independently judging clinicians. Also, our work has shown that *we are able to differentiate clearly the three groups from each other* in terms of ego function patterns, thus establishing some kind of construct validity. Table 1 summarizes these findings. We used, of course, all experimental precautions, including a small study of hospitalized nonschizophrenics to avoid contamination of the data.

I shall not go into a discussion of our definitions, or how we arrived at them, or any other technical or statistical details. Brief accounts of them are available in a variety of publications (8, 11, 15). Also, detailed manuals for interviews and interview ratings have been prepared. A monograph with all these data and a video tape for diagnostic training, are in preparation.

I suggest then that the diagnostic concept of schizophrenia can be valid and useful if: 1. this diagnosis is arrived at by an operational definition of ego functions (as we have provided) which permits interrater reliability; 2. this diagnosis allows for a socio-physio-psychodynamic conception of changes in the person over time; 3. this diagnosis defines schizophrenia as pertaining to a range of ego functions generally below seven on a scale on which 13 signifies the very best of functioning; 4. this diagnosis allows for markedly individual patterns of ego functioning primarily within the lower range of the scale; 5. this diagnosis allows

TABLE 1

EGO FUNCTIONS MEAN SCORES AND STANDARD DEVIATIONS FROM INTERVIEW MATERIAL ON SCHIZOPHRENIC, NEUROTIC AND NORMAL SUBJECTS

(100 Subjects)

Ego Function*	Schiz (50) Mean	S.D.	Neur (25) Mean	S.D.	Norm (25) Mean	S.D.	F-ratio	p value
Reality Testing	6.76	1.9	8.44	1.6	9.78	1.1	58.057	<.0001
Judgment	6.30	1.7	7.44	2.1	9.12	1.7	35.013	<.0001
Sense of Reality	5.60	1.7	7.00	1.1	9.40	1.2	88.291	<.0001
Regulation & Control of Drives	5.72	1.4	6.68	1.3	8.30	1.3	47.665	<.0001
Object Relations	5.08	1.5	6.76	1.4	8.76	1.4	71.138	<.0001
Thought Processes	6.20	2.0	8.26	1.7	9.78	.9	41.870	<.0001
ARISE	6.16	1.9	7.78	1.3	8.32	1.3	26.769	<.0001
Defensive Functions	4.86	1.4	6.94	1.4	8.66	.9	123.005	<.0001
Stimulus Barrier	6.70	1.9	7.82	1.5	9.12	1.4	28.229	<.0001
Autonomous Functions	5.84	2.0	7.68	1.9	9.32	.9	73.540	<.0001
Synthetic Functions	5.22	1.9	6.84	1.6	9.28	1.3	76.312	<.0001

* Mastery-Competence was not yet included in the tabulated material or in the profiles.

each ego function or its disturbance to be relative to the sociocultural setting of the person, i.e., the scheme should permit cross-cultural, international comparisons; 6. it is understood that a specific ego function's strength and pattern is the result of quantitatively varying and dynamic forces and therefore, is changeable to another pattern (or on another part of the continuum with the same pattern), e.g., from schizophrenic to nonschizophrenic, from character disorder to character traits, from symptom to dream manifestation; and 7. it is also understood that the dynamic constellation of forces represented in an ego function pattern tends to have a certain stability and even attains structural quality, e.g., a schizophrenic type of compromise solution or pattern of forces. More often than not the stability and permanence of such patterns, normal, neurotic or psychotic, and schizophrenic specifically is such as to make the concept of heuristic diagnostic and prognostic value. This last point holds less true in adolescents than in adults.

With these propositions in mind, I should like to present some profiles of schizophrenic ego function patterns, to illustrate the usefulness of this concept. All profiles are based on ratings of interviews, except Profile 1B which is based on ratings of psychological tests (In this chapter only the assessment of ego functions is discussed. In fact, our assessment also includes a rating scale for super ego and Id factors also.)

Ego Function Profile 1 is that of a young man in his twenties whose functions nearly all fall around or below five. The most ominous prognostic sign is probably the fact that his ratings on the psychological test performance (profile 1B) and on interview performance are almost identical. Ordinarily, the ratings on interviews are somewhat higher, reflecting the manifest clinical status, while the psychological tests show the full pathological potential. The most likely interpretation of the close similarity between the two levels in the case of this patient is that his clinical picture has leveled off at the lowest denominator and that chronicity has set in. Protracted therapeutic attention along the lines sketched by Sechehaye (18) or Freeman, Cameron and McGhie (14) might offer some hope, after very long treatment; but he has a very poor short-range as well as long-range prognosis without this intensive and extensive treatment by a maximally skilled therapist.

Profile 2 shows a patient in remission with the help of drug therapy and psychotherapy. Note that the Regulation of Drives and Object Relations are still low. When she was acutely disturbed, Reality Testing and Judgment were very low, as she was deluded and hallucinated. Thought Processes were also much lower. The still low Synthetic Function shows that so far there has been a remission only from the acute process. If one were to diagnose her at the point at which this profile was made, "borderline" condition would probably be favored. A paper by Fox (13) and some work in progress by our team will illustrate the plotting of progress in clinical status. The short-range prognosis continues to be good because the Thought Processes improved considerably but the low Synthetic Functioning suggests a fairly poor long-range prognosis.

Profile 3 is of a patient with fairly good Thought Processes who seemed a good prospect for psychotherapy, with a mixture of phenothiazine and amitryptiline providing control of drives and mood, and a rehabilitation workshop providing the general setting for a building and rebuilding of self-esteem which was poorly compensated by grandiose goals. While the cluster of high ratings for Object Relations, Thought Processes, and ARISE constitutes a basis for therapeutic optimism, the poor ratings on Regulation and Control of Drives and Defensive Functioning are liabilities. The low scores on Autonomous and Synthetic Functions are reasons for concern with regard to long-range prognosis, i.e., the ultimate stability of the improvement. The low scores for Reality Testing and Judgment reflect the acute disturbance in the form of hallucinations and delusions. This

EGO FUNCTION PROFILE #1

	Reality Testing	Judgment	Sense of Reality of Reality	Regulat. & Cont. of Drives	Object Relat.	Thought Process	ARISE	Defense Functs.	Stimulus Barrier	Auton. Functs.	Synthet. Functs.
13											
12											
11											
10											
9											
8											
7											
6											
5											
4											
3											
2											
1											

Ego Function Profile #1B

Reality Testing

Judgment

Sense of Reality of Reality

Regulat. & Cont. of Drives

Object Relat.

Thought Process

ARISE

Defense Functs.

Stimulus Barrier

Auton. Functs.

Synthet. Functs.

13
12
11
10
9
8
7
6
5
4
3
2
1

EGO FUNCTION PROFILE #2

could be a central *area* for intervention, i.e., for exploration of the dynamics of the apperceptive distortions. In this young man's prepsychotic state, his disturbance manifested itself primarily in unrealistic fantasies of achievement and in defensive denial, which were responsible sometimes for elation (and sometimes helped increase his actual achievement, although only over the short run). This profile of ego functions leads to a prediction of successful psychotherapy and a good short-range prognosis which have since been borne out.

Profile 4 is that of a severely neurotic 22-year-old female. The relatively low ratings on the triad of Reality Testing, Judgment and Sense of Reality are because of her lack of awareness of inner feelings secondary to her repressive style. Also, indications of inaccuracies in perception (vague about what day of the week it is at times) and in judgment are because of her problem of Drive Control and Defenses. Thought Processes receive a very high profile score because thinking is succinct, relevant, and clear. Attention, concentration, memory and other thought functions do not show interference. Synthetic Functioning, on the other hand, is less adaptive, in that she tends not to use past experience well in dealing with present difficulties and holds out a fairly poor prognosis for utilization of psychotherapy.

Profile 5 is that of a playwright of some modest success who seems to have too poor Thought Processes to be very promising professionally, despite a rather good ARISE. He is an overideational and very anxious person who needs high doses of tranquilizers to be able to function at all. Extensive psychotherapeutic work on his apperceptive distortions (which are associated with overwhelming anxiety, apparently induced by an extremely anxious and probably psychotic mother) appears indicated and only moderately successful even over the short term. In his case, the fairly good ability for creativity (ARISE) is offset by his poor Thought Processes and poor Defensive Functioning. His success at writing is very much of the fringe variety, and chances are that he belongs to that group of artists who have access to the unconscious in the first phases of Regression in the Service of the Ego but hardly any synthesizing-integrating ability in the second phase of the oscillation. His poor Object Relationships are a negative psychotherapeutic factor, and the low Autonomous and Synthetic Functions are poor long-range prognostic signs for this schizophrenic person.

Ego Function Profile #3

	Reality Testing	Judgment	Sense of Reality of Reality	Regulat. & Cont. of Drives	Object Relat.	Thought Process	ARISE	Defense Functs.	Stimulus Barrier	Auton. Functs.	Synthet. Functs.
13											
12											
11											
10											
9											
8						•					
7							•		•		
6					•						
5								•		•	
4	•	•	•	•							
3											•
2											
1											

Ego Function Profile #4

Reality Testing	Judgment	Sense of Reality of Reality	Regulat. & Cont. of Drives	Object Relat.	Thought Process	ARISE	Defense Functs.	Stimulus Barrier	Auton. Functs.	Synthet. Functs.

EGO FUNCTION PROFILE #5

Profile 6, for a cheerful comparison, is that of a normal person. It is a hospital worker who was interviewed and rated by people who did not know her previously. Several of us on the project knew her fairly well for a couple of years and suggested her for the normal sample. As can be seen, only her ARISE, her creativity potential, is fairly low, which is quite consistent with the social impression she makes of living happily without too great a spark of inspiration.

Hopefully, it was demonstrated that the diagnosis of schizophrenia can be made usefully and reliably. While the nomothetic use of the term seems justified by defining the schizophrenic syndrome as lying at the low end of a range of ego functions, the individual idiographic, highly personal constellation is emphasized. It may remain useful to add to the ego-psychological statements and diagnostic formulations some descriptive terms such as acute, subacute, chronic, as well as such terms as catatonic symptomatology, paranoid ideation, etc.

The ego-psychological conception of the schizophrenic syndrome permits us to understand the coexistence of neurotic symptoms; also, as the system of forces affecting the ego function balance changes, the result may be a hysterical, obsessive, compulsive, or other syndrome. The forces involved may be a change in the neurogenic factors, e.g., as modified by psychotropic drugs, or a change in the psychogenic factors brought about by a spontaneous or planned modification of the milieu or by insight psychotherapy.

The ego function approach to diagnosis has the further advantage that it is part of a larger dynamic conceptual scheme that permits us to understand not only movement from one diagnostic syndrome to another, but also the *coexistence* of supposedly discrete phenomena, such as obsessions, phobias, and hysterical symptoms in someone primarily diagnosed as showing the schizophrenic syndrome. This approach allows us to understand that the various symptoms are merely different dynamic attempts at conflict resolutions.

The ego-psychological definition of the schizophrenic syndrome, by clearly stated, ratable criteria, should improve inter-rater reliability. An ego-psychological diagnosis has the advantage *vis-à-vis* the traditional "mental status" diagnosis by signs and symptoms in the fact that signs and symptoms are discontinuous, but ego functions are continuous (16). The stability of the diagnostic implications, as mentioned earlier in reference to Beck's paper (1), has to be understood as possibly a pseudo-problem. The patient has no obligation to remain schizophrenic and this

EGO FUNCTION PROFILE #6

| Reality Testing | Judgment | Sense of Reality of Self & Object World | Regulat. & Cont. of Drives | Object Relat. | Thought Process | ARISE | Defense Functs. | Stimulus Barrier | Auton. Functs. | Synthet. Functs. |

13
12
11
10
9
8
7
6
5
4
3
2
1

conceptualization helps us understand why he may move to other parts of the diagnostic continuum, including normality.

I certainly believe that some schizophrenics are curable, i.e., reversible to where by any method the personality is not distinguishable from the relatively normal. In some schizophrenics this reversal may be of a reasonable stability and one may expect as much stability from it as from any process, including the psychodynamic constellations in "normal" people (20). Many other schizophrenics reach either only a partial reversibility or, if full reversibility, one of a less stable nature.

Nevertheless, the nomothetic connotation "schizophrenic syndrome" remains useful. There are enough *intragroup similarities among people at a point diagnosed as schizophrenic* to differentiate them, on the basis of intergroup differences, from other groups of people.

Having said earlier that I do not believe "once a schizophrenic, always a schizophrenic," and having given reasons for this view, I regretfully also add that to overstate this position would be a mistake. The unfortunate reality at present is that the majority of people with schizophrenic personalities do not get into treatment anywhere. If they do get into a hospital there is little chance for them to get the sort of treatment likely to reverse the process. Even more unfortunately, not all the schizophrenic people treated by the best available means and people become non-schizophrenic forever, or even at all. Therefore, the diagnostic concept of the schizophrenic syndrome, realistically speaking (even allowing for some spontaneous cures) is still useful for conveying the information that once schizophrenic, one is extremely likely to retain—or regress again to—schizophrenic or other severe psychopathology. To say anything else for the majority of the population involved would be a pipe dream. It will be our job to change this dream into reality by research and by community mental health measures which should go a long way towards prevention of at least manifestly severe disorders and/or their earlier treatment and greater reversibility.

ACKNOWLEDGMENTS

This chapter is part of a study "Ego Function Patterns in Schizophrenia," supported by NIMH Grant MH 14260, carried out under the auspices of the Postdoctoral Program for Study and Research in Psychology, New York University—Leopold Bellak, M.D., Principal Investigator. I wish to acknowledge with appreciation the cooperation of the Psychiatry Departments, The Roosevelt Hospital, New York City, Gracie Square Hospital, New York City, and the Lincoln Institute for Psychotherapy, New York City, in making their clinical facilities available for this project.

I acknowledge with thanks the contributions of the other members of the research team to the work reported in this paper: Marvin Hurvich, Ph.D., Helen Gediman, Ph.D., Patricia Crawford, B.A., Jacob Cohen, Ph.D., Morris Eagle, Ph.D., Nancy Edwards, Ph.D., Stanley Grand, Ph.D., Nancy Israel, Ph.D., David Jacobs, Ph.D., Milton Kapit, Ph.D., Rose Kent, Ph.D., Frances Lippman, Ph.D., Mark Silvan, Ph.D., Lloyd Silverman, Ph.D., Stephen Silverman, Ph.D., Paul Wachtel, Ph.D., and Paula Wieluns, M.S.

REFERENCES

1. Beck, A.: Reliability of Psychiatric Diagnoses: I. A Critique of Systematic Studies. *American Journal of Psychiatry*, 119:210-216, 1962.
2. Bellak, L.: A Multiple-Factor Psychosomatic Theory of Schizophrenia. *Psychiatric Quarterly*, 23:738-755, 1949.
3. Bellak, L.: *Manic-Depressive Psychosis and Allied Conditions*. New York: Grune and Stratton, 1952.
4. Bellak, L.: Toward a Unified Concept of Schizophrenia. *Journal of Nervous and Mental Disease*, 121:60-66, 1955.
5. Bellak, L. (Ed.): *Schizophrenia: A Review of the Syndrome*. New York: Logos Press, 1958.
6. Bellak, L.: The Treatment of Schizophrenia and Psychoanalytic Theory. *Journal of Nervous and Mental Disease*, 131:39-46, 1960.
7. Bellak, L.: Methodology and Research in the Psychotherapy of Psychoses. *American Psychiatric Association Research Report No. 17*, 1963.
8. Bellak, L. and Hurvich, M.: A Systematic Study of Ego Functions. *Journal of Nervous and Mental Disease*, 148:569-588, 1969.
9. Bellak, L., Hurvich, M. and Crawford, P.: Psychotic Egos. *Psychoanalytic Review*, in press.
10. Bellak, L., Hurvich, M., Silvan, M. and Jacobs, D.: Toward an Ego-Psychological Appraisal of Drug Effects. *American Journal of Psychiatry*, 125:593-604, 1968.
11. Bellak, L. and Loeb, L. (Eds.): *The Schizophrenic Syndrome*. New York: Grune and Stratton, 1969.
12. Cancro, R. and Pruyser, P.: A Historical Review of the Development of the Concept. In Cancro, R. (Ed.), *The Schizophrenic Reactions: A Critique of the Concept, Hospital Treatment, and Current Research*. New York: Brunner/Mazel, Inc., 1969.
13. Fox, M.: An Ego-Psychological Approach to Therapy with Adolescents. Paper submitted in partial fulfillment of requirements for graduation, Postdoctoral Program, Department of Psychology, New York University, 1969.
14. Freeman, T., Cameron, J. L. and McGhie, A.: *Chronic Schizophrenia*. New York: International Universities Press, 1958.
15. Hurvich, M. and Bellak, L.: Ego Function Patterns in Schizophrenics. *Psychological Reports*, 22:299-308, 1968.
16. Hurvich, M.: Personal Communication.

17. Menninger, K., Mayman, M. and Pruyser, P.: *The Vital Balance.* New York: Viking Press, 1963.
18. Sechehaye, M. A.: *Symbolic Realization.* New York: International Universities Press, 1951.
19. Silvan, M., Jacobs, D., Bellak, L. and Crawford, P.: An Experimental Study of Ego Functions. Paper presented at Mid-winter meeting, American Psychoanalytic Association, New York, 1967.
20. Spence, D. (Ed.) : *The Broad Scope of Psychoanalysis: Selected Papers of Leopold Bellak.* New York: Grune and Stratton, 1967.

5

Diagnosis and Schizophrenia

ROY R. GRINKER, SR., M.D.

THE TITLE OF THIS SECTION of the book indicates that consideration is being given to the general usefulness, reliability, and validity of psychiatric diagnosis with special reference to schizophrenia. This evokes again the worn out topic of the medical or disease-entity model vs. the social model applied to psychological and behavioral deviance. The recent intense interest in contrasting these models does not indicate a commitment to understanding but: 1. a pragmatic approach for the nonmedical psychotherapists who try to avoid the illegitimate role of doctor by semantic escape hatches; and 2. the extreme human-rights advocates who contend that psychiatrists have no role as agents of society and, unlike physicians involved in infectious and contagious diseases, should not be permitted to isolate the destructive and self-destructive psychotic.

The diagnostic dilemma has revolved in circles for more than a century although the shifts have different sequences. The history of psychiatry presented by Alexander and Selesnick (1) clearly indicates how feelings and attitudes toward the deviances of behavior and their treatments reflect the value systems and ethics of the contemporary culture. It cannot be said that chaos existed for lack of classification and diagnoses before Morel (13) described dementia praecox in 1860, or Kraepelin's attempt (10) at total classification of mental disorders in 1883. Yet the latter caught on throughout all of its revisions until after World War II, when a group of military psychiatrists under the leadership of William Menninger revised, but did not essentially alter, the nosological classification.

The major emphasis on diagnosis, before the zenith of Freudian psychiatry, was stimulated by the legalities associated with commitment procedures and the failure of a wide variety of etiological and other than

59

"moral" therapeutic approaches to the psychoses. When dynamic psychiatry took hold in the United States and with the development of ego psychology, emphasis shifted to the understanding of individual patients and their problems with a corresponding neglect of scientific psychiatry as represented by diagnosis and classification.

In the 1950's and 1960's, psychiatry became recognized as a conglomerate of many sciences, all ultimately focusing on human mental problems. Therapies extended beyond the individual to families, groups and milieu, lobotomy, insulin, metrazol and electric shock were tried and were transiently popularized. Pharmacotherapy and behavioral therapy received great impetus and hypnotherapy was revived with new emphases. All these required, in this more sophisticated era, systems of evaluation based on diagnostic accuracy, rating scales, statistical reliability, and efforts at validation.

In addition, the component sciences of psychiatry (such as: biogenetics, neurochemistry, endocrinology, neurophysiology; information, communication and perceptual psychology; as well as the social sciences) offered new insights into the systems of cause, course and outcome which transcended dynamic psychology. When individual psychology, especially psychoanalysis, lost its dominant position as the sole explanation of etiology, the debate between proponents of the biomedical and those of the social model became redundant and obsolete. It became apparent that the many-sided, multifactorial, psychosomatic systems approaches (3) which include motivational or dynamic subsystems as a part only, require a basic sense of commonality of what is being studied. Diagnosis and classification as the first, albeit tottering, steps toward a scientific psychiatry became a necessity, and the humanistic brush-off had to be ignored despite dedicated therapeutic approaches to our individual patients. It matters not at all, at least to me, whether the labels applied are disease, disorder, deviance, faulty behavior, or even degrees of faulty education or stupidity, diagnosis has become a necessity for progress for every aspect of the large extended field that we call psychiatry.

Psychiatry in its role as a branch of medicine or as an applied science is concerned with diagnosis and various forms of therapy. This field is and has been extremely confused ever since man began to function as a medicine-man healer. It is only lately that scientific methods have been applied in an attempt to understand the rationale, methods, and results of psychotherapy. If we dodge the issue that there are categories of mental disturbances with specific course and prognosis, we have no science. There can be no scientific therapy without clinical categories as guidelines to facilitate the study of the life history of specific disturbances, their spontaneous course, and the interrelationships among causative factors. Studies of the various treatments for mentally ill patients require establishing diagnostic categories, defining the methods applicable to each, and developing criteria for results (3).

The scientific attitude is characterized by curiosity expressed in the form of three questions: What, how, and why? The order of these questions is important since causes (*how*) and purposes (*why*) are not understandable unless we know *what* we are studying or talking about. The means by which we ascertain the *what* are truly important but at least by any method the scientist attempts to define the *whats*, placing them in some system of classification.

In psychiatry the sterility of descriptive and nosological psychiatry led to its abandonment when psychoanalysis overpromised answers to *how* and *why* questions through its emphasis on motivation and meaning. The underemphasis and derogation of clinical observations of behavior was associated with a studied neglect of diagnosis and classification. Such negative approaches will always obstruct sound clinical research and, inevitably, studies of causal relations.

Paul Meehl (11), a distinguished psychologist, critically states: "Rather than decrying nosology, we should become masters of it, recognizing that some of our psychiatric colleagues have in recent times become careless and even unskilled in the art of formal diagnosis." The philosopher Kaplan (9) indicates how every classification serves some purpose to disclose relationships that must be taken into account, no matter what.

Why is it true that diagnosis is important for progress? The traditional method in medicine is history-taking and examination leading to diagnosis preceding treatment. Difficulties in developing an adequate nosological classification have resulted in lack of agreement on the value of specific treatments. Recent studies have demonstrated the wide variations of diagnosis among psychiatrists from various countries. The diagnosis of schizophrenia in the United States is made many times more often than in the United Kingdom where the manic-depressive label is used ten times more frequently. For the borderline syndrome I have found that there are about a dozen synonyms used in various psychiatric centers, perhaps because the borderline has no position in our official classification as yet (7).

In general, it is proper to ask, "Diagnosis for what?" Any set of diagnostic categories should add valid predictive variance but not necessarily for all (6). Depending on the purposes of diagnosis, the traits might vary, excluding the legalities and the secondary rationalizations made post hoc to justify procedures. Thus, salient attributes of a patient are utilized for various purposes.

A skilled observer sat in on many of my diagnostic conferences to observe the process prior to discussing my methods with me and to attempt a discrimination between the use of a matching vs. a clustering model. At first glance, matching symptoms with stereotypes seems to dominate since quantification is crude if at all possible. Actually, the clinician operates more with clustering than with matching techniques. Suppose we observe a pervasive (high quality) A, with which associated traits of a, b, c, . . . n, would be expected, a cluster would be formed. One can work either way: first, find the big piece of the jig-saw puzzle and *then* the small pieces, or second, observe the small pieces to cohere into a larger gestalt. When traits are not associated or are negatively correlated with the lead trait, the clustering of the original gestalt is broken and traits are clustered around a new lead trait. This process can go on until the best cluster of traits is found. Thus clustering is associated with weighing of traits.

I believe that most well-trained and experienced clinicians utilize this process, sometimes automatically, in the function of their internal computers. In simple language and programming, the clinicians' internal processes correspond to the highly complicated statistical processes fed into computers for clustering procedures and multiple discriminant-function analyses which should fit, and in the borderline case (7) did, with traits retranslated back into ego functions. Given a common language and agreed-upon definitions, psychodiagnosis should reach good reliability.

The hitch is not only in definition but the exclusion of much data even among pure clinicians. The dynamic school overlooks much of behavior and the behaviorally-oriented school ignores large amounts of data about feelings and concerns. Both have a tendency to overlook biogenetic, family, communication, biochemical, and physiological systems of data which are becoming increasingly available and valid. Psychodiagnosis in one- to two-hour sessions may be a brilliant narcissistic exercise for the professor to astound his students, but we know the results are not impressive over the long run. Criticisms of diagnostic reliability and hence usefulness should not result in abandoning the process, but lead to inclusion of extended areas of information requiring much more time than an interview and/or a conference.

When we survey various diagnostic classifications of which there are many for psychiatric disturbances, we find about fifty percent are still extant. They all have some kind of logic such as Kraepelin's similar cause, course, and outcome in imitation of Koch's postulates. A few other dimensions may be mentioned such as exogenous-endogenous, acute-chronic, organic-functional, hereditary-environment, disease-reactive, etc.

Referral of patients to clinical psychologists for testing when uncertainty reaches the psychiatrists' threshold has decreased in the last decade. Although psychometrics, including the Rorschach and T.A.T., do add considerable content, they constitute the framework within which the psychologist essentially conducts a clinical interview not much different than does the psychiatrist and with far less skill in differentiating common human qualities from psychopathology.

There are three purposes for diagnosis: to develop a scientific etiology, to establish prognosis, and for clinical purposes to reflect the proper treatment. To deny diagnosis because it places a "pejorative externally damning label" on a person and to decry objective scientific attitudes is to carry the humanistic and admirable concepts of love and hope to extremes.

Good diagnostic systems require unbiased theoretical orientations, simplicity, reliability and consistency over time, acceptability in relation to processes that can elicit traits, such as interviewing technique, and comprehensiveness or culture-free criteria (5). In truth, our reliability is low and our measures of validity are still embryonic. Furthermore, although our central themes on which diagnosis are based are increasingly sophisticated, they are still limited to specific foci as, for example, to disorders of communications, perceptions, behaviors, clinical symptoms, patient-family transactions, levels of regression or coping devices.

The clinician uses any one or all of these sources that are available to him. His diagnostic acumen is based on his capacity to utilize the essence from all sources with which to build a gestalt, characteristic of a symptom-complex currently generally recognized and labelled. Such a technique does not, however, suffice as a method for scientific studies, for example, to delineate a new category or to develop subcategories or typologies.

In general, scientific information is obtained by collecting observations and measurements under specific conditions, encoding the data in terms characteristic of the statistical model to be used, processing the data, and checking the results again against the original events. Royce (14) exemplifies this in terms applicable to clinical research: 1. Standard conditions of observations as on a nursing unit; 2. under specified conditions even though the variables are not controlled; 3. by many persons; 4. observing specified variables; 5. repetitive observations; 6. statistical analyses leading to the determination of the contribution of each variable. To this we must add the checking of results for their logical relationship with clinical experience.

Shakow (15), who has spent most of his life investigating schizophrenia and has developed new theories, indicates that classification is absolutely necessary. This requires an accurate description of a variety of phenomena, their syndromization and the assignment of patients to categories or subgroups. He also points out that a multifactorial process requires a multidisciplinary approach. The methods of approach, the investigators' mode or biases, the stimuli utilized may consist of a wide set of variables, most of which are without merit. Most important is the differentiation between the trivial and the important, a value judgment that is difficult to make. One of Shakow's dichotomies which I have also presented is the difficulty of discriminating between schizophrenia as a qualitative or quantitative process in relation to normality. Whether one discusses anxiety, associations, behaviors, perceptions, etc., or differentiates between regression as in dreams or childishness, the problem is the same. It is the basis of the controversy between continuity and discontinuity within the field of mental illness.

Nevertheless, whenever we reach a compromise indicating unity and use such terms as holistic, process or global, we become satisfied, sense closure, and flee from the operational. Empirical research requires the observation of symptoms, behaviors, or functions but these are far from fundamental causes. The sociologist looks outward to the social world of experience with his special techniques. The psychologist looks inward at processes that he terms intervening variables and the biologist, all too frequently reductionistic, searches for genic, biochemical, or physiological deficits. Yet each focus constitutes a transacting part of the larger field from which hypothetical constructs or theory may be developed and tested. Actually a nosological and classificatory focus of the interdisciplinary components of psychiatry may facilitate their articulation.

In the early days of psychoanalysis in this country, there was a general air of caution about analyzing persons whose egos could collapse under the strain of the therapy. Psychological tests were employed to give the analyst a quick look at the patient's ego strength. When the various schools of therapy began to use their techniques for all cases, disregarding any warning, trouble began. I speak not only of psychoanalysis, but also of hypnotherapy, Rogerian therapy, etc., applied to prepsychotic or latent psychotics, the results of which I have seen for myself.

Many psychiatrists say they want to protect the patient from being labelled and thereby ruined in his social, work, and family life. We succumbed during the war and said our patients had operational fatigue. Are the standard terms any worse than one which defines levels of dyscontrol? This, despite Karl Menninger's struggle against diagnosis (12), is a system of diagnosis based on degrees of release of aggression—a system of classification based on depth of regression.

Man is not the only animal capable of symbolic representation, but this function achieved its highest development in a jump-step to what we call humanness. How far down the evolutionary scale do living beings recognize signs for categories of dangerous or supportive elements in the environment is not known. But man has developed logical structure that enables him to classify and categorize symbolically, resulting in a vast economy of energy through the creation of systems of communication. We need not attribute this function to a later developing scientific method— we call it ordinary common sense, absent in the defective or mentally retardate. In stages of schizophrenia of some types, regression is associated with prelogical thinking or, according to Arieti (2), paleological thinking, desymbolization, desocialization, and retreat from emotion.

In our quest for certainty, however, we have almost automatically forced natural phenomena and the laws pertaining to them into the straitjacket of continuity. We tend to close the arc of open circles and demand universal laws because of our abhorrence of discontinuities, belying our empirical information, and our concepts become comfortably uniform. This may be one of the reasons why some psychiatrists obliterate obvious differences and try to make of all psychopathology one disease.

Let us suppose that all psychological, mental, or behavioral deviations —for this imaginative purpose the name is not important—are phenomena resulting from problems of living. These could be called uneconomical ways of adaptation, adjustment, or coping to life stresses. Then these responses could be categorized, classified, and named according to the observable stress-stimuli, the degree of regression or the coping devices. Unfortunately, it is not the stress-stimuli that are specific but instead the stress-response to whatever stimuli. Thus the permanent question remains: Why does one person respond differently than another? I direct this question, not alone to the schizophrenic, but also to neuroses, character and personality disorders, and nonschizophrenic psychoses.

It is not sufficient to state, as many do categorically, that the significant variable is the mother-child relationship, the family deviations, communication or social reinforcing techniques, or traumatic experiences, etc.

No significant relationships have even been established between psychopathology or its type with specific early experiences. Other factors are biogenetic factors such as drive strength, neurogenic hyperexcitability eventuating in unendurable anxiety, amine transmethylation, autoimmune allergic processes, elevated lactate-pyruvic acid ratios, etc. Add on to these, triggering early and even late stressful experiences of one type or another in family, group, and social living and we have a biopsychosocial etiological gestalt.

How, then, can we classify psychiatric illness? Certainly not by means of symptoms and not by isolated etiological factors that exclude all others. Ideally, diagnoses should only be made after an exhaustive search for all possible contributing etiological factors. This requires too much time and expense and also delays the scientific purposes of diagnostic classification: to enable a wide variety of disciplines to study the "what," to test a wide variety of treatments, including the natural spontaneous course, and to determine the life history to the final end.

In the meantime, we should abstain from diagnostic nihilism, grand holistic generalizations, and minute classifications. Granted that something in between is temporary and imperfect, but applying eponyms to syndromes is only an old-fashioned childish game.

It seems as if the need to place the "conglomerate" schizophrenia into the framework of a system were a new enterprise. Actually the now vanished great naturalists of the early twentieth century were able to visualize the relationships of many foci of knowledge within a broad field. They, too, did not deal only in analogies and homologies, but also in dynamic relationships of part-functions, differentiation, gradients, and homeostasis.

Today, thanks to the ability of von Bertalanffy (4) to synthesize, entities—rather than conglomerations of parts—have been considered as systems. Living systems have been characterized as open with organizations that maintain wholeness, regulate parts, seek goals, change goals, and differentiate in growth. A system may be real, conceptual, or theoretical.

A by-product has been the application of systems theory to all sciences in an attempt to develop isomorphism and thus unification of science. The application of common and essential dynamic processes from cells to culture, in fact applicable to all levels whether molecular or molar, coincides with the idea of continuity of all mental illness held by some psychiatrists. I have spoken before of the attempt to close gaps and prefer to consider the possibility of discontinuities that include degrees of commonalities while at the same time not excluding individual properties at various levels. I feel more comfortable in conceptualizing hierarchical levels in transaction with each other.

Cybernetic feedback and homeostatic steady states do not sufficiently emphasize the principles of differentiation, growth, and creativity. For such evolutionary processes first clearly communicated for neurophysiology by Hughlings Jackson and for psychology by Sigmund Freud, there is the opposite of devolution and regression which enables us to understand better disease as a loss of higher function (a negative) and the release of lower level processes (a positive). Disease then is just those characteristics. In my opinion, any understanding of typologies of dysfunction requires more knowledge of phases of the life cycle, each of which has its own process characteristics, its own vulnerability, its own coping devices, and its own regression patterns.

Systems require several conceptual approaches, such as the constitutional which studies structure and function, and the integrative which considers integrative processes and resistances against disintegration and determinants that are disclosed in its functions and purposes as a whole in transactions with other systems. Thus, sophisticated theories or operations are multivariate rather than two variable or linear cause and effect. Multiple observers at different positions are needed.

Psychopathology, thus, is a system disturbance, never loss of a single function. It is only by viewing psychopathology in this manner as a system that we can establish diagnostic criteria and analyze the "what," for example, of schizophrenia.

If we consider ourselves as humanists who are devoted to the loving care of our patients (as all good physicians should) and approach schizophrenia or for that matter any category of behavior deviance as psychotherapists, we are not scientists. If we intend to further our understanding in the hope that better understanding of the human condition under stress will lead to the development of more effective therapies, then we need more than love and hope. In truth, we require a sound systems approach; multidisciplinary consciences, if not operations and capacity to endure contemporary uncertainty to arrive eventually at a better concept of growth, differentiation, and disease.

Ordinarily, we attempt to reach a diagnosis quickly, sometimes after one to several interviews. The therapist then chooses the place for and the type of treatment best suited for amelioration or rehabilitation. Should one method fail, another may be tried although some therapists continue their efforts using the one therapy they are familiar with for years with faith and sincerity.

It is clear that he uses clinical phenomena reported by informants and the patient himself and the behavior demonstrated by the patient. He has no time nor instruments nor skill to elicit factors not demonstrable in these final common pathways. His view is of the top of the iceberg, what is visible on the surface. Through years of experience, with success and failure, he learns the salient features of schizophrenia and its types. This kind of research produces results for the programming of his internal computer which has no voice, rarely can transmit its programs to others and dies with him.

For *research* the problem is somewhat different. Diagnosis is followed by a careful study of component parts of the system schizophrenia on which he wishes to focus. He has to choose the *what* of schizophrenia to prepare a way to his investigating and finding a more correct and more extensive definition of *what*. This is somewhat like trying to dry one's self with a wet towel. His *not-what* is not entirely useless since these form the background noise (or what we call controls) against which he can recognize the messages of the *what*.

Can we recognize by clinical means the particular *whats* even if only tentatively? This has been the problem of classifications, the usefulness of which are not nullified by their variety since the classification of schizophrenia has many purposes and these vary with observer position, intent and bias. The essential element is that there is a line of logic as the basis of any classification.

For example, Kraepelin used a modification of Koch's postulates: similar cause, course, and outcome. Wrong though this turned out to be, it served heuristic purposes for decades. Bleuler used a system of primary symptoms. Others have used informational processes, qualities of anxiety, perceptual feedback, set, etc. Some, like Shakow, have combined a variety of detailed variables, others enunciate global statements such as deficiency in organizational principle.

These all represent beginnings or attempts at finding leverage on the many variables or subsystems of the larger system schizophrenia. The process is difficult because many passes have to be made or what Freedman and Rubin call hill-climbing procedures to develop not one but several dominant hills (7). Utilizing measurements of many subsystems as traits derived from many disciplines, all using the same clinical material defining the *what*, as we "know" it now, we can develop boundaries and categories. Then and only then can we talk about multiple causes, temporal relationship, and outcome.

I believe that the concept schizophrenia has considerable proven validity if we recognize that we are confronted with a group of processes having common features but many subcategorical differences and that the purposes of these diagnoses are the practical determinants of subsequent therapy. For an understanding of the several schizophrenic processes the validity of the concept is deficient because of the existence of gaps in our knowledge of many parts of the whole system.

Actually we are accustomed to validate the concept largely by means of the study of psychological and behavioral phenomena either in a specific cross-sectional slice of time or in truncated longitudinal sections. Variability of behavior or response is now not discarded as an interfering artifact but as an essential characteristic requiring repetitive tests; and studies under so-called resting or idling situations need amplification by means of well-defined challenges and designs oriented toward recording categories of responses (8).

Modern psychological research has been effective in moving our interest in diagnosis from the primary and secondary symptoms of schizophrenia to more sophisticated approaches. To name only a few contributors to this volume, Holzman focuses on a defect in perceptual feedback. Spohn finds a deficiency in information processes because of inconstant attention. Burnham has studied inadequate differentiation and integration leading to faulty object relations, lack of autonomy and unreliable reality constructs. Shakow discusses neophobia, lack of spontaneity, faulty scanning and articulation, etc. It is interesting that most of these investigators attempt to articulate their interpretations with biological, especially autonomic, failures. It may be generalized that weak central control and organizational abnormalities should be closely related with pervasive qualitatively deficient homeostatic regulation.

What we as psychologists and psychiatrists study are the psychological and behavioral emergent manifestations of primary, i.e., basic, biological defects. From these emergent phenomena clues may be obtained that point to variables in schizophrenia which can round out or fill the gaps of the total schizophrenic concept and its subcategories. Basically this is a systems approach from which concepts of the schizophrenias may be improved beyond the simple-minded diagnoses for clinical purposes.

REFERENCES

1. Alexander, F. G. and Selesnick, S. T.: *The History of Psychiatry*. New York: Harper and Row, 1966.
2. Arieti, S.: *Interpretation of Schizophrenia*. New York: Brunner, 1955.

3. Bellak, L. (Ed.): *Schizophrenia: A Review of the Syndrome.* New York: Logos, 1958.
4. Bertalanffy, L. von: *General System Theory.* New York: Braziller, 1968.
5. Eron, L. D.: *The Classification of Behavior Disorders.* Chicago: Aldine, 1966.
6. Grinker, R. R., Sr. and Nunnally, J. C.: The Phenomena of Depression. In Katz, M. M., Cole, J. O., and Barton, W. E. (Eds.), *The Role and Methodology of Classification in Psychiatry and Psychopathology.* Washington, D.C.: U. S. Government Printing Office, 1967.
7. Grinker, R. R., Sr., Werble, B., and Drye, R. C.: *The Borderline Syndrome.* New York: Basic Books, 1968.
8. Grinker, R. R., Sr.: An Essay on Schizophrenia and Science. *Archives of General Psychiatry,* 20:1-24, 1969.
9. Kaplan, A.: *The Conduct of Inquiry.* San Francisco: Chandler, 1964.
10. Kraepelin, E.: *Dementia Praecox and Paraphrenia.* Edinburgh: Livingstone, 1919.
11. Meehl, P. E.: Some Ruminations on the Validation of Clinical Procedures. *Canadian Journal of Psychology,* 13:102-128, 1959.
12. Menninger, K. A., Mayman, M. and Pruyser, P.: *The Vital Balance.* New York: Viking, 1963.
13. Morel, B. A.: *Traité des Maladies Mentales.* Paris: Masson, 1860.
14. Royce, J. R.: *Psychology and the Symbol.* New York: Random House, 1965.
15. Shakow, D.: Understanding Normal Psychological Function: Contributions from Schizophrenia. *Archives of General Psychiatry,* 17:306-319, 1967.

6

Syndrome, Yes; Disease Entity, No

KARL MENNINGER, M.D.

DOCTOR CANCRO AND COLLEAGUES, authoritative colleagues, and wistful learners and listeners: I address all of you with a feeling of personal gratitude for the honor to me that Doctor Cancro announced in his introduction. I thank him too for letting me come last on the program so that I will not have to be blind in my attacks upon my fellow speakers. I'll have the benefit of having heard all the brilliant things that they have said.

I was thinking in preparation for coming here of the Zurich Conference, which some of us attended in 1957. I got out the four volumes of that International Congress for Psychiatry (5), as it was called, where there were so many meetings in so many parts of town and so many different points of view expressed. Doctor Bleuler (2) drew the very apt conclusion that what we discovered was that we had no agreement on anything except that this was a very important topic which deserved the concentration and further study of all of us. I remembered Omar Khayyám's comment (3),

> "Myself when young did eagerly frequent
> Doctor and Saint, and heard great argument
>   About it and about: but evermore
> Came out by the same door where in I went. . . .
> There was the Door to which I found no Key;
> There was the Veil through which I might not see."

I remind myself—and my audience—that these things were not said specifically about the syndrome that we are talking about today. But perhaps. . . .

71

Doctor Grinker makes a little fun of what he regards as the prevalent Topeka point of view. I don't know that he is accurate. It's *my* point of view that he is attacking, and Doctor Pruyser's. I don't think that all others at the Menninger Clinic can be accused of the childishness, stubbornness, and scientific stupidity which seem to be attached to our views. Just me. And if anyone puts any reliance on hope and love in the therapy of their patients, let him not do so with the understanding that this is generally recognized or approved; it's only something that I have suggested. How effective it will be depends upon the particular individual using it.

Now Doctor Grinker's jokes are not meant unkindly, nor do I take them with any offense or discouragement. My confidence in the persistence of hope is such that I recall an encounter with Doctor Grinker on the Midway of the University of Chicago campus on a chilly September day in 1930. Doctor Bartemeier and I were seeking a place to have lunch, having been in the city only a day or two, when we encountered Doctor Grinker. He was most cordial and having welcomed us to Chicago, he asked us what we were doing there. We told him we had come to undertake psychoanalytic training. This was the wrong thing for us to have said! Doctor Grinker, I know, will laughingly recall that he burst into a scornful tirade at this absurd project. He wondered how intelligent scientists could become interested in such a ridiculous and time-wasting process. This was a little discouraging to us, since we had come to Chicago at considerable trouble and expense, hoping that this venture in further professional training would turn out well. For the professor to indicate his high disapproval of it was dismaying.

A few years later, I think about four, when Doctor Alexander, Doctor Bartemeier, Doctor Blitzsten, I, and a few others had collaborated on establishing the Chicago Psychoanalytic Institute, we were very proud to discover among our most distinguished and promising candidates the same Doctor Roy R. Grinker. Now if this 180-degree shift could occur about one matter, it might occur about another. So hope seems to well up in my heart, in spite of its impropriety, and I shall blithely proceed.

I was looking over some notes on what would be appropriate and interesting to say in these last few minutes of a most interesting and stimulating morning, during which a lot of thinking has been brought forth by Doctor Altschule, Doctor Arieti, Doctor Bellak, and Doctor Grinker. What could I say in closing that would not be tedious, would not be flippant, would not be tiresome, would not tax your patience? I got to thinking how it was that I developed misgivings about schizophrenia

after having considered myself for a few years a schizophrenia expert!
(I had contributed copiously to the Association for Research in Nervous
and Mental Diseases, and to numerous professional journals.) Aschaffenburg's *Handbuch* (1) had just brought out Bleuler's *Gruppe der Schizophrenien,* and I had read it in German, which was quite a job, and
discussed it lengthily in English, which was easier. We had become excited
over what seemed to be a great new idea, not realizing that the idea was
changing right under our very noses at that very moment. Just at that
time, however, our studies of the literature were somewhat interrupted
by a practical event of great world significance, namely, the influenza
epidemic of 1918-1920. We soon had little time to read anything; people
were dying all around us and even among us. Not only that, but there
were constantly coming into the hospital—the psychiatric hospital then
called the Boston Psychopathic Hospital—patients whose story was that
the mental illness now manifested as a reason for admission had begun
more or less directly in connection with a recent attack of influenza,
usually a few days or weeks afterward. Naturally these cases were more
frequent toward the latter part of the epidemic, but they started coming
almost at the very beginning.

Doctor Lowrey and I, and some others observed a great many of
these patients and made a great many notes, some of which I still have and
some of which I have published. The point of interest now is that in a
large number of these patients we discovered, with our diagnostic routines
and acumen, clear and definite and obvious and classical pictures of
what we then called dementia praecox. (We were then changing this
name and calling it Schizophrenia. It became a taboo thing for anybody
on the staff to say dementia praecox, because it indicated that he had
not read Bleuler's article.) We made careful, competent diagnostic studies.
Doctor Roy does me wrong, unintentionally I am sure, when he says that I
do not believe in diagnosis; it's just that we have a little different definition of the word diagnosis. Certainly we made every effort in those days
to make a diagnosis according to established criteria, modalities, and
procedures. We came to the conclusion that a large number of the cases
we saw following the influenza epidemic were clearly and definitely
Schizophrenia. Some of them were hebephrenic, some were catatonic, and
some were a half a dozen other kinds of Schizophrenia which we were
beginning to recognize.

Some five years later, I employed a social worker in Boston to follow
up all the cases that we had seen during the influenza epidemic, especially
those that we had called Schizophrenia. They had been sent to Westboro,

Danvers, and other state hospitals. The astonishing discovery was that almost none of these cases could be found in the hospitals. They had nearly all recovered and—for the most part—gone home. Now, you must remember this was at a time when a case of Schizophrenia which recovered had been misdiagnosed, prima facie! There is—or was—no equivocation and no joke about this. We were informed by the officials of the various state hospitals (which were well equipped then with good psychiatrists) that our diagnoses had been in error—that this or that case was *not* schizophrenia, as we had assumed, but either manic-depressive psychosis or amentia or some other benign condition which *did* recover. The fact that these patients recovered demonstrated only that our diagnosis in the Boston Psychopathic Hospital had been wrong.

Well, my narcissism was considerably injured by this discovery, but it got me thinking. What was the *real* mistake we had made? Was it a mistake in observation, or a mistake in conceptualizing, or a mistake in labelling? I have kept on thinking about these questions ever since.

My objection to the standard view, you see, is not that there is no well-known combination of impaired associations with withdrawn cathexis, or of emotional flattening and disharmony. I point out, as do others, that this is at best a *disjunctive* syndrome; many cases with two or three pathognomic symptoms are lacking the other two or three! But my real point of difference is that to me these syndromes seem to be transient, changing, and variable. I began to go through the same psychological process that Bleuler did. Remember that he swayed to the right and he swayed to the left, and he swayed toward Freud's psychodynamic conceptions, and then he swayed away from that back to the Kraepelinian notion of an essentially organic condition. Then you remember that he ended up thinking, "Well, there are many different kinds of schizophrenias and perhaps we should have designations for each of them, and only a general formulation for all of them."

I think nobody denies the schizophrenic syndrome as a matter of agreed description. But to say that this is a reified creature, a *Disease,* is to make all its multiformity correspond to somebody's precise (and to my notion artificial) definition. The assumption that we *know* so definitely that a *disease* by the name of *Schizophrenia* (with a capital *S*) exists and persists, implies a certainty of knowledge that none of us possesses. If one uses the word *disease* in its commonly accepted sense, then the reification of the schizophrenic pictures as all being phases or aspects of this "disease" is unsupportable. It is accordingly seen by various colleagues in the same country and by colleagues in different countries quite differently, as Doctor Grinker pointed out.

In the third place, in spite of all that has been said, the name *and* the naming of it, an instance of Schizophrenia implies a hopelessness of outcome which has a derogatory effect on the patient. This is an important consideration because we are speaking of a psychological disease. To be told that one has cancer is discouraging, I concede, but the designation of cancer, the psychological effect of being told that one has it, does not in itself materially affect the disease (in most cases) and may lead to corrective steps. In a psychological disease, on the other hand, the individual is nearly always negatively affected by the knowledge and the tendency toward the establishment of a self-fulfilling prophesy develops. The name spells great knowledge and great pessimism, neither of which the doctor may have. But the patient, knowing the prevalent opinion about such a disease, begins to feel pessimistic. So do those about him, and all begin to fulfill these expectations.

It seems to me that we saw a demonstration of all this on a grand scale in the old state hospital situation, where nobody expected the patients to get well and almost none did. The doctors didn't expect them to get well, and this fact was soon communicated to relatives, and likewise to the patients. Nobody expected anybody to get well, and the tendency was for a lot of patients to do what was expected of them.

As soon as the whole attitude and the expectations of the doctors and relatives changed, the prognosis began to change. Doctors began to be interested in the possibilities of cure; more doctors began to appear on the scene; more personnel began to work hopefully with the patients; and more recoveries began to occur. I don't think this was because the later doctors were any better than the earlier doctors, but you later doctors certainly have a very much more positive and expectant attitude towards the possible courses of the schizophrenic (and other) syndromes than we earlier doctors did.

Finally, then, it seems to me that the diagnosis of schizophrenia has become pejorative and *declassé*. Just *because* of the public's superstitions, just because of our early medical ignorance, just because of a lot of historical and social things, I think it is simply not realistic to go on believing that the public can hear a word like Schizophrenia applied to oneself, or to one's child, or to one's wife with complete objectivity. You may say that we shouldn't be influenced by historical and social factors, but we *are* influenced by them, and patients are influenced by them, and our work is affected by them.

Let me follow the magnificent example of Doctors Bellak and Grinker and try to condense the rest of what I had planned to say. I share with Doctors Cancro and Pruyser the belief that the new official nosology of the American Psychiatric Association represents a regressive step. The adoption of the Meyerian concept of classification was a progressive move and to discard it after these years of struggle is tragic. Adolf Meyer was at a different medical school from mine and was held by us in high suspicion. Students of Doctor Southard regarded him no doubt as I am looked upon by the students of Doctor Grinker. We thought that no possible good could come out of Johns Hopkins. How could it be better illustrated than by this preposterous, nonsensical, absurd business of ergasiology and reaction syndrome? But I have come to recognize that Meyer's contribution was one of the greatest ever made to American psychiatry, equal, in fact, to anything that my own beloved Ernest Southard did. Adolf Meyer had a great idea; he wanted to get away, as George Engel has put it, from the stultifying influence of the Kraepelinian pigeonholes. He proposed "reaction types" for a way of viewing various psychiatric pictures. Now these reaction types have been abandoned in favor of some crystallized disease entities with fancy Greek names reminiscent of the Kraepelinian and pre-Kraepelinian epoch.

I am deeply flattered to learn that the Palo Alto Conference caught up with us in the idea of seeing coping devices in a continuum, and proposing this continuum as the basis for a better description of human error. I looked again at Chapter Seven of *The Vital Balance* (4) and was pleased to think that perhaps it had had some seed influence at that Conference. Doctor Grinker will remember this chapter in the book, for he referred to it; it deals with coping measures made by human beings grouped and arranged on an increasing (or decreasing) scale from better to worse. Instead of saying a patient is healthier, or better, one could say he is coping at a higher level. One could say that he is less depressed or less discouraged or less schizophrenic. But surely it is common knowledge that we all do better at some times than at other times, that we are less *invested* on some days than on others, that our thought processes are less disjunctive on some days than others, and so on. This is my way of looking at these cases—indeed, at all cases!

I really haven't anything new to contribute to this discussion. I believe everything I heard this morning. I liked everything I heard. (I just did not *understand* everything I heard.) I felt like Bleuler, swaying from one side to the other as I heard those able presentations.

But I still don't think diagnosis should be a matter of calling people names. I don't think diagnosis is distribution by labels, like a postal clerk tossing letters. If what comes out of the diagnostic process consigns an individual to condemnation, discourages him and dehumanizes him, it is not a true or proper medical diagnosis. I think it is a sort of twentieth-century version of witchcraft.

Remember, the witchcraft described and classified in the *Malleus Maleficarum* was a system, an elaborate and detailed classification. It had a logical theme. It said that such and such symptoms indicated the presence of a witch, Witch Type A, Witch Type B, etc. If the right symptoms were present, the name was forthcoming; the decision was made.

Now it's true that what we would do about the person who has this "Schizophrenia Type C" is different from what we did with those who had "Witch Type B." My point is that the tendency for human beings to generalize and categorize is *menschlich, menschlich, all zu menschlich.* We can't seem to *avoid* doing it. "He is a Negro." "She is a Jewess." "He is a Communist." "She is a criminal." This tendency to put labels on people is *human* enough, heaven knows, but it isn't *scientific* enough! None of these words really mean what the public thinks they mean. Suppose you have one-sixteenth Negro blood; are you a Negro? Suppose you once forged a check; are you a criminal? Well, the classification problems in psychiatry are far more difficult than these.

Of course there is a schizophrenic picture or syndrome, one which we see every day and which may or may not be synonymous with what some people call "psychosis" and with what some people call "dysorganization," and with what some people call "dyscontrol," or with what some people call other things that Doctor Grinker mentioned. There *is* such a syndrome and there is this tendency in everybody to "split," and to become disorganized and detached. There is not a person in the room whose behavior wouldn't at some moment of his existence reveal, to the right kind of scrutiny, the presence of some of this kind of behavior. But it takes not one but a sufficient number of swallows to make a summer and even swallows are migratory and can disappear. But this syndrome should not be given the designation of a disease as if it were a thing, a fixed thing, a thing which only a few unfortunate, stupid or otherwise unlucky individuals happen to get. For an individual so labelled is no longer a patient, a troubled individual seeking help. He is now a person announced as belonging to a special class of people to be feared, to be scorned, to be pitied, to be avoided, to be treated, perhaps, but always degraded, always remaining suspect in regard to predictability, adaptability, and competence. He is stigmatized even if he ceases to have any of the symptoms upon which the original disease labelling was established. It's like a cattle brand, or a slave brand.

It seems to me that that's what such pejorative labelling tends to do. I think that this is wrong, and I do see it as a matter of morality, a matter of ethics. I think it is not right for any of us to do this to any of us. Especially *we* who profess and strive to help people should avoid doing anything that, instead of helping, harms the individual who has come to us for help. *Nihil nocere.*

REFERENCES

1. Bleuler, E.: Dementia Praecox oder die Gruppe der Schizophrenien. In Aschaffenburg, G. (Ed.), *Handbuch der Psychiatrie*. Leipzig: Deuticke, 1911.
2. Bleuler, M.: Personal communication, 1957.
3. Khayyám, O.: The Rubáiyát. In Bartlett, J., *Familiar Quotations*, 11th Edition. Boston: Little, Brown & Co., 1946.
4. Menninger, K., Mayman, M., and Pruyser, P.: *The Vital Balance*. New York: Viking Press, 1963.
5. Stoll, W. A. (Ed.): Congress Report. Second International Congress of Psychiatry, Zurich, 1957. Zurich: Füssli, 1959.

7

Some General Comments and Introductory Remarks to the Panel Discussion

DAVID SHAKOW, Ph.D.

ON A RECENT OCCASION when I participated in a symposium on a topic like today's, I introduced my comments with a three-quarter-century-old quotation from D. Hack Tuke's *Dictionary of Psychological Medicine* (5). In his article on "Classification" in this compendium, Tuke said: "The wit of man has rarely been more exercised than in the attempt to classify the morbid mental phenomena covered by the term insanity. The result has been disappointing." A glance at the Appendix of the Menninger, Mayman, Pruyser volume (3) which presents such classifications in historical sequence only corroborates this judgment. Neither do I detect in any of our panelists an overwhelming passion for our present classification system.

Kluckhohn, Mowrer and Murray's simplification (1, 2) about the individual has always appealed to me. Their epitome is so felicitously phrased that it is difficult to be critical of it. They hold that any single personality comprises some characteristics like *all* other persons, some like *some* other persons, and some like *no* other person. It is this distinction among *universal, type,* and *individual* characteristics which touches centrally on our topic of today. The universal qualities in human personality are, of course, not at issue among our participants. It is in relation to the latter two aspects of the Kluckhohn, Mowrer and Murray classification —type versus individual—however, that we encounter disagreement among the panelists. At one end of the continuum, I suppose, we would have to place Karl Menninger, who holds forth in so positive and understanding a manner for the individual, idiosyncratic qualities in patients.

Doctor Altschule, in the context of a scholarly presentation of the problem of classification from the biological standpoint, also emphasizes the importance of diversity and individual reaction patterns. He believes, however, that for scientific purposes it would be necessary to invent the schizophrenia concept if it did not already exist. Classification may be absurd, but it is unavoidable. He holds, nevertheless, that the term schizophrenia itself should be abandoned, preferring the much older "Pinel's syndrome."

Doctor Arieti accepts the general notion of schizophrenia as a more or less homogeneous core, despite much in it that is variable, inconstant, and accessory. He redefines schizophrenia mainly around a concept of progressive teleologic regression, which involves: 1. a concretization of the concept; 2. a paleologic notion of thinking, which he develops on the groundwork laid by Levy-Bruhl and von Domarus; 3. desymbolization and desocialization; and 4. motor dysfunctions.

Doctor Bellak also accepts the usefulness of schizophrenia as a bio-psychosocial concept—at least at the heuristic level. He emphasizes the ego aspect and presents a technique for the more objective evaluation of schizophrenic characteristics by means of a combination of approaches. These are based on clinical and psychometric studies in which the various symptoms and traits are subsumed under twelve categories of ego functioning. He thus reworks the usual symptom-syndrome approach into an ego function approach in a dynamic way.

Doctor Grinker, in his customary forthright manner, looks behind some of the attempts to provide different models in this area and raises his eyebrows about some of the motivations. On the major issue I agree with him—it matters not from which branch of study one comes, the important point is the expertness and knowledge that entitles a person to make judgments in an area in which knowledge is at best partial. As to who is a behavioral scientist—I have long held the view that it is not a matter of *Fach* but of competence—it includes all of those who are qualified by knowledge, experience, and personality for dealing with behavior. Doctor Grinker argues for the view that diagnosis and classification are necessities for a scientific psychiatry. He is not deceived by the semantic traps which lie in the variety of labels that are used: disease, disorder, deviance, faulty education. He recognizes the legitimacy of much of the criticism of diagnostic reliability, but sees this as a challenge for doing more, rather than as a reason for abandoning such attempts. The loving care of patients has its own important place (in therapy, I presume), but for a science we need more than love and hope. His major suggestion for achieving the goal of a scientific psychiatry lies in open systems, in a sound systems approach along both constitutional and integrative lines. The approach also emphasizes ego functions traced out through both the internal computer of the experienced clinician and the external computer of multivariate, rather than linear, analysis deriving from the cooperative effort of many disciplines.

Now, let me state my own position. But first, my reactions to the panel presentations. I am highly sympathetic with Doctor Menninger's humanistic approach—not because it disregards the more conventional type of classification, but for two other reasons. The first lies in his attempt to deal with the problem dynamically and developmentally in terms of ego function in the handling of aggressivity. (In his emphasis on ego function he is in harmony with most of our other panelists.) The other contribution is the working through of what he has called his own "obsession" of collecting and presenting the trend of change in classification. The seventy-page Appendix of his book which has resulted from this pathology can only be characterized as I have once termed it, a *mitzvah*—a deed of great value—for which we are all indebted to him. Because the function of controversy in science is so important, his emphasis on the dynamics and the stages of ego dysfunction have undoubtedly had their influence on many of us whose predilection is for the more conventional handling of the problem.

But I do wish to raise a question about Doctor Menninger's moderately nihilistic attitude to classification. In this respect he is not like his teacher, Southard, although in so many other respects he is. I like to think of Doctor Menninger's approach in the context of his beloved trees—especially that 300-foot Topeka *ulmus* of which young Karl and his brothers were so proud. He was probably willing to accept it as an *ulmus americana* (if *that* really was its species). With his expertness he was, I am sure, even able to give it its *varietal* designation—*Topekaniana* perhaps? (In the Menninger youngsters' eyes I am sure there could be no other name!) However, I am sure that as he later traveled around Kansas and the rest of the world, he must have found other specimens so close to the *Topekaniana* that he would have accepted *ulmus americana topekaniana* (*Menn*) as a useful botanical *class*—even though not *every* characteristic —especially size—was identical in the other members of this species and variety.

What about my own views? Since I am only half a panelist I'll keep what I have to say brief. We can then proceed with the adversary fire-works by the panel members you have all been led to expect.

I, too, am not satisfied with the present situation. After some eighty years, it is hard to deny the essential correctness of Tuke's judgment. I do not, however, think that the solution lies in throwing over classification systems or even the present classification system. I believe it is worth salvaging because it contains so much of the high-level expert clinician's internal computer work of which Doctor Grinker has spoken. Rather I hold that we have to tackle more seriously the many difficulties which inhere in the process of classification in this especially complex area of behavior.

First, we must be willing to invest the arduous work which improved classification requires if it is to achieve some semblance of satisfactoriness. This will entail improvement in each of the three phases of classification: the initial description of the phenomena, the accurate syndromization of the characteristics, and the careful diagnosis of the patients.

This task requires that we use multiple trained observers (or observers we ourselves train), develop with care suitable rating scales for the symptoms and personality characteristics, systematically check out agreements and disagreements about the definitions and the syndromes, and avoid the contaminations of diagnosis which so frequently occur, through the use of anonymity and other devices.

A second major need lies in the wider use of dynamic concepts in the process. We have seen that several of our panelists point up this need in their emphasis on ego rather than id functioning. I may add a little from our own experience. We obtained a correlation of .89 between an index score, based on reaction time functioning, and ego strength as rated by both psychiatrists and ward personnel (4). I interpreted the index score to reflect well the ability of the patient to maintain a generalized set—what I consider in my own theoretical formulation to be the acme of ego functioning. The paths to such a goal are, of course, many: it may be Bellak's, or Arieti's, or Grinker's, or Menninger's categories; they are all useful.

And third, improved classification also calls for the increased use of statistical and computer *aids*. You will notice that I have said *aids*. These I consider to be important, but not primary. I believe that it is only when we have already laid the groundwork for such use in carefully collected basic data, that statistics and computers can be useful. Under these circumstances the "organized complexity" of the data that our field provides through the work of many groups of investigators may possibly be reduced to a reasonable, encompassable level.

But let's leave the rest for the ensuing high and low words!

REFERENCES

1. Kluckhohn, C., and Mowrer, O. H.: Culture and Personality: A Conceptual Schema. *American Anthropology*, New Series, 46:1-29, 1944.
2. Kluckhohn, C., and Murray, H. A.: Personality Formation: The Determinants. In Kluckhohn, C. and Murray, H. A. with the collaboration of Schneider, D. M. (Eds.), *Personality in Nature, Society and Culture*, 2nd ed. New York: Alfred A. Knopf, 1953.
3. Menninger, K., Mayman, M. and Pruyser, P.: *The Vital Balance*. New York: Viking, 1963.
4. Rosenthal, D., Lawlor, W. G., Zahn, T. P. and Shakow, D.: The Relationship of Some Aspects of Mental Set to Degree of Schizophrenic Disorganization. *Journal of Personality*, 28:26-38, 1960.
5. Tuke, D. H.: *A Dictionary of Psychological Medicine*. Philadelphia: Blakiston, 1892.

8

Panel Discussion
on the Validity of the Concept

DAVID SHAKOW, Ph.D., MARK D. ALTSCHULE, M.D.
SILVANO ARIETI, M.D., LEOPOLD BELLAK, M.D.,
ROY R. GRINKER, SR., M.D., KARL MENNINGER, M.D.

Doctor Shakow: I shall call on the various members of the panel to give any reactions they have to what the other members have said.

Doctor Bellak: A very brief reaction to this morning's presentations: If you look in Doctor Menninger's *Vital Balance,* you will find on page 33 that unlike his statement today he says he has nothing against the designation "schizophrenic syndrome." All he means to speak out against is the reification of the concept. I am sure we can all agree that reification is not a good thing, so that we have a baseline of agreement from which to start out. I am sure we could also agree that just because certain language habits lead to confusion and to difficulties in communication is not a reason for discarding language. In essence the extension of Doctor Menninger's idea that it is a bad thing to say somebody suffers from the schizophrenic syndrome (as he suggested today) would be similar to giving up the usefulness of semantics altogether. If Doctor Menninger is right that the term "schizophrenic syndrome," like "schizophrenia," carries a pejorative connotation, I think all of us would be willing to call it anything from XYZ syndrome to something else. I should hope that in the long run we shall have a better basis for calling it something else.

In the research in which we are now engaged, we hope to demonstrate eventually that in a large schizophrenic population you can show that a proportion of them is primarily implicated by neurogenic factors, others

84

primarily by psychogenic factors, others primarily by chemogenic factors, and others by primarily genogenic factors. It might eventually be possible to identify the disorder by some designation referring to the particular primary pathogenic or etiologic factor.

Doctor Menninger started talking about the "influenza" epidemic and did not quite get to finish his point: I wonder if it was not the thought that some of the postencephalitics exhibited schizophrenic symptoms just as I once upon a time was struck by the fact that some patients who had been diagnosed as "schizophrenic" were identified as having paresis when they finally had a spinal tap. I suppose at least if one has a certain premorbid personality various neurological problems can lead to a manifestation of what we call the schizophrenic syndrome or later the XYZ syndrome.

My main point, which was not in the version of the paper that Doctor Shakow had to read, was that even though we're speaking about specific dynamic constellations, they may at some point really take on *structural* characteristics. In terms of attaining structural characteristics they may deserve special designation as schizophrenic, neurotic, or something else, because that special dynamic constellation which has frozen into something structural has a particular predictive or other value.

Doctor Arieti had an interesting point with regard to qualitative differences in schizophrenia which I recall giving thought to in my own conceptualization. He spoke about the change in water that takes place from 33° to 32° when it freezes, something that Hegel has discussed as the change from quantity into quality. I think we can conceive of that in terms of gestalt psychology. At a point the whole is indeed more than the sum of its parts. Then you have the emergence of the new gestalt which under certain circumstances, speaking of ego functions and their deficiencies, may manifest itself as something relatively unique on this continuum of ego functions and their disturbances, namely a "schizophrenic" quality rather than a neurotic one. I recognize a qualitative change aside from a quantitative change, though still insisting that in many instances such a qualitative change might be reversible—back to the neurotic.

Doctor Altschule: You'll all be relieved to learn that I can't read most of the notes that I made this morning. I should like, however, to thank my fellow panelists for having so strongly supported my point which was that schizophrenia is an entirely personal diagnosis. As I said in my talk, there should be some sort of a name for what we are talking about, but it should be a name that has a definitive meaning. The reason I like the term Pinel

Syndrome or Pinel-Haslam Syndrome is that if I say Pinel Syndrome, all you have to do is look at what Pinel wrote. It's a very short paragraph. But when Doctor Arieti says schizophrenia to me, I now know what he means, I didn't yesterday. When Doctor Bellak says schizophrenia I now know what he means, but—through my own neglect I'm sure—I didn't know yesterday. And you see the same thing wherever you go. The word is used in an intensely personal way.

The word, I'm sorry to say, will probably last forever for two reasons. One is that it's meaningless and the other is that it's euphonious. The combination of euphony and lack of meaning is unbeatable. So that I'm perfectly happy and delighted to let people use the word schizophrenia in whatever personal sense they prefer, but when they talk to me about a syndrome that a patient shows I wish they'd say Pinel-Haslam Syndrome because then I'll be sure what they're talking about.

The main problem, of course, or one of the main problems is that in psychiatry, as in all of medicine, there are two kinds of syndromes—stable syndromes and unstable syndromes. When Aretaeus described the manic-depressive syndrome in 190 A.D. he set a pattern which has not been changed—but for language—except for the worse, I might add. So that if Aretaeus were to come back today and read Kraepelin he would say, "Kraepelin stole my words," because the syndrome hasn't changed. And you take a syndrome like acedia concerning which most of you, I'm sure, have heard nothing. That was a stable syndrome which referred to a peculiar bored, anxious depression that monks had. The syndrome disappeared when monks disappeared. On the other hand, you take syndromes like hysteria or schizophrenia, their meaning varies according to the context in which the person who uses those words wants to use them. Actually I understand that the term hysteria is now illegal. It's not a legal diagnosis although we use the word every day in our conversations. I hope that the same thing might happen to schizophrenia, that it becomes an illegal, underground diagnosis which we continue to use in the friendliest fashion in talking to each other.

The difference between me and this overwhelming group on my left here is one of focus. Now I happen to have a divergent strabismus so that what I look at is a very broad field and since I am seeing it, everything has to be included. As it happens the people on my left are all eminent specialists in what is a relatively narrow field—psychiatry. My field is internal medicine which means all the diseases of the skin and its contents. In the course of my work I see dozens of patients who are indistinguishable from those that Doctors Arieti, Bellak, and everybody else describes as schizophrenic except that some had a great loss of sodium because an overenthusiastic physician threw the book at them when they had congestive failure. Or they may have myxedema madness which is a paranoid schizophrenic syndrome, but the psychiatrist rarely sees it. A great majority of the patients I see with schizophrenic syndromes don't have the idiopathic, endogenous, or whatever you want to call it—socially generated—schizophrenia. They have a metabolic or other disease or some organic lesion in the brain which for the most part we recognize and treat immediately so that it goes away.

Well then, what justification do we have for calling these patients schizophrenic? I don't doubt the validity of that diagnosis. The diagnosis is a good one. I think the point is that it's a syndrome that can occur in a wide variety of different physiologic, biologic, and sociologic situations and therefore to give it a name that means dissociation between content and affect is not at all reasonable. What's happened here is that we're all saying the same thing, but it's my divergent squint that gives me a somewhat broader view.

Doctor Shakow: I trust some of the psychiatrists on the panel will really take up Doctor Altschule's challenge. I'm sure Doctor Grinker will and I hope Doctor Arieti will because Doctor Altschule has uttered all kinds of well, nonorthodoxies, let's say—heterodoxies.

Doctor Arieti: Well, I shall start by saying that I like what Doctor Bellak said at the beginning of his comments. I believe that none of us believes in schizophrenia as a disease entity, as we might think of pneumonia or of chicken pox. None of us believes in the existence of a schizococcus or of a psychological schizococcus. We speak about a syndrome and go a little further than just using the word syndrome as a constellation of symptoms. It is not a constellation of symptoms at random. If we believe what we have learned in our biological studies, we must believe that there is some integration or some connection between these symptoms which appear so disparate. Doctor Altschule rightly reminded us that there are over thirty types of diabetes. If we call all of them diabetes they must have some characteristics in common. So it's really not useless to use the word diabetes. I think the use of such words is helpful because it enables the physician to deal with a certain constellation of symptoms and to see the relations among them. Treatment, of course, will have to be modified according to the individual characteristics of each patient.

Now I think that Doctor Bellak this morning really showed us an important contribution he has made to the field of psychiatry. Not only has he shown the defects in ego functions of the schizophrenic, but he has also shown that they are reversible. When the patient recovers, the ego defect disappears. It is not true that once a person is a schizophrenic he will be a schizophrenic forever. Doctor Bellak, in certain ways, works from a slant different from mine. Whereas he shows predominantly the defects of the secondary process, I emphasize the reemergence of the primary process and how the primary process affects the defective secondary process, thereby giving the schizophrenic syndrome its characteristic, peculiar clinical picture.

Now as to Doctor Menninger, a big part of his comments were really about moral issues. He felt that schizophrenia is a pejorative term which should not be used. I respect his desire not to hurt the human soul, and I agree entirely with him on this matter, but I believe that his solution to the problem is not the right one. I believe that if a certain concept has acquired an emotional meaning or an emotional load which is negative, we should remove the emotional load and not abolish the concept. Otherwise we revert to a preconceptual way of thinking. Doctor Menninger gave as examples of such groupings of peoples Jews, Catholics, and Negroes. We should not ask these people to give up their Negro identity, or their Jewish identity—this is immoral in my opinion. I think we should teach people, on the other hand, to respect the individuality of man, to respect the diversities and consider ourselves humanly equal even if we're different. This goes for the schizophrenic too, of course. Now I agree that perhaps schizophrenia has acquired a pejorative connotation. We must do our very best to remove this pejorative quality by showing first of all our sense of respect for the mentally ill, and secondly by not having a pessimistic point of view as far as therapy is concerned. We all know that schizophrenics do recover. We must do our very best to improve the prognosis. As a matter of fact, certain diseases in the past had a very poor prognosis and now have a good prognosis, and therefore their names have lost the negative emotional power which they had in the past. But, moreover, I feel that if we should really follow Doctor Menninger and not call the schizophrenic patient schizophrenic anymore, but for instance call him either grade five of dyscontrol as he does, or XYZ as Doctor Bellak has suggested, soon the terminology—dyscontrol grade five or XYZ—would acquire a pejorative connotation unless the whole attitude toward the mentally ill changes.

Doctor Shakow: Doctor Arieti has given the two other panelists an opportunity now to say something.

Doctor Grinker: I was asked by Doctor Cancro as the Director of this Conference to assist in making it an adversary kind of discussion. I didn't need his invitation. It seems it has automatically become so. I'm not going to talk about my agreements, I'm going to talk about my disagreements. In the first place, we were given a historical basis for classification by Doctors Cancro and Pruyser. I think what is extremely important in what they said is that our emphasis on words whose meanings have changed does not really presuppose that when the meanings change the words always change. Many words in the English language persist with different meanings and the same is true of our scientific jargon. We use professional terms even though there are shifts in the meaning of those terms. They are not easily displaced, they are not easily changed. Dementia praecox is still used although it has been largely abandoned for the term schizophrenia. In an attempt to change the notion of mental health as something that had a positive and defined value system, I used the term homoclite in studying a group of YMCA college students. It is a Greek term and nobody knows its meaning. I only know its meaning because a Greek scholar gave it to me. Unfortunately, this term is never used, and I doubt whether it will ever be of common usage. Nevertheless, the term coping which has been modestly used by psychologists, social scientists, and psychiatrists now seems to be in the forefront. It avoids any misconceptions that there is such a think as a positive mental health, which notion we have attempted to discard for many years. The term "borderline" we used to describe a group of patients who represent a particular kind of behavior and a particular kind of course. But the borderline had previously referred to something in between psychosis and neurosis, and I doubt whether that name can be replaced, therefore we can only redefine it. Dewey and Bentley sometime ago pointed out that naming is knowing, and we can also reverse this equation by saying knowing is naming. If we keep a clear notion of what we are talking about through the use of appropriate names which can be communicated one to another without the use of paragraphs or pages, we may someday be talking about the same thing.

There is, however, a great danger and this danger doesn't apply only to the name schizophrenia. It applies to concepts applied to a name. During the height of the so-called breakthrough in psychosomatic medicine when Alexander postulated a specific emotional constellation behind a particular psychosomatic disturbance, all of our residents had a series of electric light bulbs turn on when a patient would come in with a presenting complaint. If a patient came in with a complaint of peptic ulcer, the associations were obvious that this was somebody suffering from ungratified dependency, or anger because of ungratified dependency, and the resident would find all this material in the record to the exclusion of all others. Not that he falsified, but you can find this kind of unsatisfied dependency in anyone. Stereotypes were also associated if hypertension was the complaint. It doesn't make any difference what the names are, we'll develop stereotypes; we'll develop concepts which themselves must be changed even though the name cannot be changed. It is sad that the International classification has persisted as it has in the second edition of the DSM. That was because the United States government entered into a treaty—imagine, a treaty—for classification of mental illness with other countries. We were bound by the treaty, and therefore the American Psychiatric Association has distributed a manual of definitions with the Gold Book. Now that manual of definitions isn't very good, but nevertheless, it does in some way counteract the effect of the classification. Doctor Menninger extols the Meyerian classification. I spent a good deal of time in Baltimore listening to Adolf Meyer and I'll be damned if I could remember much less spell the names. It is obvious that his classification couldn't take hold.

Now, a statement has been made that we should have different kinds of concepts for diagnosis and classification. I just simply don't understand how we can make different diagnoses in a taxonomic classification that emphasizes individual differences. It is the nature of any scientific endeavor that we know that nobody has all the attributes of a syndrome. If these form the larger bit around which other contributory bits can be congregated, we say we have a gestalt which has the pluses and the minuses which are characteristic of that gestalt. If we should develop diagnoses in terms of therapy—apart from classification—we should really be suffering from a kind of verbal schizophrenia.

Now, let me go on to Doctor Altschule. I guarantee that my first-year residents can differentiate the psychotic behavior of people with thyroid disease or LSD or what not from that of acute schizophrenics, and characteristically label them as psychotic but not as schizophrenic. He also said psychiatry is a narrow field. He meant that as a joke, but actually what I've been trying to say constantly is that psychiatry is not a narrow field. It's a conglomerate. As a science it's a conglomerate of many fields and those of us who want to contribute to the development of this field must know the contributory sciences.

Now there are a number of ways of classifying schizophrenia, which also take into account the fact that it is an adaptive attempt to establish a new equilibrium at a lower level after a regression. This equilibrium varies over time. For example, Manfred Bleuler has recently tried to classify schizophrenia in terms of the course of the illness. To use an eponym is against the trend in modern medicine and an eponym will soon become evaluated just like any other name. I have no love for the term schizophrenia, I should just as soon have it changed to anything in the world. But to use Pinel Syndrome we shall soon find our patients responding by saying, "there's nothing wrong with my penis, the penile syndrome is not mine." If we are going to continue this kind of adaptation to the misinformation of the lay people, we have to look to where that misinformation came from. When psychiatrists behave like authorities on every subject and communicate to the people who write for the slick magazines that schizophrenia is a hopeless disease, that its prognosis is terrible, that people who once have it are never freed from proneness to subsequent attacks, and so on, the public naturally accepts that as true. They will accept it no matter what you call this syndrome—schizophrenia or Pinel's Syndrome.

Now, I agree with Doctor Arieti when he talked about the lack of specificity. The disease is not within the cells but is in the total gestalt and, as Doctor Altschule has predicted, the specific biochemical changes may—and I'm not sure about this because I'm not enough of a biochemist—also turn out to be nonspecific.

When Doctor Arieti talks about the primary process prevailing in conflict areas, and that these should be studied from a cognitive point of view, he is approaching this in a logical manner from one frame of reference. You can approach this disturbance from other frames of reference. One could approach the schizophrenic in terms of anxiety, and this is particularly important from a biological point of view because it seems, at least to me, that either the basic anxiety in the schizophrenic is overwhelming in quantity, or it is different in quality and may be related to some basic biological process.

I have pretty good agreement with Doctor Bellak, which is unusual. I particularly like his emphasis on the fact that in the diagnostic classifications there are both nomothetic and idiographic elements. A patient who is labeled as belonging to a syndrome shares the characteristics of that syndrome with many people, but he also brings to that syndrome his individuality in terms of his background—both biological and experiential—and this is important for us to understand.

Now, one last remark of an antagonistic nature. I am a little bit shocked that in 1969 we are close to the twenty-first century and are still arguing about and still have to teach that there are no single etiological factors, that there is more than one disease participating in a collection of syndromes, and that there are transactions among parts of a total system. That this should still have to be emphasized to avoid reductionism on the one hand and humanism on the other hand, which represent polarities of restricted ideologies, is shocking. I think by this time we all should realize that we are dealing with total gestalts, we are dealing with multiple systems, we are dealing with parts in relation to each other, we are dealing with individual laws, and we are dealing with regulation of levels as well as isomorphism. These are common knowledge today in our field, and if we don't hold to that then we have missed the boat.

Doctor Shakow: Doctor Menninger, I heard some remonstrations before to some of the things that were said. I'm sure you want to deal with some of the problems.

Doctor Menninger: Well, Doctor Arieti misunderstood me, so maybe others did. I do believe there is such a thing as mental illness, I don't think it's a myth. I think some of the forms of it should be called schizophrenic syndrome and not schizophrenia. I was comparing the naming of some forms of mental illness to the naming of people. I was trying to indicate that there is a difference between the naming of a syndrome and making it into a category on the one hand, and naming somebody like a Philippino, or a Catholic, or a Missourian. There may be people in Kansas who might have a little prejudice against the Missourians, but in general, to say a man is a Missourian is not to judge him. It is not pejorative. He can say, "Well I was a Missourian but I moved away." None of this really affects his social status and so forth and so on. What you call a thing does make a difference. I was trying to indicate that it doesn't seem to me that the name of a disease is like the name of a category which involves one's geography or one's religion, or one's national origin or something of that kind. I was trying to express a distinction and not a similarity. I'm glad you gave me a chance to correct that. It would sound very stupid the other way. But while I'm on that, some of us were taught by our parents to call dark-skinned people, colored people. It was the only polite thing to do. To refer to them as Negroes was very haughty and to say niggers was unthinkable. Well, now as everybody knows, some of the people I'm talking about don't want to be called colored people. One of my Negro employees said, "I don't want to be called a colored person." I said, "I was always taught that was the polite way to refer to you." She said, "Well, that means a lot of different things, that means the

American Indians for example, and another thing, I'm not colored." I said, "Well, what are you? Do you want me to say you are a Negro?" "No," she said, "say I'm black." It just happens that this employee isn't a bit black objectively. I said, "I shall, but it's confusing."

I think whether I categorize her as black, or Negro, or even as a colored person, wouldn't cause me too much personnel difficulty, but I'm sure that she would feel very badly and probably not want to work there any more if I applied some of the other terms to her that have been applied to colored people in the past. Now I think the word schizophrenia has gotten a bad name. I agree with Doctor Grinker that we shouldn't be too much influenced by the misled public. In actuality, the public gets misled by somebody, whether it's by us or by the magazine writers he describes. The public has its mind made up, it knows all about this dreadful thing. The relatives wait around to ask, "Is it schizophrenia? Has he got it?" It is like waiting for a Wasserman test, either you have got it or you haven't. This seems dreadful to me. One can say to a parent, "He has a lot of schizophrenic trends or traits, but so do I, depending on the day of the week." We can then add that, "In the case of your child, they are rather numerous and ominous. I don't know how far this is going, but I think it's a good thing to get treatment started." Now, I want to say no to people who ask, "Well is this that thing called schizophrenia?" I want to say these are schizophrenic symptoms, but schizophrenic symptoms happen to a lot of people in a lot of different conditions and it is not a disease. It is an aspect of mental illness that some people think of as a disease. I am really concerned about this because we can say as often as we like that the public ought not to determine what things are called, but the public does determine what things are called. Even illness. In the last analysis, we don't decide what illness is. Illness can only be operationally defined as conditions in which people think the doctor ought to do something. How can you make an adequate definition of illness in any other way? You can say discomfort and those other words, but all of those are like sieves, they are full of so many logical holes. It gets back to the fact that operationally, this is what the public thinks. There was a time when certain things were not considered illness, which we now think are. Well, who decides that? We doctors don't.

There was a time when do you know what it meant to make a diagnosis of dementia praecox? (We didn't say schizophrenia at first, but later we got to saying it.) That meant call the dentist. Now you don't remember that, you don't even know it. That meant call the dentist and have all their teeth taken out. I have seen this happen to scores of patients, not because there was anything wrong with the teeth that we knew of, but because the origin of schizophrenia was the foci of infection at the roots. Then we had a very obstreperous surgeon on the staff of one place where I was who said it's not their teeth you need to take out, but their gall bladders and irrigate their colons! So patients would get put on the table, we would do a colostomy and run water through the large intestine for twenty-four hours. That was considered treatment. And that's what it meant if you had a diagnosis of schizophrenia.

Somebody said once that we ought to encourage all the young people to write medical literature, because it's already been ruined and they can't make it any worse. Well, I think diagnosis has, in a sense, already been brought to a point where we have got to do something different about it. You remember that even God changed his name two or three times. Once in a discussion he had, I believe, with Jacob, a little bit later in a discussion he had with Moses, and subsequently in a discussion he seems to have had with the High Priests who didn't record the particular interlocutor. But at any rate, if God can change his name, I should think we could change the name of schizophrenia. I don't mean this irreverently. God changed his name according to the early theologians because it was a new concept. It was no longer the punishing God, it was no longer the jealous God who visited punishment upon everybody right and left and hurled thunderbolts and vindictiveness around. And in order to indicate this change in the character of what was talked about, theologians changed his name. But other than this, I really have no quarrel with all my colleagues, this is a dreadful situation, we might get to agreeing, then . . .

Doctor Shakow: I won't let that happen! How do you get around the point that Doctor Arieti made that in the end any term can take on this pejorative connotation?

Doctor Menninger: No, I don't think so. Take syphilis for example. There was a time in the old days, when I was a newspaper reporter, that they would not allow the word syphilis to appear in print. At the Massachusetts General we never used the word on the syphilis service. We always referred to it as SP, the specific disease. This was because if a patient learned he had syphilis, he might go out and commit suicide. You must remember at that time there was no known cure for syphilis. We gave them mercury, but didn't expect it to do any good. It kept the patient busy though, and they had some improvement in symptoms. Then we also gave them iodide because that kept them busy counting. But seriously, we did not expect this to affect very much tissue change. When arsphenamine came in the whole thing took a different turn. Syphilis was a curable disease and, in fact, the more syphilitics you could discover, the more therapeutic possibilities you had in your practice. I can remember very well when routine lumbar punctures were instituted in Boston on every patient that was admitted, because we all hoped that they would have syphilis. If they had syphilis they had a chance, if they didn't have syphilis it probably meant dementia praecox and they had no chance.

Doctor Arieti: Doctor Menninger, we have to do for schizophrenia what we did for syphilis.

Doctor Menninger: Very well, if you think it's in the same class. Now you see syphilis is a disease in my opinion in the sense that it definitely . . .

Doctor Arieti: I am referring to the name and its connotation.

Doctor Menninger: I think you already have. I think most people with this syndrome get well, don't they? What do you think? He says yes, and you say no, and I don't know. But I thought that quite a lot of them got well. All right, you've already got a great therapeutic result and yet I don't think we've changed the social reactions and connotations to the name. I'm talking too much, Mr. Chairman, I'd rather know what the audience thinks.

Doctor Shakow: We shall call on the audience pretty soon, but I just want to bring up an example from my own experience and that was at Worcester. We had a notion that catatonic schizophrenia was decidedly the form of schizophrenia that had the best prognosis. We'd tell the relatives that this was the way we felt, so there wasn't this pejorative attitude towards it. On the other hand, at Boston State Hospital, where May was the superintendent, they stuck very closely to the Kraepelinian notion that if it was dementia praecox, the diagnosis being made on the basis of prognosis, if a patient got well, then this patient was not a catatonic, he was manic-depressive. His attitude also got across to the relatives. If the diagnosis was manic-depressive, it called for a good prognosis; if it was dementia praecox, a bad prognosis. And you get this pejorative connotation. This is where I raise the question about how much we have built into it. We are dealing with a serious disorder but it doesn't necessarily follow that it always has a bad prognosis. I think that as psychiatry has tended to move off into the outpatient area and get away from state hospitals, the notion has been perpetuated that what is in the state hospital is sort of hopeless.

Well, I'll put the question to Doctor Altschule. Do you really think that the diagnosis of schizophrenia, the way it is carried out by competent psychiatrists working with patients, doesn't make a distinction between the passing disorders which come with drugs or with some special intercurrent medical condition?

Doctor Altschule: I evidently failed this time to make the particular point that the patients, in whose cases the psychiatrists are called in, are patients who have already been screened for the most part. There are a few who get to a psychiatrist first, but the overwhelming majority, I would say 99.99%, of the patients who come to most mental hospitals have already been screened. This kind of screened patient only very rarely would be misdiagnosed. I'm talking about what the general practitioner and the internist or surgeon in the general hospital sees. He sees patients who develop schizophrenic syndromes and they are curable. In fact, they are very quickly curable for the most part. Then there is another group of patients who have taken something, and that is not immediately known. For example, several physicians have collected small groups of patients who had what seemed to be—at least by local standards— typical schizophrenia. It developed later that they all fell into a fairly homogeneous group. They were young students who had taken sleeping pills because they got all wound up before their examinations and couldn't sleep after the examinations and they took something which contains scopolamine. Not only was the clinical impression paranoid schizophrenia, but psychological testing showed changes consistent with that diagnosis. The condition remitted within a matter of a few days or a few weeks. Now, that experience some of our residents had with that very small group of patients was a very good thing for them, because when they go out into the community and see patients who seem to be typical schizophrenics, they've learned that things are not always what they seem. I should agree, in fact insist, that my colleagues to the left of me have substantiated very forcibly what I have said, and have done it beautifully, using orthodox terminology which of course I couldn't. Hence I don't see any serious disagreements, but the point I wish to make is that the kind of practice one does determines what one looks at and hence what one sees. In a practice that consists almost entirely of screened patients, what I'm talking about would be relatively—almost completely —meaningless. In the case of the physician who first sees the patient, what I've said is far from meaningless.

Doctor Shakow: One of the questions from the floor asks the panel to comment on the views of Tom Szasz about schizophrenia or mental illness as a myth.

Doctor Grinker: The difficulty in talking about Szasz's views is that they are oriented toward a particular goal. He is not so much a psychiatric as a political writer. The concept of mental illness as a myth depends upon your definition of illness. I am perfectly willing to accept any statement with the word disturbance, disorder, deviance, or anything else, but schizophrenics do exist. What Szasz is concerned about is what do we do with these people, where are their determinants, where is their will? His typical statement begins, "Whose agent is the psychiatrist, or the judge, or the jury?" So it is a political concept. Szasz is a professor of psychiatry in a reputable medical school, but he's more concerned with civil liberties and the political status of patients. What I should say in this respect is we still have a number of people who are so disturbed or whatever you want to call them that they cannot be entrusted with their own or with other lives and have to be protected through some adjudication. According to Szasz that is entirely wrong. We are already seeing through our revolving-door policy of treating schizophrenics with phenothiazines and sending them rapidly out of the hospital without adequate outpatient treatment, that they quickly come back. During their stay outside the hospital they are somewhat dangerous to themselves and to others. This is not a scientific or psychiatric problem in any respect, it's a political problem.

Doctor Menninger: I think I speak for most of us here who feel that some patients not only can be treated against their will but must be. Now there's a certain position, which Doctor Grinker referred to, that says if a man doesn't want to be treated he shouldn't be obliged to be. They have qualified that now and say that at least he shouldn't be obliged to take treatment against his will if any other method is successful. Now, who's going to say if any other method is successful? I feel that this is a very loaded and complicated political-social question. I'm just an old-fashioned doctor who thinks that some people are going to have treatment whether they want it or not. Just what technical and legal procedures are necessary for that I'm not really sure about. I'm not in a position yet to say nobody should be treated against his will. Doctor Grinker and I have seen in Chicago some individuals who very much need medical treatment, and yet who say they won't accept it. Not because they're Christian Scientists, but sometimes because they feel that they would not be fairly treated by people of our color and sometimes because they feel they have been so badly treated by some of our colleagues in certain institutions that they fear all treatment. We see this very paradoxical thing, but none of this makes mental illness a myth in my opinion.

Doctor Shakow: This is a question addressed to Doctor Bellak. Do you have profiles on nonschizophrenic, psychotic patients, and can they be distinguished from schizophrenic patients? What aspects of the profiles predict short- and long-term prognosis and how are they determined?

Doctor Bellak: To start with the easier part, the second one, mostly the variables on the right side of the scheme, i.e., the autonomous and synthetic functions, determine, I believe, the long-range prognosis. The synthetic function is probably the one which correlates most highly with the concept of ego strength per se. If the synthetic function is poor and if the autonomous functions are poor, then I tend to think that the long-range prognosis is poor. With regard to differentiating schizophrenic and nonschizophrenic psychotic patients we are still in a process of factor analyzing a great many ego function patterns in our population. We not only hope to be able to differentiate schizophrenic and nonschizophrenic psychotics, but also hope to find a variety of syndrome patterns within the schizophrenic group. If things work out nicely, which maybe is expecting too much, I should hope that eventually groups which are primarily— let me put a heavy emphasis on *primarily*—psychogenic, neurogenic, chemogenic, or genogenic might have specific ego function patterns. Logically they do not necessarily need to do this, and I'm sure there will be many overlaps. By the same token, I hope that we'll be able to show that schizophrenic and nonschizophrenic psychotics can be differentiated but I cannot show you convincing profiles at this point.

Doctor Shakow: This question is directed to Doctor Arieti. Your excellent and comprehensive application of primary process cognition reemergence in the face of progressive destruction of self is completely understandable, but what about crisis situations? For instance, World War II or starvation, in which the need for survival reopened the system by giving the person a more simple and direct goal that blasted the cognitive jungle.

Doctor Arieti: Situations of crisis such as the ones which you have mentioned may actually help the individual from the point of view of fighting schizophrenia. You see, we have to distinguish two different types of threats, or anxieties, or dangers—the external dangers and the internal.

A war or a military defeat may promote a feeling of solidarity, or the feeling that the military defeat is not the responsibility of the individual. The danger then remains external. It's not an attack to the individual's self-esteem. The attack to the individual's self-esteem is much more important in the etiology of schizophrenia. As a matter of fact, this is one of the fundamental points in the psychodynamics of schizophrenia. What does the schizophrenic patient do? He tries—I'm talking now in particular of the paranoid patient—to change an inner danger into an external one. For instance, instead of thinking badly about himself, he sees dangers outside in the environment. So, realistic dangers are not the ones which generally lead to schizophrenia, only those which injure the self.

Doctor Shakow: This one is a loaded question and I'll put it to all members of the panel except myself. For those of you treating patients with a schizophrenic syndrome, how do you handle therapeutic interruptions such as coming to a conference like this?

Doctor Arieti: Well, I prepare the patient. The interruption is not really very long, just two or three days, and I think even the sickest patient is able to tolerate this if we prepare him in advance and if we reassure him that we shall be back. I have also not eliminated some other possibilities. For instance, I tell some patients where I am and if they want to contact me by phone they can do so. Occasionally they have done that. I have found that to give them the opportunity to reach me by phone gives a feeling of reassurance which is really very welcome. The patients are very grateful and, as I said before, very seldom use this prerogative.

Doctor Shakow: Doctor Bellak, would you like to comment on this?

Doctor Bellak: I do about the same things Doctor Arieti does. There are, of course, many other possibilities which I'm sure he's also aware of and often uses. You can use this instance (of variation) for a matter of reality testing. You can use it for reaffirming to the patient that he is not so sick and dependent that he needs you constantly. You can make provisions for somebody else to be available, a family member and/or a colleague.

Doctor Grinker: Well, you've heard the traditional ways of dealing with the problem. I'd like to make some general comments. One of the reasons, I think, for gaining a feeling of the delicacy of the schizophrenic patient, that he has got to be handled in such a way which implies that he is constantly in a delicate balance, is just that we treat him that way.

In any dyadic relationship, whether it be psychotherapy or psychoanalysis, the patient brings into the therapeutic situation, almost invariably, his liabilities, his distresses, his difficulties, his troubles. We do not get a good view of his assets. His assets are expressed in behavior in his community —hospital or otherwise. It seems to me that what we are confronted with in studying our patients is exactly what the experimental psychologists have recently learned—they cannot understand the basic behaviors of their experimental animals so long as they are in laboratory cages. The primatologists have moved out into the natural field and observe the apes within their troops, and how they behave in the presence of dangers, and how they deal with their young and all kinds of social activities which are not demonstrable in the cage. Our cage is the interviewing or therapy room. The patient cannot exhibit much behavior. By virtue of coming to a doctor, and in some way or other paying for it, he wants to talk about his troubles and he doesn't give us an adequate idea of his assets. Now it seems to me that we should do more in the way of leaving and testing our patients in the community. Not only because we want to keep the families in touch with them so that they know some day they're going to return to family life and work life, but also as a continual kind of testing of assets. We've been on the side of pathology, we have not been on the side of successful coping and I think we ought to move more in that direction in our therapeutic procedures.

Doctor Shakow: There is a question addressed to Doctor Bellak. Do figure drawings substantially assist in designating the schizophrenic reaction?

Doctor Bellak: In general the answer is a yes. In our psychological battery we include many different tests. If the schizophrenic syndrome is a many faceted syndrome, it takes a many faceted approach to tap the various aspects. Some test procedures, like figure drawings, particularly bring out disturbances of body image. Others bring out different aspects, like thought disorder.

Doctor Shakow: What relationship, if any, do you see between the works of Mahler, Bender, Thomas, and so on delimiting interactional patterns of constitutional givens and environment and your understanding of predisposition for schizophrenic syndrome later in life?

Doctor Grinker: I think that all of the people who have been devout hereditarians and those who have been devout environmentalists are moving closer together, to recognize that even the highest genetic loading requires an environmental experience to bring it out. The people who are loaded highest in their genetic background require less in the way of deleterious experience to bring out the syndrome and those who have less genetic background require a much greater amount of stress to evoke the syndrome. So that I think the concept of a dichotomy is fast disappearing. So much so that, in the Foundations' Fund for Research in Psychiatry's Conference in Puerto Rico two years ago on schizophrenia, instead of talking about the etiology of schizophrenia, they talked about the transmission of schizophrenia. Now we don't know the specific genic disturbance, and it's not known whether it's one gene or multiple genes or whether the genes have multiple potentialities for disturbances. We certainly don't know what early experiences are specific for schizophrenia. We don't know what the systems of communication are, we don't know what the family constellation is, although there have been people who have said that the schizophrenic system of communication is this, that, and the other. It depends on whether you want to talk about the families that Lidz has been describing or the families of Wynne and Singer. So that there are individual theoretical positions but all of them are now moving closer together and eventually we'll hear no more of this nature-nurture business.

Doctor Shakow: Thank you, the panel has indicated to me that they're reaching their tolerance limit so let me take this last question. I should like some discussion of the concept of latent, covert, prepsychotic or sub-clinical schizophrenia. I think some of the people on the panel have had particular experience with this. Doctor Grinker, do you want to say something about that? It begins to touch on some of your borderline conditions, doesn't it?

Doctor Grinker: Well, the implications of these names are that eventually the person is capable of or will develop an overt schizophrenic syndrome. This has never been proven. Working with the borderline syndrome I find that there are about ten diagnoses that are used: chronic undifferentiated schizophrenia, psychopathological disturbances, character disturbances, latent schizophrenia, covert schizophrenia, subclinical schizophrenia, and prepsychotic schizophrenia. Each institution has its favorite term which it uses when the diagnosis of schizophrenia cannot be made, but there are certain characterological elements that seem to indicate that there are restrictive and constrictive developments which cannot be diagnosed as a neurosis. So we've taken these people and put them together, finding the common features of the total syndrome. There are at least four subcategories which fit into what these diagnoses assume. The patients with this diagnosis of the borderline syndrome do not become schizophrenic. We have followed these people now for up to five years and they are not becoming schizophrenic. So we have some confidence in the reliability of this diagnosis. I think that there are certainly some characteristics of the schizophrenic syndrome that lead one to make this kind of a subdiagnosis. When one puts together all the other elements in the structure of the syndrome, it becomes clear that it is not schizophrenia.

Doctor Shakow: All right. We end on that note. Thank you.

Section II

THE INDICATIONS FOR AND VALUE OF HOSPITAL TREATMENT

9

Hospital Treatment in Schizophrenia: An Overview

HERBERT C. MODLIN, M.D.

THE THINKING OF THE CONCEPTUALIZERS is expressed in Section I of this volume; in Section II the interveners speak. These two categories of endeavor are not mutually exclusive and, in the context of the chapters to follow, we may expect further thoughtful and clarifying contributions toward understanding of the schizophrenic process.

The role of the mental hospital in the management of schizophrenic syndromes has a lengthy and complex history, a distinguished as well as a pathetic past. Fortunately, space limitation impels me to spare you a detailed recital of the past. Sketchily hitting the high spots is seldom fruitful; therefore I shall present only a brief resumé of where we seem to be now with what we may call the traditional uses of the mental hospital. I hope, by clearing some brush, to bring into more prominent view scrubby trees reaching for light through the umbrella of giants towering above them which the other contributors to this section will demarcate additionally.

Among the several considerations recommending hospitalization of the seriously disturbed, the first and paramount focus should be on the patient's welfare. Changing the environment from extramural to intramural often effects a salubrious diminution of stress; and in a relatively undemanding and empathic setting reparative processes are better able to occur. Use of the hospital can serve as a splint, or even a plaster cast, for a fractured ego. Reinforcement of the patient's failing functions is frequently the treatment of immediate choice. If duly enlightened and experienced and discerning personnel can temporarily take over and exercise for him some aspects of his essential psychological operations—such as rational perception, delay, judgment, decision-making and self-preservation—then a patient's confusion, fear, despair or withdrawal may be lessened.

Hospitalization also facilitates expedient, energetic and continuous application of direct attacks on psychopathology through modalities such as constant observation, psychopharmacology, milieu management and psychotherapy. The drastic change in environment may offer the failing organism, which is our patient, a sufficient break with the immediate past that a kind of new start becomes possible. He may, by benefit of properly dosed therapeusis in a controlled setting, have a chance to reorder his existence so that he ends up better equipped than ever before to confront reality. The goal here is ambitious: not just symptom remission but psychological growth.

A second consideration in prescribing hospitalization is benefit to the patient's family. Removing the patient temporarily may aid in breaking up a pathological intertwining of static, damaging relationships and permit a reorganization of family behaviors and resources. Such a move may also afford the family needed respite from the unnerving, fear generating tyranny of the patient's illness and provide them an opportunity to gain improved perspectives of their duties, obligations, sacrifices and responsibilities. It may halt their exploitation of the patient's illness to solve or to evade pertinent family issues and problems.

A third benefit is to the larger group, the community or society. Hospitalization of a person manifesting the strange, the weird, the threatening, the irrational, the "devil-possessed" may accomplish reduction of community anxiety. It reassures that viable agencies do exist for presumably humane management of severe misfits and that, generally speaking, all is still right with the world.

Frequently omitted from lists such as this is a fourth possible benefit of hospitalization: to the psychiatric professional. Idealistic and humanistic though we may strive to be, some mundane aspects of psychiatric practice cannot be ignored; the psychosocial rehabilitator has needs too. There are professionals who perform most comfortably, confidently, and productively in certain settings, in a professional environment of their own choosing. They may realistically expect to be accused of having erected a Procrustean bed. Most of us, however, do not achieve the envied flexibility of the genital character. We have our limitations as well as our special assets. It is incumbent upon the professional who undertakes helping the sickest among us to apply the methods and employ the tools which best augment his particular skills. The mental hospital may constitute one of these. Work with the extremely disturbed is in some ways our most stressful venture; it is understandable that we may feel the need to band together as a hospital staff for mutual support, reassurance and the sharing of responsibility in an awesome and sometimes not very apparently rewarding task.

We should now consider the contraindications to hospitalization. I could start over with my outline and present the reverse argument for most of the subheadings. I shall not belabor this kind of repetition; but some reflection must be given lest we neglect disciplined scrutiny of our therapeutic endeavors, lest we stagnate in our uncritical, unthinking adherence to the familiar, the customary or the traditional.

In the patient's interest, through nonhospital treatment we may more nearly successfully encourage his coping with a demanding environment to which he can yet respond by exercising his healthy, uncontaminated personality functions. If the demands be less than overwhelming he may continue in sustaining productivity, and reparative processes may be stimulated in him even while active pathology still obtains.

Negative effects of incarceration (known as "hospitalism") that are commonly engendered by understaffed, underbudgeted, underinnovative institutions can be avoided in community-based treatment. There are hospitals and hospitals. Regrettably a double standard of psychiatric practice prevails—for the haves and the have-nots—and consequently a great number of our schizophrenic sufferers are candidates for minimal hospital treatment.

Removing the patient from his family and his community can foster the retention or the development of attitudes which in the long run may handicap therapeutic efforts. Hospitalization of the patient may serve to confirm the family's or the community's conviction that only the patient is at fault, may free them of the onus to participate in the discovery and consideration of why the patient fell ill or how he can be helped, may verify their belief that severe mental illness is solely a responsibility of the state. Sometimes when the family is difficult, demanding and intrusive or when several members seem ill themselves, the family's relinquishment of responsibility for the one member now labeled "patient" may be abetted by the psychiatric hospital professionals.

Convenience may be one indication for hospitalization. In a recent paper by Mendel and Rapport (1), the factors dictating institutionalization of the seriously disturbed in a large city were analyzed. The data revealed that most recommendations for hospitalization occurred between

5:00 p.m. and 8:00 a.m. and on week-ends. Discussed as determining factors were the concerns of a probate judge, the anger of a family and the apprehensions of neighbors. We do have variable standards of clinical practice in most communities, some of them, it must be acknowledged, second rate. Numerous psychiatric professionals may intend by prescribing hospitalization to relieve the doctor as well as the patient. I assume the implications and vicissitudes of this factor need no further exposition.

The advent of community psychiatry, social psychiatry and public health psychiatry was in part motivated by profound discouragement over the general quality of mental hospital treatment. The alternative, avoiding the public mental hospital whenever possible, is now considered the treatment of choice by many. According to these critics, we may no longer perfunctorily recommend inpatient status; we are called upon to vindicate it in every case and to prove that other settings would not suffice. In my view these critics have some justification since they are attacking essentially second- and third-rate psychiatric practice. This does not automatically mean that hospitalization is an anachronism; it cannot mean that all psychiatric hospitals are *passé*; it does mean that poor hospitals practice poor medicine. The contributors to Section II do not represent inferior institutions. On the contrary, their contributions were solicited because they represent excellence in hospital practice. Thus, I feel that the loaded question, "Aren't all hospitals by their very nature bad hospitals?" need play little part in these specific deliberations.

To complete my resumé of standard issues influencing decisions to hospitalize the schizophrenic citizen, I must turn briefly from the contemplative to the clinical. There are tried and true language symbols we can use which connote qualitative and quantitative measurements. Is the patient's illness acute or chronic, progressive or static? Is his symptom picture mainly paranoid or nonparanoid? Is he dangerous to himself or others? Is he young or well past youth? Does he have recourse to a functioning family or is he alone? Was his premorbid adjustment adequate or faulty? How does he fare in relation to the twelve ego functions Dr. Bellak described in Chapter 4?

Some methods of the best treatment we now know for the schizophrenic sufferer are possible only within a hospital setting, and some are most effective when the patient remains in the family and community. For some approaches there is an option, and compromises such as day hospital or foster home care are feasible. Although some therapeutic interventions can be tried while the patient struggles with the larger environment they can be carried out more effectively, at less overall cost and in a shorter time with hospitalization as an adjunct.

I anticipate that knotty issues in the ensuing chapters will be not merely raised but will be tackled with vigor. Again regarding the trees, now is an opportune time to remove deadwood from the forest and possibly to relandscape it, to identify those sturdy, deep-rooted evergreens against which we can lean with confidence, to mark those damaged and diseased trees which should be chopped down, and to tag those straight saplings which should be nurtured.

REFERENCES

1. Mendel, W. S. and Rapport, S.: Determinants of the Decision for Psychiatric Hospitalization. *Archives of General Psychiatry*, 20:321-28, 1969.

10

The Hospital Treatment of the Schizophrenic Syndrome; The Role of Object Relations

ROBERT W. GIBSON, M.D.

A FUNDAMENTAL DISTURBANCE in human relationships is characteristic of the schizophrenic syndrome. This disturbance, because of its particular nature, is the major obstacle to successful treatment.

Psychotherapy, one of the most powerful tools for modifying interpersonal relations, was at first thought unsuitable in the treatment of the schizophrenic syndrome. By now it has been repeatedly demonstrated that the patient suffering from this disorder can develop a transference relationship permitting the full range of psychotherapeutic interventions including interpretation of resistance and the various transference manifestations.

But the psychotherapeutic work with such patients has many special features. To establish contact the therapist must be more active, he must go to the patient. The therapist may become important to the patient as an object in his own right activating the patient's fears of object relations and precipitating difficult management problems. The therapist must be more open and by providing a model encourage the patient to expose himself to what he has found to be the hazards of human relationships. At times the therapist must even share and live through the patient's conflicts. Only in these ways can the therapist establish what for the patient is a new experience—a relationship that nurtures ego growth.

Such therapeutic work is done most effectively in a hospital setting that offers the patient opportunities for relationships. Problems that develop as treatment progresses can be managed so that the patient's total experience will encourage and support his struggle to establish new object relations. The hospital staff must have the understanding and support needed to handle the inevitable anxiety aroused in relating to the severely ill person. Such a treatment effort requires a high level of collaboration as illustrated by the following clinical example.

A male patient with predominately paranoid symptoms became withdrawn, less communicative, and abruptly stopped eating. His general nutrition was good and he took adequate fluids but despite all encouragement would not eat. During one of several hall discussions about this patient an aide noted that the patient occasionally tried to smell the food offered. This led to speculation that he might fear that the food had been poisoned. The therapist recalled that just prior to his refusal to eat the patient had been more open in discussions about himself and had then become hostile and suspicious. From his knowledge of the patient's history based on discussions with the parents, the therapist suggested that experiences involving intrusiveness and excessive control during the patient's early years might have made him experience closeness as dangerous—poisonous. Out of this discussion came a working hypothesis that the patient might be less threatened if allowed control over his intake by observing his own food in preparation. An hour or so before meals he was taken on a tour of the kitchen, saw the food in preparation, and apparently his fears were relieved because he promptly began to eat.

This symptom might have been handled through the use of tube feeding, drug therapy or even electroshock. Such measures of direct external control would probably have reinforced the patient's fears of being influenced and poisoned. Instead, after first determining the patient was in no physical danger, the staff, through discussion of their observations about the patient's behavior pooled with the information from the therapist, arrived at a plausible hypothesis about the causes of the symptom. From this, an approach was developed that not only relieved the symptom but increased the patient's trust and strengthened his relationship to the staff.

This clinical illustration is taken from experiences on a research project conducted several years ago at Chestnut Lodge under a Ford Foundation grant. A detailed presentation of this work has been published (1969) by International Universities Press under the title *Schizophrenia and the Need-Fear Dilemma*, by Donald L. Burnham, M.D., Arthur I. Gladstone, Ph.D., and myself. Drawing on some of the concepts developed during the course of this work, I should like to present a conceptual framework for the hospital treatment of patients suffering from the schizophrenic syndrome.

The term "need-fear dilemma" is a kind of shorthand designation for the patient's conflict in his object relations. He needs objects to strengthen a weakened ego but simultaneously finds the same objects threatening to his ego integrity. Although a basic problem for all persons capable of object relations, the dilemma has a particularly damaging effect on the patient we call schizophrenic, intruding into almost all aspects of his life experience.

This dilemma is the end result of disturbances of ego development that have caused deficits in at least three areas of function: 1. executive functions of the ego are vulnerable to disorganization; 2. the ego is relatively lacking in autonomy from internal drives and external stimuli; 3. the ego lacks ability to maintain a reliable and enduring reality construct. These disturbances are interrelated and tend to influence each other. For example, the inability to control drives may have a disorganizing effect on the executive functions of the ego; faulty reality testing hampers the sorting of external stimuli from internal drives, making the task of control more difficult; and so forth.

The patient's vulnerability to disorganization of ego function leads to a desperate need for objects to give support and structure to his weakened ego. He finds objects frightening and potentially dominating because he lacks ego autonomy. All object relations are distorted by his poor reality testing. The total effect of these disturbances of ego functioning is to make the schizophrenic person particularly dependent on objects, but simultaneously threatened by them.

Patients try to solve the need-fear dilemma by adopting three major patterns in their object relations: 1. clinging to objects to gain support of an auxiliary ego; 2. avoiding objects to escape the fear of control and engulfment by the object; 3. redefining objects so that need fulfilling qualities are retained and fear inducing qualities are excluded. The various patterns (1. object clinging; 2. object avoidance; 3. object redefinition) are not static and may shift quite suddenly, leading to the ambivalence of object relations so characteristic of patients manifesting the schizophrenic syndrome.

Before discussing specific problems encountered in clinging, avoidance, and redefinition, I should like briefly to restate my position thus far. The patient suffering from the schizophrenic syndrome is confronted by a serious dilemma in his object relations. He needs objects for ego support but finds they evoke painful feelings that threaten his autonomy. In response he may relate to objects by clinging, by avoidance, or by redefinition. Object relations are fundamental to ego growth making it necessary in the treatment process first to establish a relationship; second, to modify the basic character of object relations by working through, corrective experience and new identifications; and third, to relinquish the objects involved in the treatment process, opening the way to new relationships.

The patient for whom object clinging has been a characteristic response to the need-fear dilemma, usually has a history of one or two highly dependent relationships. Disruption of these relationships is often the precipitating factor for psychotic disorganization and hospitalization. Symptomatic improvement frequently occurs quite promptly with hospitalization particularly if the patient is returning to a setting with which he is familiar. The organization of the patient's external environment provided by the institution substitutes for the patient's weakened internal ego organization, making it easy for the staff to establish a relationship.

There are some patients, however, who desperately seek an object relationship in such a fashion that it drives the staff away. I recall a 30-year-old woman who had been severely ill for many years. She moved toward people with a shuffling sideways gait. Her posture was stooped and she shrugged her shoulders and arms in a supplicating gesture. Her facial grimacing was continuous as she strained to speak. Hair and clothing were in disarray, soiled by food and grime. The total impact was of something subhuman.

My first contact with this woman came in the winter when she had a chronic upper respiratory infection. She rubbed a thick mucous discharge about her face in a most distressing fashion. All of us found it impossible to see her as anything but a loathesome creature. Nevertheless over a period of months she tried to establish a relationship with me. The most dramatic attempt came when she gave me a badly soiled candy bar she had clutched for hours. I accepted the melted piece of chocolate, but I suspect my revulsion must have been apparent. All of the staff struggled with similar experiences.

It was possible for us to overcome our problem only by instituting a project to improve the patient's personal appearance. The staff selected sport clothes that were more becoming to the patient, and lavished time on her hair and makeup. Naturally her appearance improved immeasurably but, more important, the plan made it possible to establish object relations with several people even though at a primitive level. This in itself was not curative but it did provide a setting in which a psychotherapeutic effort had some chance for success.

It may become extremely difficult for staff members to maintain a relationship with a patient who engages in object clinging over a prolonged period of time. The patient inevitably has constant reminders that he cannot have total possession of the object and as a consequence may be beset by feelings of helplessness and rage. The intensity of the patient's needs place a heavy burden on the person who is the object and may become so taxing that he will break off the relationship.

We might hope that with experience the therapist and other staff members could better tolerate the demands of the object clinging patient. Unfortunately, experience may just sensitize them to the problem. For example, along with almost everyone else in the hospital, I once observed two withdrawn teenage patients improve remarkably in what appeared to be a romantic involvement. It was a pleasure to watch this shy courtship as it led to their first date. But something went terribly wrong on this date and the girl returned in a state of severe psychotic disorganization from which, so far as I know, she never recovered. I offer no explanation for this sequence of events but mention it only as the kind of incident that makes one feel an awesome responsibility in establishing a close relationship with a schizophrenic patient.

In a hospital setting this heavy responsibility can be shared among several significant people in the patient's environment. Staff members can get considerable support from discussions of their work with the patient. The patient may feel less threatened because the hospital offers greater promise of meeting his needs than any individual can. The nonhuman environment may become extremely important. The hospital is always there; it has a visible structure; it provides a vast array of routines, policies, regulations and traditions.

For example, a young girl who had emerged from a schizophrenic reaction asked with great apprehension if Sheppard Pratt was going to be sold to a neighboring college. She urged me not to let this happen, explaining that prior to coming to Sheppard she had been on a unit of a newly-built general hospital. This fine modern plant was efficient but she experienced it as cold and impersonal. She described herself as an interchangeable part in a large machine. As best she could describe during her psychotic state she felt that Sheppard Pratt, its buildings, including their inadequacies, the staff, the way of doing things had a personality of warmth and friendliness. The patient's reactions were no doubt overdetermined but are worthy of serious thought in this era of efficiency and rapidly expanding treatment facilities.

Paradoxically these very advantages that the hospital has in making it possible to establish and maintain relationships become disadvantages as the patient tries to move beyond object clinging. Understandably he is reluctant to give up relationships to the hospital staff; he seldom finds people outside a therapeutic setting who make such a concerted effort to maintain a relationship. Staff members, too, may find it difficult to end the relationship; the person who can persist through the ordeal of relating to the regressed patient must be getting some fulfillment of his own needs.

While helping a patient through the separation phase the staff may be called upon to make difficult judgments and take calculated risks. Patients who function remarkably well within the structure of the hospital may still have great difficulty as they move into unstructured situations. The ability to plan and order life is one of the last steps of ego growth in the resolution of the schizophrenic syndrome. When a patient shows reluctance to face new demands it may be the result of an accurate appraisal of a persisting ego deficit; he really isn't ready. On the other hand, moving into new situations almost always causes anxiety and we must be prepared to live through the experience with the patient; most of all we must not abandon the effort even though the patient shows regression in the face of this challenge. If possible, the patient should never be forced to relinquish a significant relationship until he has established a new relationship that shows some promise of taking its place. One of the most effective ways to accomplish this is by providing a range from full hospitalization, through partial hospitalization, to outpatient care.

If the patient's fear of objects predominates, he may try to solve his dilemma by avoidance. Because of his deficit of ego function, he perceives all objects as threatening to his autonomy. In some patients a sense of helplessness can evoke extreme rage leading the patient to project his destructive impulses so that all objects are seen as dangerous. He avoids relationships by physical threat and assaultiveness.

A therapist, sensitive to the patient's needs and fears, may establish contact with the assaultive patient and hopefully create a bridge to additional relationships that will lead to ego growth. But the pattern of hostile isolation often leads to a particularly malignant interaction. The patient's rejecting behavior creates fear and resentment, discouraging staff efforts to make contact. The staff sees the patient as dangerous and because he lacks a well-defined ego structure he is quite susceptible to such suggestions; he tends to fulfill the staff's expectations by continued assaults. The psychosocial forces may become so powerful that nothing short of a transfer to another institution can interrupt them.

The use of tranquilizing drugs for assaultiveness is sometimes opposed on the grounds that symptoms may be resolved without understanding of the underlying causes. It is suggested that feelings of rage are repressed and isolated, perpetuating ego fragmentation. To some extent these objections are valid.

By utilizing the controls and protection of the hospital setting it may be possible to establish a relationship to the assaultive patient without the use of tranquilizing drugs. But if the reputation of dangerousness and assaultiveness begins to develop, with all its antitherapeutic consequences, then drugs are indicated to break the vicious circle of assaultiveness and fear. The patient's communications often become more intelligible, he is less threatening, and the staff less fearful. This encourages the staff to reach out to the patient, making it possible to interact in more positive ways that promote the development of an increasing circle of object relations. When used in this way, the tranquilizing medications can offer valuable assistance in the overall effort to establish relationships that will help the patient achieve further corrective experiences and ego growth.

Avoidance by simple withdrawal, catatonic stupor being an extreme example, can be a most formidable obstacle to the establishment of object relations. Staff members often seem reluctant to approach the patient actively, particularly if they feel that in so doing they will be behaving like an intrusive, controlling parent. The staff, believing they are treating the patient with dignity and respect, may adopt a permissive attitude, giving a minimum of direction. Carried to an extreme, staff may ignore personal hygiene and dress and may even be reluctant to tube feed a patient who refuses to eat.

A gentle, nonthreatening approach to the withdrawn patient may do much to allay his fears and has much to offer. But as an attempt to convey respect for the patient's integrity it is probably missing the point. The patient is in desperate need of object relations that can provide sufficient structure and direction for his deficiencies of ego organization. Furthermore, if a passive attitude leads to what amounts to neglect, the patient may interpret this as indifference or even an affirmation of his own feeling that he is not fit for contact with other humans.

For example, a patient had, during a two-year stay at another hospital, remained in his room and seldom permitted anyone to enter. He had bathed not at all; he had been unwilling to shave or cut his hair. Since the staff had been unwilling to force these issues, he had acquired a luxuriant beard and growth of hair to his shoulders. For this patient, the two-year experience of gentle persuasion had made no noticeable change in his pattern of object avoidance. In response to a more vigorous approach including insistence that he bathe, shave, get a haircut and come out of his room, he became threatening and delusional; beliefs that he controlled the world reappeared. Nevertheless, he did interact with the staff in a matter of weeks and a workable, though sometimes stormy, relationship was achieved.

The specific techniques used for achieving a relationship with a withdrawn patient may be dictated by the personality and the experience of the staff member. But whatever the approach, the staff must be prepared to go to the patient. Any interaction, even if it is stormy and angry, is better than none. The most damaging thing that can occur is the establishment of a hostile truce in which patient and staff tacitly agree to keep their distance so that the painful feelings and disturbed behavior can be avoided.

Some patients attempt to solve the need-fear dilemma by what we have chosen to call object redefinition. In schematic terms, object clinging can be viewed as a movement toward an object, while object avoidance is a movement away from an object. Still a third alternative is for the patient to alter his percept of the object so that the need fulfilling characteristics are accepted but the fear provoking characteristics are excluded from awareness. Object redefinition may be achieved simply through selective inattention alone, or through a variety of defense mechanisms, including denial, displacement and projection. In more extreme situations redefinition of the object world requires delusional thinking.

For example, one patient believed that a malevolent "Mr. Jones," whom she had never seen, was controlling her life by contacting her therapist and for that matter all of her acquaintances. Whenever hostile feelings appeared in any relationship, she concluded that the other person was acting under instructions from "Mr. Jones." Thus disturbing feelings could be excluded from all personal relationships, permitting her to retain a view of the object as friendly and supportive.

Within a hospital setting, patients often divide the staff into good and bad objects, attributing to the good objects need fulfilling qualities, supportiveness, dependability, permissiveness, and to the bad objects fear producing qualities of demandingness, intrusiveness, coerciveness. There is some tendency in most hospitals, whether by formal design or informal practice, to divide responsibility between therapeutic and clinical administrative considerations. Such a division makes it easier for the patient to divide the object world into good and bad, to maintain a position of object redefinition, and to avoid the painful recognition of ambivalent feelings.

Object redefinition as a kind of compromise solution to the need-fear dilemma can, in the initial phases of treatment, make it easier to establish relationships both for the staff as well as the patient. It can be easier tolerated than the painful extremes of clinging or avoidance. As efforts are made to alter the patient's fundamental disturbance in object relations, the hospital staff may be repeatedly confronted by a difficult choice between two alternatives: to preserve the relationship they accept the patient's distortions, running the risk of perpetuating the patient's defenses and underlying conflict; to improve reality testing, they confront the patient with his distortions but risk driving him into a state of object avoidance.

Object redefinition serves as a resistance against feelings of hostility aroused by the need-fear dilemma. As the resistance is exposed, the patient inevitably experiences anxiety which may lead to increased expressions of hostility along with exacerbations of other symptoms. It is taxing enough to work with a patient's resistance within the limits of a psychotherapeutic session, but even more difficult for nursing staff to handle in their daily contacts with patients in relatively unstructured situations often involving not just the individual patient, but a larger group.

The psychotherapist's efforts at clarification of behavior patterns and interpretation of genetic links are in themselves not enough for the severely ill schizophrenic. By redefining the psychotherapeutic relationship itself, the patient may set up an impregnable defense against all interpretations. In a hospital setting it is possible for the therapist to get adequate information about the patient's object relations and to exert sufficient influence over these relations so that object redefinition can be constructively modified.

It is difficult to do justice to this kind of therapeutic intervention in a condensed clinical illustration, but I want to try. A 22-year-old girl, with a diagnosis of Schizophrenic Reaction, Chronic Undifferentiated Type, was transferred to Sheppard Pratt from another hospital because after two years of intensive effort they felt at a complete impasse.

After about six months it appeared that we were well on the way to the same result. The patient was generally quite withdrawn. She made superficial but repeated scratches over her entire body, many of which became infected. She made some mild suicidal attempts and was considered by the staff to be the number one problem on the hall. Of particular concern was a growing antagonism toward the patient shared by most of the staff. The many judgmental attitudes expressed toward the patient were a measure of this; her demands interfered with the care of other patients, she was manipulative, possibly malingering, and so forth.

From a series of discussions with the hall staff, therapist and others, the following pattern emerged. Typically the patient had shown interest in a particular person, often a newly arrived student nurse. The nurse was soon made to feel that she alone could understand the patient and that the other staff members were cruel and unsympathetic. The patient sought exclusive possession of the chosen nurse and could not tolerate any display of interest in another patient. If the nurse made the slightest suggestion that she thought the patient was improving, the relationship came to an abrupt and stormy end, often with multiple self-inflicted wounds. The patient assigned the nurse to the category of bad, demanding objects. By that time the nurse was usually glad to join, having found her own estrangement from the rest of the staff taxing, and the patient's hostile dependency a heavy burden.

During this same period the patient had gradually developed a strong attachment to her psychotherapist. She tried to keep this relationship a very private affair and had successfully interfered with communication between therapist and staff. She had insisted that all material from the therapy sessions be held in strict confidence even if it concerned matters of vital importance to the staff such as a current plan to injure herself. The therapist had not agreed to this but had certainly been influenced by the sharp drop that occurred in the patient's communications whenever he entered into discussions with the staff.

The consensus of staff discussions was that the patient's need for relationships was so great that anything but total possession was threatening. The nature of her contacts with the nursing staff inevitably led to fears of loss, with feelings of helplessness and rage. These feelings were in part expressed by her self-mutilative attempts but the main response was to reclassify the people from the good, need-fulfilling category to the bad, demanding. The structured nature of the psychotherapeutic process had allowed the patient to retain the therapist as a need-fulfilling object though even this was often precarious.

As an outgrowth of these discussions, the therapist, with several members of the hall staff, met with the patient. As each told how the patient, by her rejection, had made them feel hurt, guilty, helpless, and finally angry, the patient listened intently. She was amazed to see that her actions had been such a determining influence on the staff response. No longer could she hold the view that she was a passive victim. In succeeding weeks, she reestablished more positive relationships with several staff members, altering her position on the hall and the whole feeling tone. By sharing information and utilizing it in a collaborative approach, the way was opened for object relations on a more constructive basis.

The promotion of positive personality growth in the patient suffering from the schizophrenic syndrome can rarely be accomplished by a psychotherapist alone. In the therapeutic relationship the patient is apt to experience the full range of his conflictual feelings with the therapist as object. Time and again he must face both horns of a dilemma—need and fear—with the ever present danger of psychotic disorganization. Unless the patient has sufficient resources to cope with this anxiety, hospitalization is indicated.

It follows that the core problem, in the treatment of the schizophrenic syndrome, is to establish and maintain object relations despite the presence of the need-fear dilemma. To accomplish this goal, the hospital must provide the opportunity for significant relationships with many people in the environment. The treatment program must provide necessary external control and regulation while simultaneously facilitating development of internal controls and regulatory capacities. In other words, the hospital must provide support to the patient's weakened ego and at the same time confront him with the challenges and opportunities needed for ego growth.

11

Hospital Treatment in Schizophrenia: The Indications for and the Value of Hospital Treatment

ERNEST M. GRUENBERG, M.D.

YOU MIGHT VERY WELL expect me, as an advocate of community care, to say that there are no valid indications for hospitalizing people exhibiting the schizophrenic syndrome. Indeed, as our newer and better patterns of patient care have developed, we find ever larger proportions of hospitalized schizophrenic patients suitable for placement outside the hospital. This has become especially the case with the increasing availability of more numerous and flexible transient forms of care—hostels, halfway houses, family care, patient clubs, etc. Simultaneously, larger numbers of candidates for hospitalization are being cared for without hospitalization as a result of the inauguration of precare consultations and the introduction of strenuous efforts to gain the patient's cooperation, or at least his passive acquiescence, in treatment (11, 19).

When surrounded by all these indications of progress, inevitably one begins to ask, "Where will it all end?" Is it really necessary to hospitalize any patient with the schizophrenic syndrome when so many appropriate alternate modes of care are available? It is attractive to conclude from successes of the recent past that if we become good enough at providing emergency and routine precare alternatives we shall arrive at the point where no cases will require hospitalization.

I myself have come to the opposite conclusion. It may be worthwhile pointing out that following World War II, the rapid expansion of both outpatient services and private office practice coincided in time with a most rapid increase in the proportion of the whole population being cared for in mental hospitals. Many advocates of extending "community services," as the community outpatient clinics were called, often stated that such expanded services would relieve the government of the cost of providing increased numbers of mental hospital beds. The flaw in this argument was that those communities which had had the most outpatient facilities for the longest period of time were the same communities with the highest bed occupancy rates in the mental hospitals. Further, during the early 1950's, when irresistible pressures had resulted in a rapid expansion of outpatient facilities, the number of mental hospital beds occupied in New York State alone was rising at the rate of 3,000 additional patients per year.

I am convinced that we shall need hospital treatment as part of the psychiatrist's armamentarium until such time as we are able to prevent the schizophrenic syndrome from occurring or until we discover means of aborting psychotic episodes quickly and effectively with a highly portable treatment that is suitable for use any place in the community.

However, I see no point in discussing indications for hospitalization in situations where a good treatment program is not available. Nor would it be fruitful even to consider the indications for using the hospital that takes on the characteristics of a prison-asylum as a consequence of the absence of the other parts of the community service network. As we all know, such a situation leads first to overutilization of the hospital and subsequently to underutilization, since sending a person to the hospital then becomes a form of community rejection.

Therefore, I am assuming, in presenting indications for hospitalization, that hospitalization is an integral part of the total complex of care which ranges from occasional consultation with the family physician to intensive outpatient treatment, hostel arrangements and day and night hospital care, through full intense hospitalization with continuous observation. I am also assuming that a single team provides care to the person with a chronic incurable disorder throughout all phases of his difficulties and in each facility as indicated. Of the greatest importance, I am assuming that the mental hospital is much less the isolated institution common a decade or two ago than a modern mental hospital with drastically reduced barriers between itself and the rest of the community (13). That is, I view the modern mental hospital as much less a total institution in Goffman's sense (6) than as one part in the network of community services. From my own observations at the Dutchess County Unit of Hudson River State Hospital and elsewhere, I have concluded that barriers between hospital and community can be done away with through the use of informal admission and release, the elimination of locks and bars and other symbols of isolation, the incorporation of the hospital's services into a full spectrum of community care, the removal of barriers to visitors, and the reliance on the patients themselves to take care of all their own needs to the maximum extent that they are capable of doing (2, 20).

I also want to make it clear that I believe hospitalization should end when the indications for admission to hospital no longer exist. Most of the following indications for inpatient treatment specify hospitalization under conditions far more relaxed than those generally accepted. While indications for hospitalization fall into two groups—short-term hospitalization (less than a day to less than half a year) and longer-term hospital care—I shall only discuss indications for short-term care.

The indications for short-term hospital treatment are:

1. To provide a treatment which cannot be given on an outpatient basis, for example: when dangerous drugs requiring continuous observation for safe administration are indicated; when either frequency of drug dosages or other factors make outpatient treatment unduly hazardous; when electroshock and similar treatments are indicated.

2. To protect the patient from his own uncontrolled dangerous impulses or the consequences of self-neglect. You will recognize this as the old legal justification for involuntary certification, that the patient is a danger to himself or others.

3. To remove a person temporarily from an environmental stress during a period when he cannot cope with the stress or be helped to cope with it successfully.

4. To provide a temporary relief for the patient's associates who are managing to live with him but at a significant cost to themselves. These costs include the loss of the caretakers' free time and the emotional energy which is mortgaged from other potential forms of emotional investment.

5. When a form of communication needs to be established between patient and hospital. Two ideas are frequently communicated by the process of hospitalization of the patient: the patient's difficulties are because of sickness; and, the hospital is available to the patient and to his family for assistance in the course of their living with a chronic incurable disorder.

I should like to discuss further the fourth and fifth indications. I have stated that hospitalization should be available as a temporary respite to those caring for the patient in the community. Clinical staff should stay alert to the emotional burdens shouldered by the people who keep chronically handicapped patients in the community. It is always wrong for the staff to wait for a crisis before suggesting rehospitalization, and it is sometimes wrong to wait until rehospitalization is demanded by patients or relatives. The clinician should feel able to insure, for example, that members of a patient's family can take an annual vacation free from the excessive emotional strain of taking the patient along with them. Again, physical illness or a pregnancy in a family member should suggest an indication for rehospitalization. While family indications are too numerous to list, some of the more common and recognizable ones include painting of a house, natural disasters such as floods, or when a youngster is preparing for college entrance examinations.

I do not wish to suggest that a family cannot have a pleasant holiday with a person who has a schizophrenic syndrome, or that people with a schizophrenic syndrome are never helpful in times of family crises. Indeed, severely disturbed people often improve remarkably under the pressure of a real need for their help. But such positive aspects should not blind us to the fact that not all patients respond positively. Frequently a patient's ability to live within the family is based on a fragile adaptation by both sides, with the supporting family members experiencing strains of which they may or may not be aware. It is part of the clinician's job to recognize such strains and do what he can to prevent them from becoming expressed by a rejection of the patient. One of his tools is judicious use of the hospital to temporarily relieve the family of its burden.

In developing a community placement as an aid in maintaining stability for the patient, the hospital must see itself as having to share the burden of caring for the chronically handicapped and sometimes troublesome individual. Ordinarily there should be common consent and common recognition between all three parties regarding what is occurring, i.e., both patient and family should know that the hospital can and will provide this kind of relief for a week or two as part of its responsibilities in caring for the patient. However, should such an understanding be misread by the patient as a declaration that he is more of a burden to his family than he is prepared to admit, or be seen by the family as a statement that they are less omnipotent than they like to think—or that their relative is sicker than they are prepared to acknowledge—it is not necessary to insist that a respite is the reason for rehospitalization. The patient and his family should, instead, be permitted to think that there is a need to readjust drug dosages or that diagnostic studies are required or that some new treatment directed at a target symptom be attempted. Indeed, a specific reason for rehospitalization may not always be clear, even to the clinical staff.

While I prefer to look on this sort of temporary rehospitalization as part of the hospital's contract with the family to share in the patient's care, others may view holiday and family illness readmissions as prophylactic, i.e., as a means of preventing the family from decompensating in its ability to care for the handicapped relative. I find this prophylactic argument unwholesome, for it tends, first, to deny that an immediate benefit is being sought; second, to distract attention away from making the hospital stay a constructive experience for the patient; and third, to put the family in the role of tools to the clinician. Therefore, I prefer to specify the fourth indication for hospitalization as a positive treatment in offering temporary relief to those who make community care possible.

My fifth indication for hospitalization is based on the need to communicate to all concerned the absolute availability of the hospital's services, for the very act of hospitalization is often the most effective means of reassurance. Hospitalization is the classic way of indicating that the medical profession recognizes the presence of a disorder (thus eliminating blame); that the clinicians assume responsibility; and that the person who is not functioning well must be seen as a patient (8). This can sometimes help the family accept the presence of illness, and the patient accept the sick role without exaggerating his disability.

For example, some outpatients are extremely fearful and have a sensation that they are falling apart and cannot continue to exist. Not infrequently they ask directly or indirectly if the therapist does not think they are crazy and should be locked up. For such patients the mental hospital is symbolic of total collapse and helplessness, and a short-term period in a good mental hospital can indeed be salubrious. Again, I am talking about the mental hospital which does not lock patients in a padded cell and which deals with them in such a way as to maximize their own decision-making in the details of daily living. Experience in such a hospital can offer the patient reassurance that his fantasies of total disintegration are unreal and that he is not as sick, as helpless or as hopeless as he had imagined. And that nobody else is either.

For those patients with a tenuous grasp on life who can be urged to make out as best they can in the community, the assurance that the hospital stands behind them and will help whenever it is needed is often crucial. However, a number of such patients are only persuaded of the truth of this flexible relationship through experimentation. We have all met the suspicious patient who, told that he need not stay in the hospital unless he wants its benefits, will feel the need to prove the truth of the matter by insisting, apparently irrationally and unwisely, on leaving the hospital—just to find out that he really will be permitted to leave. In the same way, the insecure and uncertain patient sometimes needs to reassure himself that the hospital will be there if needed by insisting, seemingly unwisely and irrelevantly, that he be hospitalized. I believe that patients need to test their ability to manipulate the hospital's admission and release practices to assure themselves that the policy really is flexible. It is important, therefore, for the staff to recognize not only that this testing is occurring, but to use these experiments to help the patient gain a conscious sense of assurance that the hospital's thresholds are really what the staff says they are.

Families, community agencies and general practitioners are also frequently uncertain of the response for demands for help through brief hospitalization. While some can be reassured via the investment of consultative time, at other times the easiest way to allay doubts is to permit hospitalization without resentment or argument. However, the staff must be careful not to mistake family efforts at rejecting the patient for demands for this type of experimentation.

It is one thing to list five indications for hospital treatment in the presence of a schizophrenic syndrome. It is quite another to explain the reasoning behind my views. I want to underline that I do not think that these indications for hospitalization have always been found acceptable, nor do I believe they have any abstract virtue. They represent my current views as to what hospitalization in the best comprehensive community programs can do for the patient with a schizophrenic syndrome. Since these indications will certainly be modified in the future as our knowledge changes and our technology improves, perhaps the best way to explain my reasons is to trace historically the relationship between the concept of schizophrenia and hospital care for the mentally ill.

The efforts by clinicians to classify what is wrong with the alienated in institutions are competently summarized in the Appendix of Dr. Karl Menninger's *Vital Balance* (14). We must start by recognizing that the very concept of schizophrenia emerged out of the mental hospital. Kraepelin's concept of dementia praecox was an obvious analogy to late dementias and in obvious contrast to congenital defects of mental life. Perhaps he was attempting to mimic, with insufficient data, the advances made when general paresis and Bright's disease were recognized. At any rate, Kraepelin was preoccupied with the concept of using the course of disorders as a major characteristic to differentiate one type of disorder from another. And dementia was by its nature a progressive condition.

However, as outpatient clinics became more common towards the end of the last century, psychiatrists began to encounter a wider range of dementia praecox cases than had previously been seen in hospitals. This led to an ever-increasing confusion regarding the diagnostic classification of mental disorders—a confusion still with us—since it became more and more apparent that cases of dementia praecox did not have a uniformly dementing course. In addition, with the beginnings of office practice, the psychiatrist began to recognize that the effects of the interpersonal interactions between himself and the patient had an effect on symptoms and complaints. Eugen Bleuler decided that dementia praecox was no longer a viable concept in his brilliant treatise on the group of schizophrenias in 1911; Janet, Charcot, Freud and Jung all affected his thinking. In contrast to Kraepelin's fatalistic notion that both course and manifestations were predetermined and imposed themselves on a helpless victim, Bleuler reformulated the syndrome as the consequence of a struggle between the patient and a disorder. By reorienting us to a dynamic interactive orientation, Bleuler was moving in the same direction as Freud and Adolf Meyer. Thus the concept of a simple few categories of dementia praecox with uniform course was reformulated as a heterogeneous group of syndromes with shifting manifestations and extremely varied courses. There is nothing like a broadened exposure for breaking up hardened categories.

Not only did Bleuler describe the schizophrenias as varied in nature and course; in specifying what makes it difficult for the patient to pursue his life, he also made a sharp distinction between the primary disorder and the secondary psychogenic defensive responses. This fundamental distinction has permeated all subsequent work on the schizophrenic syndrome, but unfortunately we have often been lax in our efforts to specify what we think is primary and what we think is secondary about the schizophrenic picture. When using Freud's outstanding elaboration of the mental mechanisms underlying symptom formation, we tend to account for therapeutic ineffectiveness by focusing attention on the symbolic content of symptoms on the one hand and by referring vaguely to "thought disorder" and "depersonalization" on the other. It would be wiser, however, to keep in mind the often-repeated observation that the patients who most dramatically illustrate Freud's mental mechanisms in their purest forms are more likely than not to reveal evidence of a schizophrenic syndrome. All of this insight tends to become another example of the great pathologist von Haller's observation, that pathology illuminates physiology. Disorders bring normal physiological mechanisms into increased action as a consequence of the organism's efforts to adapt to the new state of affairs. These increased activities of normal mechanisms make them easier to observe. Thus the normal cardiac contractions when increased in amplitude with a fever become the obvious palpitations often observable by the patient himself.

We sometimes have difficulty remembering that the patient with a schizophrenic syndrome shows evidence of excessive use of some mental mechanisms just because he *is* a distressed person; the mechanisms the patient is using are the same as those of anyone else, but he is overusing them to deal with his problems. The use of these mechanisms is not the source of his distress, only a symptom of it.

Advances in psychological and psychotherapeutic insight coincided with the radical transformation of the doctor-patient relationship which developed as a result of the expanded outpatient and private practice of psychiatry. In this outpatient context, very many cases of schizophrenic syndromes were seen where there were no indications for hospitalization. It thus became fashionable to consider a diagnosis of "schizophrenia" as not being sufficient indication for hospitalization, with psychotherapeutic techniques being used to treat schizophrenic outpatients.

While psychotherapeutic techniques had been developed and first used in office practice, these techniques soon began to penetrate the psychiatric hospital. Some hospital psychiatrists, more often at first those in the private rather than public hospitals, mastered and began using these techniques. Other psychiatrists in office practice brought psychotherapeutic techniques into the hospitals when they wanted to be able to continue treatment with a patient who became too disturbed to remain an outpatient. These introductions have lead to considerable interesting work with psychotherapy on extremely disturbed patients showing a schizophrenic syndrome, a development that other contributors to this volume have more clinical experience with than I. My own experience is confined to a single study in a university medical center—Columbia-Presbyterian Medical Center—where the psychotherapeutic technique was being transmitted to its residents in training. The results of the study make me doubt the efficacy of long-term inpatient treatment using psychotherapeutic techniques with schizophrenic patients (9).

The study focused on 200 consecutive schizophrenic patients who lived in the immediate vicinity of the Center and who developed psychotic decompensations of such severity that immediate hospitalization was required. The patients were randomly assigned either to the Center's Psychiatric Institute or to the usual treatment facility available to residents of the Center's service area—the Psychiatric Division of Bellevue Hospital.

The initial intent of the study was to demonstrate what the Center's full range of comprehensive neighborhood services which provided continuity of care could do for schizophrenic patients, as opposed to the one-shot, no follow-up, short-term care offered by Bellevue. The study did, in fact, provide another opportunity, that of observing the course of events in two comparable groups of patients, one of which was treated with long-term psychotherapeutic techniques as contrasted with another treated on a short-term basis. For while the psychiatrists in both institutions were predominantly psychoanalysts or analysts in training, the Center had decided advantages over the usual treatment facility.

Bellevue, a university-affiliated city psychopathic hospital, is basically designed only for triage and acute treatment. It has no facilities for follow-up care. Its plant is dilapidated; it is poorly financed. It is chronically overcrowded and understaffed. And its staff is under constant pressure to make a disposition of patients either to state hospitals or by discharge home with no subsequent outpatient services.

In contrast, the Medical Center's Psychiatric Institute, a university-affiliated state hospital and teaching resource, is basically designed for research and teaching. It has almost no restrictions on length of stay or types of range of services it can offer. Its plant is modern and well polished. It is well financed. It is never overcrowded. It is chronically overstaffed. And its staff is under no pressure to make any disposition of patients.

So strong was the Center's dedication to teaching psychotherapeutic methods with inpatients that the bulk of those patients in a study based on comprehensive psychiatric services who were being treated at the Center were kept in hospital for many months, even though neighborhood outpatient services were provided by the Center and despite the fact that almost all the patients lived within a 15-minute walk of the hospital. Conversely, the bulk of those sent to the city hospital were released within a few weeks and returned home to their previous mode of functioning.

Comparison of short-term differences in the patients was difficult to evaluate, since it is almost impossible to compare the functioning of patients still in the hospital with the functioning of patients back at home and at work. We can, however, make long-term comparisons, for after two years almost every person of both groups had been released from their respective hospitals. At that point in time there was little to distinguish them. If anything, those who went to the overcrowded city hospital with minimum treatment facilities appeared to be functioning somewhat better than those treated in the seemingly more desirable circumstances of the Psychiatric Institute. Or, to put it more exactly, fewer of them were functioning extremely badly. (Parenthetically, I should say that all the original diagnoses and the follow-up evaluations in this study were made by research personnel not responsible for the patients' care. I am convinced that their mixed biases about the study did not determine the pattern of the findings.)

By and large, then, it would appear that in general little if anything can be gained by introducing prolonged intensive inpatient psychotherapy with schizophrenic patients who have had psychotic breakdowns. This, of course, does not rule out the possibility that psychotherapeutic efforts conducted in hospitals can help schizophrenic patients in some instances and under some conditions. But the data from this study put a heavy burden of proof on those who advocate the general extension of psychotherapeutic measures to hospitalized schizophrenic patients on the basis that these measures will make a large difference in the recovery rate.

While psychotherapeutic techniques were coming into vogue in American mental hospitals, some exciting things were beginning to happen in British mental hospitals. Not in all British mental hospitals but in a few. Some British psychiatrists had been impressed by their surprising experiences at the time of forced hospital evacuations and severe staff shortages during World War II (15, 16). Not only did patients not take advantage of ample opportunities to escape, but many responded positively to wartime crises by helping less able patients. Some of these psychiatrists knew that during the first part of the 19th century many mental hospitals, inspired by the humanism of Pinel and Tuke, had completely given up physical restraints and operated as unlocked institutions. John Conolly (3, 4) was the hero of this period, and his reports on the operation of Hanwell Asylum were reread. Three British mental hospital directors— Bell, Macmillan and Rees—pretty much independently but with encouragement from Walter Maclay (12), the Senior Psychiatrist in the Ministry of Health, began quietly experimenting to see in what ways how many of their patients could be cared for without the use of locked doors.

After a decade or more, several things were established. First, no doors needed to be locked except medicine cupboards and that holy of holies, the staff toilet. (This refers to mental hospitals for mental patients; criminals require hospital units in the prison system, not prisons in the hospital system.) Second, patients could only be kept in an unlocked hospital when there was a full activity program to engage their attention. Third, patients were best cared for outside of the hospital once the initial period of disturbance had ended, which care in turn depended upon the establishment of extended outpatient and consultation services into the fabric of community life. This community care required a most relaxed approach to rehospitalization, which made sure that everyone knew that marginally adapted patients could be rehospitalized on very short notice and without fuss and red tape. Fourth, there appeared to be a radical reduction in the rate at which new cases of chronic deterioration developed after the new open-hospital and community-care program had come into being (7, 11).

I first became aware of these developments in 1953. It took me several years, extended visits, and a chance to observe the reactions of other skeptics to overcome my own skepticism regarding these claims. But I became convinced that basically what I have described actually did occur —and it all happened before the advent of any of the tranquilizing types of drugs.

But belief remained but belief for awhile, since research data were lacking on the effects of these new programs. Because the means of achieving a reduction in chronic deterioration required community care of rather disturbed patients, the whole picture could not be conveniently got simply by studying the patients remaining in the hospital. Thus, when I was given an opportunity by Dr. Robert Hunt to study the impact of a similar transformation of patient care that he had inaugurated at Hudson River State Hospital in 1960, I seized it (17).

We wanted to find out if the number of cases becoming chronically deteriorated in personal and social functioning decreased at the time the new services were inaugurated. Therefore, it was necessary to develop a research technology to ascertain the existence of chronic deterioration and to see if the number of new chronic cases arising in the population being served did in fact drop each year. In order to do this, we had to define as objectively as we could what was meant by deteriorated personal and social functioning. This turned out to consist almost entirely of objective features of behavior: first, self-care in grooming, eating, retiring and arising, and dressing and undressing; second, doing some work of social value to others (either a paid job or a share of housecleaning and maintenance care of children or other helpless persons, etc.); and third, engagement in recreational life, e.g., reading, writing, dancing, game-playing and the other activities, which are the embroidery that makes life more than a drab, humdrum existence (18).

Deterioration is a word that is used loosely, and has both broad and narrow connotations. Therefore, we rejected it and gave our more specifically defined patterns of failure in personal and social functioning a new name, the Social Breakdown Syndrome (1). It is the chronic forms of this secondary syndrome which appear to be preventable (11). These are prevented by making the duration of hospitalization as minimal as possible, by changing the meaning of hospitalization from a negative to a positive experience and by helping the patient to use his remaining capacities to the fullest extent possible. This seems to depend upon the availability and use of a full spectrum of services rendered by a single clinical team which takes continuing responsibility throughout the course of the patient's experience with his disorder.

In addition to its preventability, the Social Breakdown Syndrome (SBS) is interesting because its form is the same regardless of the diagnosis. In our study, which focused on one county, we found that in one year only about half of the new SBS cases started in schizophrenic patients. The remaining cases were scattered among patients with many different diagnoses. The same breakdown holds equally for those with long-term (lasting one, two, three or more years) episodes and only half of these are patients with the schizophrenic syndrome. Thus, it is obvious that a person with the schizophrenic syndrome does not decompensate in his personal and social functioning differently from, say, a mentally retarded or chronically depressed or post-traumatic brain syndrome case.

Another remarkable fact about SBS is that the majority of cases begin prior to any mental hospital care and terminate very quickly following hospital admission. Thus, I might add as another indication for hospitalization, ending an episode of Social Breakdown Syndrome as quickly as possible. However, SBS has still another important characteristic: about one-third of the episodes begin and end without a hospital admission. Further, hospital admissions do not involve any episode of Social Breakdown Syndrome, either before admission or afterwards. Therefore, since many episodes of SBS can be ended without hospitalization, I shall limit my indications for hospitalization to the five discussed earlier.

This section of the volume focuses on our differing views on the indications for hospitalization in people exhibiting the schizophrenic syndrome. This is a worthwhile topic which should be pursued. Therefore I wish to discuss a few points in the hope that they will anticipate potential questions which could distract from the main theme of this section.

First, it is important to distinguish between the Social Breakdown Syndrome and institutional neurosis on the one hand and the unitary theory of mental disorders on the other. Institutional neurosis—an idea enunciated clearly by Russell Barton—described the secondary disabilities which are the consequences over a long period of time of a dehumanizing institutional life. The deterioration in the patient's personal and social functioning which occurs as the result of institutional neurosis is an example of the Social Breakdown Syndrome. But the concepts are different since SBS almost always starts outside the hospital and is often terminated by a brief hospital stay.

The unitary theory of mental disorders is also different from the SBS. As I understand it, the unitary theory of mental disorders seeks to distract attention from the standard nosological entities and to see all the symptom patterns as types and degrees of decompensation. The Social Breakdown Syndrome, however, is a concept of a secondary sociogenic form of decompensation in personal and social functioning which is the consequence of the responses of both the patient and those near to him to whatever is wrong with the patient's mental functioning. Thus the SBS concept does not replace the distinction between a ruminative tension state and a manic-depressive reaction, nor does its usefulness depend on anybody's views as to the nature of that distinction. The concept of the Social Breakdown Syndrome does provide us with a new understanding about those manifestations of mental disorders which are the most distressing to the people in the patient's environment. For we have been helped to see that many of these manifestations can be quickly relieved by modifying the behavior of those same people and by avoiding excessively intense and prolonged hospitalization.

New ways have, of course, been added to account for secondary symptom formation in the half century since Bleuler articulated the concept that psychological defense mechanisms produce many secondary symptoms seen in schizophrenic patients. I should also like to call attention to an obvious inference regarding secondary symptom formation as a topic that requires a different context for discussion. For after the Social Breakdown Syndrome was found to be preventable by changed organization of services and policies regarding staff functioning, techniques were developed for ascertaining the presence of this secondary syndrome's components. The application of these techniques showed that the same manifestations of decompensated personal functioning are not limited just to schizophrenic patients but occur as well in patients exhibiting a range of disorders. Sociology and social psychology have advanced sufficiently to provide at least tentative bases for attributing many behavior changes seen in schizophrenic patients to hitherto poorly understood sociopsychological mechanisms (9). When these insights are combined with those that have resulted from increased understanding of intrapsychic mechanisms of symptom formation, we may be able to account for as secondary almost all the features of the clinically observed schizophrenic syndrome as defined by Bleuler, including those he called "primary."

But secondary to what? Secondary to the underlying disorder, of course. But what is the underlying disorder? We know some of the things the underlying disorder is not. But we seem hardly closer than we were in 1911 to knowing what underlying defects or processes lay the ground for the multiple pictures we call the schizophrenic syndrome. However, because our capacity to account for secondary symptom formation in the schizophrenic syndrome is so greatly enlarged, it is obvious that we must again ask what the primary manifestations are.

I shall conclude by pointing out that indications for hospitalization might better be formulated if indications for terminating hospitalization were included. I remain convinced that hospitalization should last only as long as the indications for admission to the hospital continue, and should be terminated when the indications for admission are terminated.

Our main point has emerged about providing care for patients with severe disorders, and this is that when such people come to a mental hospital, "social ties are torn, habits are changed: life goes on without the usual proprieties; people are hurt by those who do not hate them; they come to obey from fear; . . . a person is stripped of the social privileges he enjoyed while in the community. . . ." (5, author's translation).

Certainly we can reduce the extent to which "coming to the hospital" wreaks havoc on the lives of the people. But we cannot prevent at least some of these effects if the patient's hospital stay is prolonged. Yet patients are still kept too long in the hospital under poor conditions and for bad reasons such as: outpatient care being unavailable from the inpatient therapist; no patient clubs exist; night and day hospitalization are not available as transient forms of care; hostels away from the patient's own family are not available; the hospital is a great distance from the patient's own home. These are the reasons why continuity of care and informal rehospitalization on short notice are difficult or impossible.

Let me add again that the goal of hospitalization is not recovery but is specified in the following five indications for hospitalization: 1. to give treatment too dangerous to be given on an outpatient basis; 2. to provide protection from the patient's own behavior; 3. to provide temporary isolation from unmanageable stress; 4. to give those providing community care a temporary respite; 5. to help communicate the fact of the hospital's availability.

REFERENCES

1. American Public Health Association: *Mental Disorders: A Guide to Control Methods.* Prepared by the Program Area Committee on Mental Health, American Public Health Association. New York: American Public Health Association, 1962.
2. Bennett, C. L.: The Dutchess County Project. In Gruenberg, E. M. (Ed.), *Evaluating the Effectiveness of Community Mental Health Services.* New York: Milbank Memorial Fund, 1966.
3. Conolly, J.: *The Fifty-Fifth Report of the Visiting Justices of the County Lunatic Asylum at Hanwell.* London: J. T. Norris, 1840.
4. Conolly, J.: *An Inquiry Concerning the Indications of Insanity* (1830). Reprinted, London: Dawsons of Pall Mall, 1964.
5. Esquirol, J. E. D.: *Des Maladies Mentales, Considérées sous les Rapports Médical, Hygiénique et Médico-Légal.* Paris: Baillère, 1838.
6. Goffman, E.: Characteristics of Total Institutions. In Walter Reed Army Institute of Research, *Symposium on Preventive and Social Psychiatry*, April 15-17, 1957. Washington, D.C.: U. S. Government Printing Office.
7. Gruenberg, E. M.: Can the Reorganization of Psychiatric Services Prevent Some Cases of Social Breakdown? In Stokes, A. B. (Ed.), *Psychiatry in Transition 1966-1967.* Toronto: University of Toronto Press, 1967.
8. Gruenberg, E. M.: The Social Breakdown Syndrome—Some Origins. *American Journal of Psychiatry*, 123:1481-1489, 1967.
9. Gruenberg, E. M.: From Practice to Theory: Community Mental Health Services and the Nature of Psychoses. *Lancet*, 1:721-724, April 5, 1969.
10. Gruenberg, E. M. and Kolb, L. C.: The Washington Heights Continuous Care Project. In press.
11. Gruenberg, E. M., Snow, H. B., and Bennett, C. L.: *Preventing the Social Breakdown Syndrome.* Baltimore: Williams and Wilkins. In press.
12. Maclay, W. S.: Experiments in Mental Hospital Organization. *Canadian Medical Association Journal*, 78:909-916, 1958.
13. Macmillan, D.: Recent Developments in Community Health. *Lancet*, 1:567-571, March 16, 1963.
14. Menninger, K., Mayman, M., and Pruyser, P. W.: *The Vital Balance.* New York: Viking Press, 1963.
15. Milbank Memorial Fund: An Approach to the Prevention of Disability from Chronic Psychoses. *Proceedings of the Thirty-Fourth Annual Conference of the Milbank Memorial Fund, 1957*, Part 1. New York: Milbank Memorial Fund, 1958.

16. Milbank Memorial Fund: Steps in the Development of Integrated Psychiatric Services. *Proceedings of the Thirty-Sixth Annual Conference of the Milbank Memorial Fund, 1959.* New York: Milbank Memorial Fund, 1960.
17. Milbank Memorial Fund: Mental Hospitals Join the Community. *Milbank Memorial Fund Quarterly,* 42:7-175, 1964.
18. Milbank Memorial Fund: Evaluating the Effectiveness of Community Mental Health Services. *Proceedings of a Round Table at the Sixtieth Anniversary Conference of Milbank Memorial Fund, 1965.* New York: Milbank Memorial Fund, 1966.
19. Morrissey, J. D.: The Chichester and District Psychiatric Service. In Gruenberg, E. M. (Ed.), *Evaluating the Effectiveness of Community Mental Health Services.* New York: Milbank Memorial Fund, 1966.
20. Snow, H. B.: The Dutchess County Project after Five Years. In Gruenberg, E. M. (Ed.), *Evaluating the Effectiveness of Community Mental Health Services.* New York: Milbank Memorial Fund, 1966.

12

Indications for Hospital Admission of Schizophrenic Patients: Some Sociopsychiatric Considerations

ALFRED H. STANTON, M.D.

A PSYCHOTIC PATIENT referred privately and treated briefly in the community may, somewhat paradoxically, prove to be helpful in indicating some special aspects of a clinical consideration of psychiatric hospital admission of schizophrenic patients. The patient was, in fact, referred because the psychiatrist was affiliated with a psychiatric hospital; the referring physician urged that consideration be given to the burden the patient's wife had tolerated increasingly for many years.

The patient was a lawyer over 70, still professionally active and in good general physical health except that he had suffered an operation which had conspicuous effects about two years before and five years earlier had suffered a myocardial infarct. For the last year his wife had not left his side, literally, giving his dependence as the reason. His wife, eight years younger than he, and also his daughter and the whole family were unusually close to him.

Their central complaint was of his jealousy. Throughout almost fifty years of marriage it had been extraordinary; on their honeymoon he had accused her of flirting because of her sitting at the hotel window. She had even left him briefly during the first year to return to her home for this reason. She was not allowed to dance with any other man throughout her marriage, could not compliment any other man either to his face or alone to her husband. Since the coronary insult, and particularly during recent months, bursts of anger and threatening had frightened everyone, and led to his consultation, with the idea of hospital care in mind.

His first interview revealed that he wished to see me in order to enlist my services—to help his wife with her trend toward unfaithfulness. A successful lawyer, he marshalled a series of about ten episodes collected over the years which indicated his wife's unfaithfulness to him; he maintained throughout the interview a guarded care, alert to whether I would accept his wife as the patient. Clearly delusional interpretations were built upon these incidents but none was close to convincing; all did suggest occasional flirtatiousness. Some were clearly complex—like her offering him only her cheek to kiss.

It will not surprise psychiatric clinicians to learn that his jealousy fed over the years upon her actual slight flirtatiousness, and that thoughts of murder, and possibly public scandal had at times been imminent. Nor will they be surprised that, since the coronary episode, both had had difficulty in intercourse, although an internist had helped by advising nitroglycerine before intercourse. A man servant, feared as a sexual rival, was described by the husband in glowing terms, particularly his physical attractiveness. The possibility of homosexuality was lightly mentioned by the husband about people in general, on the tacit assumption that no one in the room would be concerned in more than an academic way with this problem.

The family, one or the other, was seen for nine interviews. At first, in an effort to obtain emotional distance, and because of the highly cultured background, both were ordered to reread *Othello,* independently and thoughtfully. Each time the husband raised the question if he or his wife was sick, usually very subtly, it was countered by identifying his question as one of who was to blame, in the manner of an attorney, casting his psychiatrist in the role of a judge. The question was then reformulated as one of his wishing to save his marriage and his and his wife's satisfactions, and therefore what could he do—what was under his control. If something within himself contributed to the difficulty and could be identified, it would presumably strengthen his position as the guardian of the marriage. We identified the fact that he had narrowed both his wife's and his own life to such an extent that any reasonable woman would feel stifled, as indeed might he. We indicated that his constant attention to possible infidelity, and warning his wife of the attractiveness of other men, might actually tend to interest her in what he feared, and, finally, he was advised to resume certain of his activities and to insist upon his wife having a greater range of activity, unsupervised. He decided to "control himself," and a final useful hour was spent in his boring but very necessary, recounting of his achievements throughout his life because of his great self control. His family reported enormous improvement—better than for many years before the coronary, and he seemed to be taking masculine pride in his controlled restraint. He had grasped intellectually the nature of the prescription (although without knowing much about its underlying rationale) and took pride in sharing the professional role. The way was open for either or both to return if it proved wise; indirect but reliable information has indicated no recurrence of the episode for four years.

I have chosen this case report to emphasize certain aspects of the analysis of the character of schizophrenic persons' disturbances and their treatment. In this case, the only manifestations of illness, diagnosis or treatment were psychological-symbolic and interpersonal—and notwithstanding the prominence of drugs and physical therapies in psychiatric treatment, the symbolic communicated aspects of analysis of treatment are always prominent. The analysis of hospitalization and its effects must be thought of as specialized types of people's living with each other, interacting and interpreting this type of experience—not as primarily a nonsymbolizing organism in an environment.

Titchener (20) summarized the implications of Brentano's psychology —contrasting his assumptions with those of Wundt—in ways which are highly pertinent: "the phenomena (of psychology) . . . are very far from being static appearances. Generally they are activities: in the individual case they are acts. Hence, they can properly be named only by an active verb. They fall into three fundamental classes: those, namely, of Ideating (I see, I hear, I imagine), of Judging (I acknowledge, I reject, I perceive, I recall), and of Loving-Hating (I feel, I wish, I resolve, I intend, I desire). We may use substantives if we will, and may speak of sensation and idea, memory, and imagination, opinion, doubt, judgment, joy and sorrow, desire and aversion, intention and resolution; but we must always bear in mind that the psychical phenomena is active, is a sensing or a doubting or a recalling or a willing.

"It is true that we never have act without content. When we ideate, we sense or imagine something; when we judge, we perceive something, acknowledge the truth of something, recall something; when we love or hate, we take interest in something, desire or repudiate something. This, however, is precisely the difference between psychical and physical phenomena. The latter are blank and inert: the color or figure or landscape that I see, the chord that I hear, the warmth or cold or odor that I sense, the like objects that I imagine, all these things are described when their given appearance is described; their appearance sums them up and exhausts them; they have no reference, and do not carry us beyond themselves. Psychical phenomena on the other hand are precisely characterized by relation to a content, by reference to an object; they contain an object intentionally within them; and this character of immanent objectivity, in virtue of which they are active; marks them off uniquely from the physical phenomena upon which they are directed and toward which they point."

Not only are the elementary analytic concepts of Freud built upon the act as a unit (he was a student of Brentano's over some years) but those of Adolf Meyer led him to substitute the term "reaction type" for "illness" concepts which contain within them references to action and not merely to behavior, process, or disease. Modern social science may be more explicit—as in Parsons and Shils' *Toward a General Theory of Action* (17). Psychiatric disorders have to be conceived as people doing something, rather than simply as events occurring, and even where nonpersonal facts, like drug actions, require analysis, they are made manifest within a personal acting framework as well as a physiological one. Cause and effect relations in hospital practice occur as two or more people interacting, doing something with each other, on the basis of more or less shifting or stable intentions, more or less accurate information, more or less conventional or bizarre aims and premises, of more or less well or misunderstood agreements. All parties give meanings to what they are doing, and, indeed, these meanings are to some extent defined by the meanings given by the others to the transactions. People give themselves the liberty of interpreting their own and others' actions and intentions, and these meanings are inseparably part of the cause and effect sequences.

These meanings, for both observer and patient, are so dependent upon the context within which the action occurs that the psychiatrist shifts repeatedly back and forth between the detail to its context, as part of his characteristic clinical way of working. It is this habit which means that for the hospital psychiatrist the character of the hospital becomes part of the warp and woof of his understanding of his patient. To be sure, there are many times when he tries, with some success, to treat the hospital context of his patients in some static, selective, and arbitrary way (most often referring to it as "reality" as if its structure were fixed by nonhuman agencies trying to see his problem "simply").

Admission of a patient to a hospital, then, is his transfer from one type of social group (or groups) into another, whatever else it entails. And the physician's prescription should be based upon at least a partial awareness of the implications of the change of group.

Recognition of the central importance of the character of the patient's group involvement has been growing until it has almost reached the point of being overlooked as commonplace. To some extent, however, where patients are known thoroughly as may occur in intensive psychotherapy, it can never be commonplace; therapy with patients tends almost uniformly now to deal first with the patient's perceptions and interpretations of the here and now and, however much the physician may wish to avoid "interpreting reality" to the patient, he cannot avoid considering it and noting its pertinence. The growth of the confrontation therapies—group psychotherapy, family therapy, and marginal psychotherapy in connection with activities for instance—has been in part an outcome and in part a cause of this greater awareness of and focus upon what used to be called the current social field of which the patient's responses are a part. Psychoanalytic psychology has permitted the widespread recognition of indirect and disguised participation in the social group—even "withdrawal"— as what it is rather than as some "bizarre" symptom. The clear-cut observation of Doctor Schwartz (19) that even fecal smearing by each of four very chronic schizophrenic patients was uniformly a reply to a brush-off by the staff—and never occurred in group psychotherapy—was only a particularly emphatic observation of this sort. It was surprising; one had to be in a position to look at what had just happened among others than the patient.

If it be assumed, then, that a certain number of characteristically schizophrenic actions may be an unrecognized part of a long-term conversation between the patient and his personal contacts, we can identify several possibly troublesome constellations which have been suggested— either from family or hospital studies.

Doctor Schwartz and I (19) described in connection with excitement (some of it schizophrenic) a constellation of lasting covert disagreement regarding the management of the patient, between the authorities or putative authorities in charge of the patient, and its dependence, in turn, upon controversy and tension among the hospital staff. As in the group psychotherapy situation, and fecal smearing, it was possible to find evidence that the excitement was dependent for its continuing existence upon the continuation of the staff disagreement and reticence. Supported by the studies of Gladstone and Burnham (9), and by others on a more clinical level, it may also be one precipitant of schizophrenic withdrawal. Family schism indicated by Lidz, Cornelison, Fleck and Terry (15), as a situation frequently confronted by schizophrenic patients in their families prior to hospitalization is unmistakably reminiscent of the type of hospital disorder which we noted.

This type of disorder may be only one of many types of situation where patients, or people about to become patients, must confront and manage a social situation of intolerably complex demands. The paradigm of Bateson, Jackson, Haley and Weakland (4) of receiving conflicting demands, from which one cannot escape, conveyed to one at different logical levels so that the fact of their conflict cannot be noticed, has been so generally noted that it has entered the common language as the double bind. The family dedicated to pseudomutuality described by Wynne (22) and his colleagues, and tested experimentally by Lerner (14), may confront a patient with problems before which even the experienced psychotherapist has quailed after trying to "break through" such an attitude.

"Labeling" of patients, whereby parents insistently inform children about what is in the child's mind, even as they did when the child was a toddler, was found much more frequently in the families of schizophrenic patients than those of normal children by Lennard, Bernstein and Beaulieu (13). Such an education in the irrelevance of the distinction between one person and another, an affirmation of symbiosis if you will, outlines another type of complexity which, if avoided at home by the child's conforming, must lead to overwhelming handicaps outside. While we cannot yet test clearly the necessity of the latter types of social facilitation for maintaining schizophrenic experience, by interrupting or changing the situation, clinical observation in the family or on the ward convincingly supports their significance.

If characteristically schizophrenic actions, then, develop within, and may depend upon the continuation of, certain specifiable types of interpersonal dealing, the nature of the decision to hospitalize a patient will be determined by these facts. While certain obvious incompetences of the patient, like proneness to suicide, confusion, disorientation, aggression or gross inability to care for oneself, may and often do give no real choice except to find a "protected environment" even in the modern day of medications, nevertheless the decision is also one of substituting one social life for another. The social implications are likely to become prominent in a relatively few days, if the psychiatrist allows himself to consider them. Is the patient to become a "long-term" patient or are only "limited goals" appropriate? Will a threatened divorce become more or less likely? Is the patient prone to a "real regression" encouraged by hospitalization or able to "regress in the service of the treatment?" It is at this time that the diagnostician needs to formulate his real questions of which regimen of several options is the more likely to prove genuinely therapeutic the most rapidly. I believe this estimate is neither easy nor impossible; it is, I believe, usually not attempted, the problem set differently.

We have approached the decision to advise a patient's entering the hospital by considering certain social configurations which there is reason to believe may favor the development or maintenance of schizophrenic experience, configurations which may occur either inside or outside the hospital. It may be a moot decision whether they are more likely to occur within or outside the hospital. In reaching the decision, however, there are other constellations of overwhelming emotional importance which may occur within the hospital, and which are widely suspected of being nearly universal within hospitals. There are the obvious and important characteristics of the hospital—a degree of protection from violence and from losing oneself, supervision and administration of medication and other physical treatments. But other matters are as important, or often, of more importance.

Mental Disorders: A Guide to Control Methods (1) described a psychiatric disorder, the Social Breakdown Syndrome. The committee brought to bear the experience of a considerable number of distinguished scientists and physicians interested in the psychiatric field. The identifying boundaries of psychiatric disorders are not as objective and often not as clearcut as in biological disorders, and it is not surprising therefore that one cannot give to this newly identified illness a specific time, place, and agent of its discovery. Awareness of its existence and importance has been growing for some years since World War II, and it is not surprising that it was first articulated and published by a group. In 1959, Russell Barton (3) described a similar situation calling it the Institutional Neurosis. The study of it has been extended by Ernest Gruenberg whose discussion of it in Chapter 11 permits me a brevity which would otherwise be unjustified.

As the Committee describes it: "There is one type of mental malfunctioning which occurs in many different chronic mental disorders, particularly schizophrenia, mental retardation, and various organic psychoses. It is responsible for a very large part of the institutionalized mentally disordered; it is responsible for much of the other forms of extreme social disability seen in these illnesses. This form of mental reaction in the presence of mental disorders is largely a socially determined reaction pattern which the committee believes can be identified as a major target for community mental health programs today. . . . This particular reaction, made up of a number of symptom patterns, (comes) into sharp prominence because of its great commonness and its sensitivity to improved organization of services. It has not had a name in psychiatric literature in the past. . . . It is largely because of current successes in dealing with this syndrome, it is believed, that for the first time in two generations the census of patients occupying beds in mental hospitals has started to decline, in the English speaking countries."

This superimposed syndrome is characterized by a loss of interest in the outside world, a heightening of interest in trivial and immediate concrete issues, a loss or blunting of many of the relatively delicate nuances of social interchange such as wit and whimsy, interest in special characteristics of others, and the like. Apparently trivial jealousies and resentments, long feuds over almost forgotten incidents are common forms of aggressive discharge. This is the terrifying, even if common, personality disaster which is feared, with some warrant, when psychiatric hospitalization is recommended. If the conception is correct, the decision to hospitalize should indeed be approached with caution and sophistication.

There are many grounds for accepting their interpretation of the syndrome. Report after report, several from Topeka, have indicated the considerable effects of a new energetic and imaginative program instituted on a "chronic" ward. Eldred, Bell and Longabaugh (7) had the opportunity to score the number of interactions on such a ward at McLean, a hospital with a comparatively favorable staff-patient ratio, and found the number to average less than ten a day per patient, even though meals were included. Apparently with the impact of the research itself, the number increased, and sociometric estimations provided an interesting insight into the latent structure of the ward (5). (While satisfactory reliabilities could not be reached considering the small number and the degree of disturbance of the patients, staff sociometric choices and inspection of the patient choices gave indication of trends.) Patients considered the most and the least sick by the staff were selected by the staff most often; in contrast, patients selected other patients largely on the basis of how well they thought them to be. Most interaction by patients was with staff and it was overwhelmingly about local topics of concern. The first change noted in patients who were later to be discharged was found in the pattern of interaction. These fortunate patients began to deal much more with the staff and, after a period, picked another patient with whom interaction grew until it outranked that with the staff. These pairs of patients seemed to improve together and to be discharged in pairs (again the numbers are too few to be definite). The friendships did not persist significantly after discharge. Clinical condition, as reflected in a number of measures, improved considerably and notably *after* the increase in measured interaction.

Such a ward may almost be a caricature of anomie and, indeed, this sociological conception has provided the cues to intervention. Spontaneously developing informal ward structures, built around household duties, local favors, privileged positions on the wards and, in some instances, functioning as aides to the aides, have been known for some time, and show the depth of the reluctance of human beings to reach a total amorphousness. Less well recognized and appreciated have been informal economic systems, systematic instruction in how to manage getting out, comparison of various psychiatric hospitals and other matters of obvious patient importance. These structures have often had high potentialities for good and evil; instruction in how to get out may be a primitive but helpful form of psychotherapy. But suppression, sometimes brutal suppression and intimidation may also flourish.

The introduction of explicit and official group activity of many sorts, primarily after World War II and reflecting the experience of British and American military and veterans' practices, was a central and effective attack upon this anomie. It is now clear that not even in a mental hospital can one escape committee work. The introduction of the concept of community to the hospital meant that ostracism for eccentricity was likely to be temporary, that one's taking responsibility continued to be obviously valued by one's fellows, that aimlessness gave way to purpose, discussion could deal with general topics—that, in short, one continued to have some importance. As noted most emphatically by Artis (2) and his co-workers schizophrenic utterances seem to melt away in large group discussions. I recently spent two and a half hours of discussion with some forty young men and women, patients who had been admitted, in many cases, for schizophrenia; the topic (in this year 1969) was the merit of the hospital rule that patients of the opposite sex did not touch each other excepting in obviously conventional ways like dancing and shaking hands. Needless to say, not one of the young people agreed with the Establishment, but nevertheless in the whole evening only one statement was made which was not clear and pertinent; they were often skillfully pointed. None of the patients looked schizophrenic—or any more so than their age peers in Harvard Square.

There is, again, no dearth of reports which indicate the significance of this change. Kellam and Chassan's (12) observations were the first to show objectively that patients on the same ward tended to improve and get worse at the same time. The clinical impression is strong that this improvement is not merely temporary comfort or freedom from strong emotion, but improvement in whatever symptomatic disorders the various patients exhibit. A thorough study was reported by Fairweather (8) who organized one ward into many small groups and left the other more traditionally as a large single unit. The differences in discharge and in achievement after discharge were often impressive—all favored the small group organized ward. A most significant account is given of the development of a task-oriented group at the Yale Psychiatric Institute studying the use of power in the hospital; Rubenstein and Lasswell's (18) analysis and reporting of the group gives the clearest indication available of the type of group activity within which schizophrenia tends to become irrelevant, while a patient's serious citizenship is repeatedly reinforced. Normal behavior has an arena.

A partial explanation, in social terms, of the effectiveness of small group organization may be found in the notion of social bankruptcy developed from the ward analyses of Longabaugh and Eldred (16). They scored the interactions of patients in a carefully time-sampled way, counting the values transmitted or requested from one to the other in the interaction; these values were goods, information, evaluation, support, help, direction and permission; they might be offered, sought, taken, accepted, deprived, rejected, ignored or referred. From the many measurements obtained, they were able to derive a number of indices of efficiency, self-reference and the like. From it they derived a quantitative construct of "bankruptcy"—a situation where the person is perceived by others as of no value to them and where others tend to conclude that it is more costly than rewarding to maintain an interpersonal relationship with him. A number of tests of the concept proved consistent with it as characteristic of the chronic schizophrenic, with the exception that on the ward, the illness itself proved rewarding to the staff, in that their major official function was validated by the patient's illness.

In the active group situation, however, to use these economic constructs, the patient's value is quite generally increased, more or less obviously, regardless of the task of the group, and at no expense to the hospital. One might say that the group makes manifest the fact that, normally, humans are of value to each other.

We have considered a major, perhaps the major, danger of hospital social structure, approaching it from the point of view of the clinician considering the hospitalization of a patient, or his discharge. It would, therefore, be incomplete not to note that, again, while the danger has been discussed and described largely as a property of the hospital, similar circumstances often occur, and less manageably, in the outside community. The psychiatrist has in his casebook enough material so that he does not need the pungent phrase "a one-man psychiatric ward" to recognize that circumstances outside of the hospital also are often conducive to the Social Breakdown Syndrome and that, therefore, his decision cannot be made without consideration. Indeed, it is the disadvantages of the outside community that may make him consider the hospital a "therapeutic" community for his patient. Hospital discharge is not an automatic criterion of advance.

The hospital may, and should, make available to the patient both individual and group activity more easily than it is available for him in the community outside. It cannot hope to match the range and social import of all activities available outside, but within the hospital it should be easier to join in those activities which are offered.

The schizophrenic breakdown frequently occurs in persons of a particular type of personality, and a partial recovery is even more frequently followed by this type of person—the intellectually intact person who can, and does, largely conform to social expectations but in an empty, affectively detached way. Can not enforced or encouraged "groupiness" encourage such a stable maladjustment?

Indeed impersonal social activity is as common as genuinely personal relationships; the way one takes part may be as significant as the fact of taking part.

This also can be a feature of group activity which may be influenced for therapeutic ends. Following Sullivan, people may deal with each other cooperatively or collaboratively; the former he uses to cover interactions where people do what is expected, knowing correctly that their own aims will be met by fitting in with the social norms and the general expectations of those about them. The particular identity of the other is largely irrelevant, since one is dealing with him on the basis of widespread social norms. Paying one's fare to the bus driver and a thousand other actions of this sort make it possible for all of us to live in a complicated world. But often most of it is unsatisfying. Collaborative relations are those which are characterized by the fact that one takes into account the particular needs and character of the other, those characteristics which make him unique and peculiarly himself. What happens to him makes a particular, not a generalized, difference. Indeed one may characterize a relationship as loving if the pleasure of one is heightened by the knowledge of the pleasure of the other in the interaction. But be that as it may, such a relationship is always exquisitely personal, and is felt as such by the participants. It is such relationships that our schizophrenic patients who have partially recovered—"with defect"—find difficult or impossible, but continue to need nevertheless.

A part of institutional living, particularly of efficient or economical institutional living, is likely to be the prominence of impersonal interaction—dealing with others on the basis of a generalized image rather than the particular knowledge of the particular people.

Although largely avoidable, it is almost impossible to appreciate the degree to which impersonality has dominated the psychiatric, and the general, hospital. On the one hand is the fear of being personal, of intruding, or of the sexual implications of the word personal; on the other hand are a large number of social practices persistently asserting and reinforcing social distance and impersonality. Linguistic habits like "them" to refer to patients, "females" for women patients, of the classical referring to patients by diagnosis, reinforce habits of objective reference to parts of the patient systematically excluding the rest from consideration. The picture of the professional attitude is often taught as remote, objective, untouched—and untouchable—with neutral affect, if that, and certainly nothing personal. Kahne (11) quotes a nursing text to this point: "In regard to family, their members' occupations, likes and dislikes, always listen when a patient talks but be careful to avoid all judgments or comments that may add to a patient's anxiety. All the above are 'touchy' subjects and should be carefully handled." Also: "When a patient does burst forth with a confession of some feeling or experience about which he obviously feels strongly, care must be exercised not to presume on the revelation. *The patient should be treated exactly as he was previously* and mention of what was revealed should come first from the patient."

Such attitudes lead to myths like the replaceability of one nurse or physician for another, the use of staff members or patients as instruments and other silent assumptions which can collectively create a desolate hell whose shortcomings will usually be too obscure for the uninitiated patient to diagnose and cope with.

The study of Wenar (21) and his colleagues on the relation of the milieu to autistic behavior among autistic children is directly related to this point. Developing measures for both the symptomatic behavior of the children and of certain characteristics of the milieu they studied—a large custodial institution, a small active highly-planned group-organized institution, and a small day care unit organized with a psychoanalytic orientation—they met the problem straightforwardly of estimating environmental as well as symptomatic characteristics as part of the appraisal problem. The latter day care institution had a much higher adult-child ratio, more involvement of adults, consistency of care, communication and other characteristics. The active small group oriented institution was much less personal—in the terms we have been using—than even the large custodial institution. After a year, there was no change in any of the three units in the ability of the children to communicate and speak, but the day care unit proved much more helpful in all other measured effects; interestingly the more active group-oriented program, much better staffed but more impersonal, showed children who *declined* in their ability to master their environment, a sharply unsatisfactory effect even compared to the apparently warmer custodial hospital.

A special subtype of this impersonality, brought to our attention by Haycox (10), is the tendency of both staff and patients to treat each other as part objects. If one is overtaken by a policeman, one tends to respond to him, not in personal terms, but as the incarnation of judgment, pursuit, punishment—that is on the basis of only a part of his person. A sick patient is likely to see her psychiatrist in terms consistent with her felt needs to which the doctor seems pertinent—all else is likely to be unnoticed in any serious way; only later as she comes to see the place of therapy can she respond to the physician as a person and not as an embodiment. But this is even more persistent and hard to notice in the staff, particularly the psychiatrist. Its ramifications are blatant or subtle. For instance: "To say that a schizophrenic patient is capable of only a part-object relation is to have with that patient yourself only a part-object relation. It is taking a part of the patient and letting it account for the whole."(10) Doctor Haycox cites Doctor Christ (6): "She suddenly reported that she felt like *one* person. She was no longer a 'set of thoughts' or a 'bundle of feelings,' as she expressed it, but one person. We were able to review at that time how she had previously experienced other people as mere ideas, for instance, Dr. B. as the idea of restriction or her family members as incarnations of certain character properties. Her younger sister was experienced as the idea of angry aggression. This was all different now. She not only could see herself as a person but could also see other people as persons with their contradictions."

Again the same problem will be ubiquitous, perhaps more so in the nonhospital community. For a patient's behavior to fall from the personal characteristic of doing something odd into the class of the mentally ill in his social community is to not only change in status but, to some extent, to lose one's whole position as a person. And people in the hospital may on the one hand reinforce the damage, or on the other rescue the patient from it.

Planning and conducting a treatment program with a patient on a basis of knowing that particular patient, and on the basis of his total, not partial characteristics, are themselves a significant dimension of the treatment program as well as setting the stage for the rest of the program. This completely personal type of consideration is something which may be available at the psychiatric hospital, and is unlikely to occur elsewhere except in families. Its importance cannot be estimated from its inconspicuousness. It has its conditions and its favorable circumstances, so that to some extent its occurrence can be planned.

I should like to return to the nature of the decision to admit or to discharge a patient from the hospital—the transfer of the patient from one social milieu to another. For this brings to attention a major factor which has often tended to slide into obscurity—the characters of the social milieu as well as the patient. When asking psychiatrists for the indications for hospitalization, they nearly always will speak in terms of the gross conditions requiring hospitalization upon the tacit assumption that if none of these exist, hospitalization is not indicated. While there are obvious economic grounds for this assumption, to temper one's clinical analysis entirely to the "practical realities" is to allow one's very thoughts to be molded by an arbitrary if, at times, humanistic opportunism; further it may lead to the unnecessary denial of one form of treatment when the patient has presented himself for advice simply because the psychiatrist can no longer think of a more expensive regimen, or because he has misunderstood the patient's economic circumstances. I suspect that the psychiatrists I interviewed spoke only in terms of the necessities of hospitalization partly because of this tempering of their clinical analysis to the demands for the least possible expense.

But whether or not it is "practical" it is a mistake to overlook the fact that hospitalization may benefit many patients who can survive without it. Psychiatric hospitals can and do provide an atmosphere which can help a patient and therapist deal with the long, relatively symptom free post- and prepsychotic states of wooden conformist isolation; narcissistic defenses considered "impenetrable" by the individual psychotherapist may prove so irrelevant and troublesome for the patient to maintain in an appropriate group situation that they can be gradually seen and abandoned. The possibility of avoiding improvement with defect exists now and should not be overlooked.

In passing, it should be mentioned that a significant contribution to the maintenance of the patient's value is the existence in the hospital of individual psychotherapy. Here almost by necessity (but only almost— the individual therapist can manage impersonality if he tries consistently enough) individual and unique issues become significant to both, and the effect spreads to the considerations of others.

In summary: There is evidence that there exist types of social compliance with schizophrenic actions both inside and outside the psychiatric hospital. Some of these have been sketched. Aside from the obvious circumstances requiring hospital care for survival, there are grounds for assuming that hospitals have and do create circumstances where schizophrenic behavior is nonfunctional and tends to ease or disappear, often quite rapidly, as well as creating situations which tend to complicate and reinforce psychosis. The indications for hospitalization and for discharge cannot be analyzed adequately without taking these characteristics of the social circumstances into account.

REFERENCES

1. American Public Health Association: *Mental Disorders: A Guide to Control Methods.* Prepared by the Program Area Committee on Mental Health, American Public Health Association. New York: American Public Health Association, 1962.
2. Artiss, K. L.: The Symptom During Therapy. In Artiss, K. L. (Ed.), *The Symptom as Communication in Schizophrenia.* New York: Grune and Stratton, 1959.
3. Barton, R.: *Institutional Neurosis.* Bristol: John Wright and Sons, 1959.
4. Bateson, G., Jackson, D., Haley, J., and Weakland, J.: Toward a Theory of Schizophrenia. *Behavioral Science,* 1:251-264, 1956.
5. Bell, N. W., Longabaugh, R. H., and Eldred, S. H.: Sociometric Structure of a Ward for Chronic Schizophrenics. Unpublished manuscript, 1963.
6. Christ, J.: Psychoanalytical Treatment of a Dissociative State with Hallucinations. In Eldred, S. H. and Vanderpol, M. (Eds.), *Psychotherapy in the Designed Therapeutic Milieu.* Boston: Little, Brown & Company, 1968.
7. Eldred, S. H., Bell, N. W., Sherman, L. J., and Longabaugh, R. H.: Classification and Analysis of Interaction Patterns on a Ward for Chronic Schizophrenics. In Rioch, D. McK. and Weinstein, E. A. (Eds.), *Disorders of Communication.* Baltimore: Association for Research in Nervous and Mental Disease, 1964.
8. Fairweather, G. W.: *Social Psychology in Treating Mental Illness: An Experimental Approach.* New York: Wiley, 1964.

9. Gladstone, A. I. and Burnham, D. L.: A Method of Studying the Relationship Between Pathological Excitement and Hidden Staff Disagreement. *Psychiatry*, 29:339-343, 1966.

10. Haycox, J. A.: Discussion of Paper by Jacob Christ. In Eldred, S. H. and Vanderpol, M. (Eds.), *Psychotherapy in the Designed Therapeutic Milieu*. Boston: Little, Brown & Company, 1968.

11. Kahne, M. J.: Bureaucratic Structure and Impersonal Experience in Mental Hospitals. *Psychiatry*, 22:363-375, 1959.

12. Kellam, S. G. and Chassan, J. B.: Social Context and Symptom Fluctuation. *Psychiatry*, 25:370-381, 1962.

13. Lennard, H. L., Bernstein, A., and Beaulieu, M. R.: Interaction in Families with a Schizophrenic Child. In Mishler, E. and Waxler, N. (Eds.), *Family Processes and Schizophrenia*. New York: Science House, 1968.

14. Lerner, P. M.: Resolution of Intrafamilial Role Conflict in Families of Schizophrenic Patients: I. Thought Disturbance. *Journal of Nervous and Mental Disease*, 141:342-351, 1965.

15. Lidz, T., Cornelison, A., Fleck, S., and Terry, D.: The Intrafamilial Environment of Schizophrenic Patients: II. Marital Schism and Marital Skew. *American Journal of Psychiatry*, 114:241-248, 1957.

16. Longabaugh, R. H., Eldred, S. H., Bell, N. W., and Sherman, L. J.: The Interactional World of the Chronic Schizophrenic. *Psychiatry*, 29:78-99, 1966.

17. Parsons, T. and Shils, E. D. (Eds.): *Toward a General Theory of Action*. Cambridge: Harvard University Press, 1952.

18. Rubenstein, R. and Lasswell, H. D.: *The Sharing of Power in a Psychiatric Hospital*. New Haven: Yale University Press, 1966.

19. Stanton, A. H. and Schwartz, M. S.: *The Mental Hospital*. New York: Basic Books, 1954.

20. Titchener, E. B.: *Systematic Psychology: Prolegomena*. New York: Macmillan, 1929.

21. Wenar, C., Ruttenberg, B. A., Dratman, M.D., and Wolf, E. G.: Changing Autistic Behavior. *Archives of General Psychiatry*, 17:26-35, 1967.

22. Wynne, L., Ryckoff, I., Day, J., and Hirsch, S.: Pseudomutuality in the Family Relations of Schizophrenics. *Psychiatry*, 21:205-220, 1958.

13

The Psychotherapeutic Center and Schizophrenia

OTTO ALLEN WILL, JR., M.D.

THERE ARE MANY IMPORTANT ISSUES associated with psychiatric hospitalization; it would be presumptuous of me and beyond my professional competence to attempt a consideration, however brief and elementary, of more than a few of these. I am concerned here with a particular function of the hospital in the treatment of the schizophrenic person, speaking by intention from a restricted and special point of view. I shall discuss some aspects of a psychotherapeutic center in which educational and research enterprises are closely related to the treatment program. In so doing, I shall not deal with such matters as the following despite their significance: 1. The advantages and disadvantages of hospital, outpatient, halfway house, and home care; 2. the hospital as a place in which a variety of therapeutic modalities have major roles—EST, insulin coma, psychosurgery, drugs, and so on; 3. the use of the institution for brief sojourns ended by a return to the home or by transfer to another facility for more prolonged, and perhaps custodial care; 4. the organization as a socializing instrument in which emphasis is placed primarily on the effects of group relationships—as in formal group therapy, the milieu, and so on; and 5. the social pressures related to the increase in population, the numbers of so-called mentally ill, the shortage of professional personnel, the costs of care, the competing and often contradictory systems of treatment, and the inequities and general unavailability of psychiatric help.

The resort to the above exceptions might seem likely to rule out most of what is realistically of value in a commentary of this nature. However, such stringencies may be advisable in an effort to focus on a particular task and prevent involvement in issues of such magnitude and urgency that the chances of increasing understanding in a small area of interest could be lost. Thus it is that I do not seek to define or defend what may be the "best" mode of therapy or to present "solutions" for the wide range of social-psychiatric patterns of behavior that come to be labeled schizophrenic, and concerning which there is much disagreement about diagnosis, etiology, course, prognosis, and suitable intervention. Often it is difficult to specify what one holds to be professionally desirable for the particular patient, when the unmet needs of so many others are apparent and currently beyond much, if any, help. Nonetheless, certain approaches limited to a few should not be abandoned simply because they are not readily available to, or suitable for, the many; the wise study of the single case can yield data applicable more or less directly to a multitude.

When one presents ideas such as I do now, he should, perhaps, comment as best he can on what he knows of his own particular point of view or bias. I am a physician, a psychiatrist, and a psychoanalyst. Years ago I worked in hospitals housing large numbers of patients; there the primary concern of the staff was in the provision of the elements of food, clothing, shelter, and humane care, there being little energy, money, time, or personnel to do more. I have learned something about human behavior from many experts in the field, as well as from my own observations, but I cannot speak with assurance about what schizophrenia is or even know if there is such an entity in the traditional medical sense. I have seen exhibited and have myself used some of a variety of treatments—from intrathecal horse serum, insulin, metrazol, nitrogen, carbon dioxide, electroshock, prolonged sleep, lobotomy, and so on, to the drugs of this present age. I have worked with those who sought what help I could give and with others who would have had nothing to do with me or my kind were it not for the restraints of law and institutional walls. In both groups some have found profit, and others not. For reasons not at all clear to me I have often felt myself to be an outsider, living on the periphery of those activities and groups that constitute the conventionalities of our lives. I have been struck by the readiness of men to identify the outlander —the stranger who seems foreign and somehow unfit—and to push him away so that those who are left may be alike and supposedly not suffer from major differences. There are many who are placed in this category, and (again for obscure causes) I am drawn to some (not all) of those called schizophrenic. I discovered within myself no special therapeutic skills—no deep wells of empathy—but I did find something that I had not fully known and that Sullivan (5) expressed so clearly that it is worth repeating despite its deceptive simplicity. I quote ". . . there is nothing unique in the phenomena of the gravest functional illness. The most peculiar behavior of the acutely schizophrenic patient . . . is made up of interpersonal processes with which each one of us is or has been historically familiar. For the greater part of the performances, the interpersonal processes of the psychotic patient are exactly of a piece with processes which we manifest some time every twenty-four hours. In most general terms, we are all much more simply human than otherwise, be we happy and successful, contented and detached, miserable and mentally disordered, or whatever." My interest then was not so much in the treatment of a disease process known as schizophrenia but in the study of the vicissitudes encountered in forming a relationship with someone who has learned that he can expect more anxiety and hurt than good from such an involvement. Throughout the years, marked by numbers of therapeutic enthusiasms and regrets, the human relationship itself was seen to be a major force in bringing about beneficent growth or psychological disaster. Although there are other factors significant in the formation of a personality, the interpersonal influence is not only powerful but to a large extent observable. It is this influence that holds my attention and constitutes the bias which is to be taken into account in what follows.

The following brief account is presented not because it is unusual but because it is commonplace. It is a picture of the human estrangement with which we are all familiar and with which we must deal in one way or another. In this instance hospitalization was of great importance in treatment.

When I first met Miss A, she was nineteen, and I was a therapist on the staff of a small psychiatric hospital. She was brought to us from another institution by ambulance, in restraints and heavily sedated because of her assaultiveness and her efforts to mutilate and kill herself. She had a reputation for destructiveness and resistance to treatment; the person was rapidly becoming blurred and lost in the stereotyped formulation of her as a patient and a schizophrenic. Her earlier life experiences were pieced together from the hesitant, reluctantly given, and fragmentary accounts of her parents, refined by later additions given by herself, and by inferences as to what might have been, drawn from observations of our behavior together.

Miss A, the oldest of three children, was a "wanted" baby and was said to have had an uneventful and happy childhood. In her high school years she was a good student and took part in sports and other social activities. Her parents and teachers thought of her as contented, compliant, and successful. The girl herself, in contrast to these views, felt increasingly that she was out of place and unsuited to the requirements of her life. She had no close friend in whom she could confide, although she was popular in the more superficial sense of the word, went about with young men, and was looked upon as pretty and socially desirable. In her senior high school year she complained of fatigue, ate poorly, lost weight, and vaguely expressed concern that she was ugly and unwanted. Privately she felt that she was undergoing an ill-defined but dreadful change. She was tall and feared that she would not stop growing and would become monstrous. She searched her skin for imperfections and finding them was horrified at the thought that through them were about to be exposed a deeply hidden evil and a perversity that would rise to public view despite all of her efforts to conceal and restrain them. In the end she, and those upon whom she had depended (her parents in particular), would be contaminated, somehow poisoned, and destroyed. Her body to her seemed deformed, and she kept to herself as much as she could without leaving school altogether. Her efforts to speak to others about her apprehensions were futile; no words were adequate to describe her experience, and when she did speak, she was guarded and enigmatic, not wishing to reveal herself as hopelessly evil or mad. No medical explanation was found for her fatigue, a holiday was prescribed, and she was assured that all must be right for one so physically attractive, intellectually gifted, and socially competent as she. Such reassurances served only to increase Miss A's sense of aloneness and inability to make sense with others.

Being so favored by nature, as she was told, she knew guilt for making little use of her gifts and shame for concealing an evil that others did not see. Despite these increasingly unpleasant events Miss A graduated from high school and entered college. There she felt lost and isolated but made a valiant effort to keep going by increasing her activities. She studied diligently, took part in dramatics, and had a series of sexual affairs. At the end of the first year, however, she felt less secure than before. She found it difficult to concentrate on her courses, and on the stage she felt detached and lost in the portrayal of someone other than herself. Her lovers were no more than bodies, and as one replaced another, she looked upon herself as an object to be manipulated and put aside. She grew depressed, withdrew to her room, abandoned her classes, and slept fitfully, often wakening in terror from poorly remembered dreams. A persistent something—not clearly a voice—seemed to urge her to kill herself lest she destroy others. One night, alone in her room, she cut long gashes in her arms and legs, rubbing the blood over her body and wondering if its presence was a sign that she was alive or a warning that she should be dead. She felt herself to be invaded by a power beyond her control, and in response to its seeming intent, she threw herself from her window as if for the moment she were invulnerable to hurt. She fell two stories, but the impact was lessened by shrubbery, and she was not seriously injured.

Then began Miss A's career as a patient. She was hospitalized, diagnosed as schizophrenic, and during the course of the next year received deep insulin coma (fifty) and twenty electroconvulsions. She was at times quiet and withdrawn, on occasion assaultive and destructive, and frequently attempted to mutilate herself. At the end of nine months she was discharged as improved and attempted to return to school but left after a few weeks because of her fear of failing. She was seen in psychotherapy for two months but left the therapist, saying that he was personally unsuitable. Four other therapists were consulted within the next six months, and each was abandoned as somehow unsatisfactory. Miss A worked for a couple of weeks as a model, but her depression returned, and again she was hospitalized after taking an overdose of barbiturates. With the aid of ataractic drugs she returned to outpatient psychotherapy, persisting in this for three months and bringing it to a close by developing a hallucinatory episode accompanied by self-mutilation and another suicidal attempt with drugs. It was at this juncture that I met Miss A and became her therapist.

The beginning of psychotherapy with Miss A was not an uncomplicated matter; it was marked by a number of characteristics which required our attention in planning a therapeutic program. Miss A had been deeply troubled for years during which she had been able to maintain a deceptive facade of amiability and conventional success. During these years despair had increased as had the feelings of isolation and unrelatedness. Efforts at communication had not succeeded, being handicapped by the autistic nature of experience and the fear of the possible consequences of self-revelation. Speech had become more defensive than informative, and there was little hope on her part that she could make much sense with anyone.

The etiology of this increasingly disastrous behavior is unclear. Information about the early years of Miss A's life was inadequate or lacking, and no one could say with absolute assurance what events were of particular significance in forming her personality. This last is true, despite the fact that much that came to be known of her is not presented here.

As communication failed and isolation increased, Miss A made desperate attempts to maintain social contact through sexual activities, work, and so on. It was only when her behavior was troublesome to others and obviously socially deviant that action was taken and some recognition given to her condition. Her cutting herself and leaping from the window were socially unacceptable, and she was hospitalized. By this act a new role was forced upon her—that of psychiatric patient with its many implications of disgrace, failure, shame, wickedness, devil-possession, and hopelessness. Miss A's own sense of self-identity was uncertain and diffuse; the role of patient was horrifying to her, and she was left with a sense of being nothing—of having no place to go.

Miss A had no reason to have confidence in psychiatric treatment; as she well knew, she had derived no lasting profit from a variety of approaches, and she had no confidence in their advocates, just as she had little trust in any human being including herself.

At the time of our meeting Miss A wanted no part of me, refused to see me or stay in my presence, correctly asserted that she had not sought my services, protested my intrusion into her life and my coercive posture in insisting on her treatment, and predicted that our relationship could lead only to her death or our mutual destruction. She fought all my attempts to be of use to her or to have contact with her.

As for myself, I had to deal with the fact that I was in a conventional sense unwanted, and despite my advocacy of freedom I was being coercive. The history of treatment was not promising of future improvement, and the earlier difficulties that led to the first disturbed episode were complicated by later discouragements and by Miss A becoming resentfully and despairingly immersed in the role of patient with the possibility that she might come to accept this as an identity and a career. Thus my interest in being Miss A's therapist was tempered by a recognition of some of the social complexities that often modify and distort the concept of schizophrenia.

The term schizophrenia requires some definition by each one who uses it. In this chapter I refer to schizophrenic behavior as a reflection of earlier life interpersonal and social experiences, as designed to accomplish certain ends, however expensively and inadequately, and as fulfilling a role of which the culture has need. The possibility of there being an as yet unidentified biochemical factor associated with such disturbances should not reduce our interest in the clinical phenomena that are inextricably involved with early growth and development. These events reflect defects in learning, an ill-defined and unstable sense of identity, and a complication of the symbolic universe that seriously interferes with object relations and perception.

Although the basic difficulties in human relatedness probably arise from experience in the first two years of life, prior to the development of dependable concepts of self and others and of skill in the use of language, the people under discussion now have managed to get through the puberty change and into chronological early adolescence without the development of behavior so deviant as to require public notice or intervention. The schizophrenic state may be looked upon as an expression of the culmination of interpersonal insults, learning defects, and dissociations of experience vital to satisfactory adult living, uncorrected from infancy and finally brought into the open by the exigencies of a current situation believed to be of great importance for personal survival.

Miss A was unable to meet the challenges of adolescence—the establishment of a reliable sense of identity, the beginning of psychological separation from her family, the patterning of sexual behavior, the formation of a communicative and intimate relationship, the development of a personal sense of values. The behaviors, designed earlier to bolster up decreases in the sense of personal security, were often found to be handicaps in the making of needed relationships. In general, as the desire for the integration of a relationship increases, previously dissociated sentiments may be required to broaden the encounter and enrich its significance. However, as defensive operations (such as selective inattention and obsessionalism) are not so active, there may appear in awareness less refined referential processes characteristic of earlier, anxiety-laden, poorly assimilated experience, related to reverie and the dream, and accompanied by uncanny feelings of awe, dread, disgust, horror, and loathing. The imprecision of these processes is associated with a growing unclarity of self and others and a disturbing sense that meaning is spreading and cannot be localized. Concepts of space and time are no longer certain, and the person involved feels an urgent need to resolve the intolerable lack of determinacy and predictability in his life—to "make sense" of events, to bring order into what threatens to be chaos, and to recover some reminder of the familiar. In the attempt to accomplish an almost impossible task—to comprehend inadequately perceived and poorly defined events, to solve an urgent problem, to put vaguely understood autistic and dreamlike symbols into words, to maintain human contact, and to avoid appearing mad—speech becomes marked by loosely connected elements, autisms, neologisms, inexact phrases, and personal idioms. All of this is done in an effort to control the contents of awareness and to focus on what would be relevant in life were one not so vitally concerned with the shoring up of a rapidly failing self-esteem. The final disaster is experienced as a collapse of all that has been dependable and familiar, including the sense of self and important systems of value upon which some reliance has been placed. This is the state of panic, usually not long lasting, so painful as to require some early solution and influential in future developments through the anticipated horror of its possible recurrence. Resolution of panic may occur through death by exhaustion, suicide, or misadventure; through a reintegration of personality structure permitting further growth and learning; through further dissociation of aspects of the personality, the maintenance of which may require gross strictures on interpersonal development; or through the retreat to hebephrenic or paranoid ways of life that stubbornly resist all efforts at modification. Here we are concerned with a therapeutic program whereby major dissociated systems need no longer be maintained and further growth and learning be made possible as confidence, trust, and self-knowledge are increased.

Psychotherapy is an interpersonal experience, a special form of the human relationship. From the point of view that schizophrenic behavior itself reflects past experience in interpersonal and social fields and is also responsive to current events and anticipations of the future, psychotherapy would seem to be a meaningful form of intervention in an attempt to alleviate disorder. By this last I mean that both psychotherapy and schizophrenia can be looked upon as forms of interpersonal relatedness. The patient has learned that he must be cautious and suspicious and must develop elaborate modes of behavior in dealing with other people because he tends to become intolerably anxious with them at the same time that he needs them; he may also learn (as in psychotherapy) that he has generalized his fears too much, that he has exaggerated his own destructiveness, and that the present and the future need not be simple replicas of what is remembered as having been. It should be noted that the psychotherapeutic relationship—like others—is not neutral; it has consequences, and these can be constructive or destructive for both participants.

There follows a brief outline of some of the factors that constitute the forming of any potentially therapeutic relationship with particular reference to the schizophrenic person such as Miss A.

If there is to be any psychotherapy, patient and therapist must *meet with each other*. The frequency of the meetings, the length of each, and the places for them will be determined by the needs of the participants at any stage of the work. For the first few months I met with Miss A each day of the week for an hour, sometimes longer. As she would not come to my office or remain in it with me, I came to her room, sometimes locking the door to prevent her from running out. My only requirement was that we be together, recognizing the fact that in so doing we both would be anxious in differing degrees.

During these meetings the *form of contact* is far more than simply verbal. We shared the space of her room, and its size and configuration were aspects of our communication. There were long silences—perhaps a week or more of silent sessions—during which one became aware of the modalities of time, odor, vision, bodily movement, and so on, as parts of the contacts that people make with each other. On a few occasions Miss A hit me, and touch was made possible through the blow and my holding her wrists in response. Once she suddenly came to sit on my lap and weep and then to crouch on the floor beside me, holding my hand in silence.

There were times when I sat in a chair or on the floor of Miss A's room without closing its only door. She would then go out on the ward, returning at times to dismiss me or apparently to ignore me but obviously paying attention to my presence. The reports of socialization programs with animals other than humans are of interest in this regard but need not be reported here (6).

In various forms *emotional arousal* was an element of these sessions. At first Miss A was afraid that I would physically hurt her, and she expected that I would make her anxious—deliberately or by mischance. Frequently she was angry, threatening to kill me and attempting to drive me away. Again, she was depressed, sad, and able to show her great loneliness and finally, her ability for affection. In turn, I was at times bored, angry, puzzled, compassionate, discouraged, and so on. It is noteworthy that the emotional climate was never "neutral" (if there could be such a state) and that there was an increasing sense of involvement, although this was scornfully denied by Miss A who for more than two years could not recall my name and insisted that our meetings had no significance for her.

The therapeutic relationship is *transactional* in that it involves reciprocal behaviors in a social field in which the responses of each participant are to some extent governing of and governed by the behavior of the other. From this point of view the therapist is a participant in the sense that he experiences, learns, and to some extent changes in the course of his work with a patient, but he is also an expert participant-observer in that what he does is in the service of his patient.

In the above briefly noted procedures we are describing the *development of relational bonds* between two individuals—in this instance patient and therapist. The following quotation from the work of John Paul

Scott (4) is helpful here: "an individual at the proper period in life will become attached to anything in the surrounding environment, both living and nonliving. Certain behavioral processes will promote positive contact with living objects, normally members of the same species, and certain other processes will prevent such contacts as the animal grows older. In animals like dogs and people it is likely that the capacity to form these attachments is never actually lost in adult life but simply takes place more slowly, usually because of various interfering patterns of behavior. Simple as it is, this interpretation explains many of the paradoxes of human behavior, e.g., that it is possible to both love and hate the same individual."

The situation devised to foster the development of such bonds—or the beginnings of the therapeutic relationship—includes the elements noted above: (a) recurrent meetings of the participants; (b) contact of the participants with each other—verbal, visual, tactile, aural, and so on; and (c) emotional arousal. The details of the above are variable and cannot be dealt with here.

The use of *drugs* to facilitate the formation of a relationship is a subject for further careful study. A number of my associates say that psychotherapy with markedly anxious people can be improved greatly if the anxiety is reduced through the use of such agents as chlorpromazine. There is some evidence that prolonged use of phenothiazines may produce cardiac complications (1) and the effects of chronic drug usage are not yet clearly established. Of particular interest is the question of learning; that is, what is the difference in learning and experience with and without drugs? (6)

With Miss A drugs were not used. On some occasions of great disturbance she was placed in a wet sheet pack which procedure made it possible for someone to sit close beside her without injury or undue fear. Someone (usually myself) was with her during periods of her intense anxiety, remaining until she felt more at ease; occasionally we were together four or more hours at a stretch. We were attempting to help Miss A learn that whereas she could experience great discomfort with people, she could also be relieved of anxiety through human contact.

As the patient is enabled to recognize and accept dependency, he will also discover that the relationship with a therapist, while useful, is not enough. Unless the therapist has some unresolved need to hold on to his patient, the natural course of growing up will lead to *separation*.

After nearly three years of finding me unsatisfactory, threatening, and supposedly destructive, Miss A began to depend on me. We shopped together, walked in the country, and she turned only to me for advice and help. I found the change pleasant and realized that I should regret her leaving. However, she found other interests, went back to school, formed friendships more profitable than the attachment to me, and as she "grew up" left therapy for more important things in life.

The above, of course, takes place in a social-physical-cultural environment—a milieu. The hospital situation can be useful—or harmful—but not neutral. Not all living situations are suitable for all needs, and there is little likelihood—or desirability—of producing a hospital, home, or community satisfactory to all human requirements. Of the environment Cumming and Turner (3) have, in part, this to say: "The importance of the milieu . . . cannot be overemphasized. In daily interaction with the environment, the individual not only learns new concepts and new skills, but also receives new proofs of already achieved and cherished abilities and, of course, of continuing areas of ineptness . . . the social milieu continually influences individual personality functioning . . . there remains the question of what particular social structures exert important influences on what individuals." Of this, more later.

The psychotherapeutic approach to schizophrenia is one form of hard work. What virtue there may be in such efforts may be distributed under two headings: (a) the personal benefit to a few patients, and (b) the knowledge that can be gained in such encounters. These possible virtues, however, do not exert a wide appeal, and there is no general great enthusiasm about becoming involved in these enterprises. Among the reasons for this indifferent—or even negative—attitude are the following which I shall present briefly.

The therapist is often haunted by the thought that the "true cause" of schizophrenia—such as some biochemical abnormality—will be revealed with the result that his own efforts will appear as futile if not ridiculous.

The work is economically expensive, often prolonged, and very few patients are financially or otherwise eligible for it. The therapist may find it difficult to justify what he does, and he may feel guilty at what he may conceive of as his ivory tower existence and his lack of social conscience.

The greater number of practitioners probably would not consider psychotherapy the method of choice for the schizophrenic person and would select physical or pharmacological modes of intervention instead. The therapist, then, often feels that he is an outsider and an impractical, quixotic dilettante detached from psychiatric reality. A danger of this position is the development of an intense, unresolved identification with the patient.

The therapist is required to commit himself to a relationship which may be disrupted prematurely for various reasons. Treatment may seem to prosper but is accompanied by a disturbance of the family equilibrium which has been adjusted to (or required by) the sick role, and then relatives may remove the patient—often with his open or covert cooperation. Financial support runs out, the hospital group may act to extrude the troublesome patient, and other events (often unexpected) may bring to a close incomplete work. Such losses and separations are not easy to endure, as the treatment will not prosper in an impersonal atmosphere; the personal quality, however, increases the vulnerability of all concerned.

The patient himself is a problem. He usually does not follow conventional therapeutic rules and customs, he may be actually dangerous to those who try to help him, he does not show the appreciation of the therapist that the latter may desire or require, and his methods of communication are often disconcertingly obscure and unconventional. He may demand energy, interest, and time that interfere too much with the therapist's life.

The treatment is not only prolonged and marked by uncertainty, but its outcome is never fully clear-cut and satisfactory. Because of the time involved and the mutuality of the relationship, the ending (even if successful) may seem anticlimactic; many people will have participated in achieving the outcome, there is no one magical healer, and the conclusion (not a bad one) may be that one simply took part rather modestly in someone's growing up. For some therapists this procedure is lacking in drama as well as in precision.

Psychotherapy in a hospital cannot be popular with those who want to maintain a stable and somewhat peaceful setting. Physical therapies (such as EST) and heavy drug dosages are incompatible with an intensive psychotherapeutic program; therapists will turn to them when they are themselves anxious rather than working through a problem with the patient, and patients will doubt the therapist who retreats from the relationship when the going gets rough. Patients generally try to get rid of other patients who do not "fit in"—who are "too" disturbed, regressed, outspoken, crazy, or even "well." Administrators, nurses—and therapists —act in the same way. In a hospital there is always somebody—or a group—trying to push out, segregate, kill, or dispose of in some way the "undesirables."

People—and this includes almost everyone—are usually anxious with those who are schizophrenic. Messages are obscure, conventional values are questioned, "normal" behavior is caricatured, that which we wish to leave unnoticed is brought into the open, and the "unconscious" seems to be on display. Most of us withdraw from such contacts.

These are a few of the reasons why therapists of schizophrenic patients frequently give up the work, and hospital personnel have serious doubts about the advisability of supporting these programs (2).

Thus far little attention has been given here to a hospital program. I have described something of certain problems to be dealt with in such a program. Miss A was, in my opinion, best treated in a hospital, although with great effort she might have been cared for in a home. The elements of a treatment setting, as here suggested, shall now be described briefly.

I favor an environment flexible in terms of space, personnel, and social groups, adjustable to the patient's state of anxiety, and his abilities in the use of interpersonal skills. At times a person needs to be alone or with one other person or with a small group, and so on. Opportunity for the exercise, learning, and correction of childhood, juvenile, and adolescent experience should be provided.

The living group of patients should be limited to twelve or fourteen, but access to other groups should be possible as desired and needed.

Personnel—nurses, therapists, administrators, and others—should be in open communication with each other, despite the frequent painfulness resulting from such encounters.

Hopefully one therapist will carry on the major portion of the work. Change from one therapist to another after three or four months disrupts the relationship and favors discouragement.

Those who work with such patients should have a certain confidence and belief in what they do, which does not mean that they should be falsely optimistic. Pessimism and cynicism have no place in this work.

The contact with the families of patients is a vital part of this work, but the subject cannot be developed here.

The primary focus of the work done in such an organization is the planned use of the human relationship. The human transaction—in one-to-one encounters and larger groups—is the means of treatment, the subject of education and study, and the source of research.

The above is too general and too little to be of much practical use and may appear to be no more than empty platitudes. The putting of such ideas into action is dependent on the people interested in making them into realities. I can add little to what has already been written on the subject. But of this I am certain, the work in an organization of this nature is never-ending and is marked by the conflict and repeated attempts to resolve crises characteristic of any group in which growth and learning are permitted and encouraged.

In the setting briefly referred to here, certain aspects of the human predicament can be given a close look. Here we can take time to observe —and participate in—phenomena of estrangement, isolation, aggression, anxiety, fear, hatred, and love, learning something more about what we do to lead the young into paths of disaster as well as those more hopeful. Here can be studied certain of the vicissitudes associated with the development of relational ties and man's peculiar, unique, and perhaps fatal allegiance to his self-created world of symbols. Here we can learn about a certain kind of deviant—the schizophrenic outsider—and come to realize that we can help reduce his anxiety and pain without insisting on conformity, but rather valuing the differences as well as the likenesses of men.

We are concerned, irrespective of our professions, with the nature of man and the possible course of his career as a biological species. Man has the knowledge to destroy himself or to better his life. What will be done with that knowledge we cannot say, but we should never cease our efforts to increase it or to understand and improve its employment. So it is that we must dare to look at, study, and report what we do without hesitancy, pretense, or shame; it is urgently required that we learn who we are, what we can and cannot do, and whether we value ourselves and our kind sufficiently to seek seriously our preservation. In a small way, but an important one, the psychotherapeutic work with the schizophrenic person may contribute to what we must learn; he is one of the frank and brutal reflections of ourselves, and we must not fear to look at the ways in which we have been made into his image and he into ours.

REFERENCES

1. Alexander, C. S.: Report read at a meeting of The American Heart Association, Minneapolis, 1969.
2. Burton, A.: Unpublished manuscript.
3. Cumming, J. and Turner, R. J.: Social Structure and Psychiatric Disorder: A Theoretical Note. In Zubin, J. and Hunt, H. F. (Eds.), *Comparative Psychopathology, Animal and Human*. New York: Grune and Stratton, 1967.

4. Scott, J. P.: *The Process of Primary Socialization in Canine and Human Infants*, Monographs of The Society for Research in Child Development, Serial No. 85, Vol. 28, No. 1. Yellow Springs, Ohio: Antioch Press, 1963.

5. Sullivan, H. S.: *Conceptions of Modern Psychiatry*. New York: Norton, 1953.

6. Woolpy, J. H.: Socialization of Wolves. In Masserman, J. H. (Ed.), *Animal and Human*, Science and Psychoanalysis Series, Vol. XII. New York: Grune and Stratton, 1968.

14

Panel Discussion on Hospital Treatment

HERBERT C. MODLIN, M.D., ROBERT W. GIBSON, M.D.,
ERNEST M. GRUENBERG, M.D., ALFRED H. STANTON, M.D.
OTTO ALLEN WILL, JR., M.D.

Doctor Modlin: One of the issues that struck me in listening to both yesterday's and today's presentations, I might characterize as an attitude of pessimism—the unspoken attitude of "once a schizophrenic, always a schizophrenic." Therefore these people will live a schizophrenic life and our job is to help them when they undergo exacerbations. We've heard similar attitudes for a long time. I recently went to a conference in which a very energetic chap who has been doing intensive research on schizophrenia for a number of years said, "I think we should put our efforts into working with the children of schizophrenic mothers. Here is a population of high risk, here is a population that might be salvaged." He wound up saying, "I don't think there's much point in working with the mothers themselves." How do you, gentlemen of the panel, feel about this?

Doctor Gibson: On the matter of prognosis, I recall that recently we've been doing a follow-up study at our hospital. If you correlate actual outcome in rather crude terms with predicted outcome, they do seem to go together fairly nicely. The prognosis was arrived at by an experienced psychiatrist in each case, not using any very complex rating scale. It certainly is statistically significant, but if you take the poor prognosis group, you will still find a substantial number that do very well. So that I've come to the conclusion that we are fairly good at making predictions if we have a group of a thousand, and then we analyze how the different members of this group of a thousand made out. But I don't think a patient is very much interested in how a thousand make out. It is not particularly reassuring to have 90% improve if you're in the other 10%, so that while there certainly is something to prognosis, there are major exceptions to it. I shouldn't want to see an individual, in trying to work with a patient, write him off as being in a poor prognosis group. I think it was Otto Will that made the comment that you couldn't be cynical in this work or pessimistic and stick with it if you're trying to treat a patient intensively. I would certainly subscribe to that because I believe you would give up long before you got into it. I think that most people I know who have persisted in the work have developed different payoffs, if you will, for why they stay with it. They don't concern themselves that completely with the outcome. They are interested in it, of course, since everyone wants to see the patient improve, but they derive a high degree of satisfaction out of the understanding and comprehension they get of the patient. This helps them to persist. The other aspects, the learning experience for them and the type of human experience between two pople that you get out of this work becomes at least a partial payoff, and I don't think you can do this unless you do have that sort of feeling for it.

Doctor Gruenberg: I'd like to comment on that issue too from a somewhat different point of view. If the staff thinks they can predict who is not going to respond to treatment, then this tends to happen, statistically at any rate. Those who are being treated by a staff that is optimistic tend to improve. In other words, what is said to the patient, what the doctor thinks, what the staff thinks all affect the course. I think there is abundant evidence for this. Consequently, while I think it's a mistake to be rosy-eyed about what can be accomplished in "curing" schizophrenia, or resolving all their problems, or ending the state of the schizophrenic syndrome, we do know that most of them recover from their episodes of decompensation rather rapidly. Only a portion decompensate again. A significant proportion not only never decompensate again, but it's very hard to find any signs of schizophrenia five or ten years later. That the schizophrenic psychotic episode generally has a benign prognosis can be documented by dozens of studies, literally from all points of view. Many of them show clear clinical signs of schizophrenia for the rest of their lives. However, one of the real problems is that it's a mistake for staff to permit itself to think it can make a prognosis in the individual case. I'm not discouraging continued research in improving our ability to predict the course. But I think in practical clinical work, one has to adopt an optimistic atmosphere to get the best possible results for any group of patients. The remark about the low level of functioning of a large proportion of schizophrenics after they've had an acute period of illness certainly conforms with everyone's experience as far as I know. But some workers draw the inference that all schizophrenics need supervision and various kinds of special assistance indefinitely and between episodes of psychotic decompensation as well. As far as I can make out this is an error, because of cases that have not had any follow-up care a large proportion do very well. And I think one of the problems we're encountering today in the organization of good care for schizophrenic patients is that we do not know when to stop and when our efforts need to be continued. Certainly this is true for the community care of the psychotic schizophrenic patient. Once they're back in the community they do present all sorts of social and personal problems, many of which the clinical staff have never encountered before in their personal lives. They haven't had friends who have had these problems, and they see these problems as related to the schizophrenic syndrome. Many of the problems they are seeing are problems that lots of nonschizophrenics have, but the clinicians have never seen such individuals before. They don't know when the patient really needs continued attention, and as one develops a community care program, one of the hardest things we're going to have to find out about is how to judge when the patients will do just as well without our help as they will do with our help. We don't know when to stop treatment it seems to me.

Dr. Modlin: We might continue on that theme for just a moment. What are the indications for termination of treatment, or, to be a little more specific, the indications for hospital discharge, the indications for dehospitalization?

Doctor Will: Well, using the particular case already described, I'd say I had to arrive at the decision that dehospitalization was possible and then that it was desirable. In the kind of relationship discussed, that is pretty much arrived at through a consensus between the two people. It isn't that I come to a decision at some point of the work that this person should now live outside the hospital and say so. There begins to develop a series of behaviors, my own and the patient's, in the course of our work which make it much more clearly evident that the kind of dependency on the therapist, which has developed, is no longer required. The patient begins to develop other interests than the therapist, and in developing these other interests, begins to raise questions about how they can be better realized than in the current situation. I feel sometimes that is not too different, although the analogy may be a bit strange, in terms, say, of my children. I remember when one of my boys was very little, I used to take him to the zoo in Washington, which I rather enjoyed and he tolerated. Then as he got somewhat older he wanted to go to the zoo, and my enjoyment was increased, and we shared this together—this mutual pleasure. I remember very distinctly one Sunday morning telling Patrick that today we could go to the zoo. I was looking forward to it with pleasure, and he just said, "All right." I felt a little unhappy about this and added, "I just said I'd take you to the zoo, Patrick, we'll have a whale of a good time." "Well," he said, "if you want to." I had discovered, a little belatedly, that he had some friends, and he was torn between his wish to be with and please his father and his wish to be with them.

Doctor Modlin: If I heard you right you equated the end of the relationship between the therapist and the patient with leaving the hospital. Does that mean that this sort of relationship cannot be maintained after the patient has left the hospital?

Doctor Will: The type of situation I was talking about was one in which the hospital offered certain advantages—many of which have been named by members of this panel—but the time comes when those advantages are not sufficient. I should hope that I can continue therapy with the patient, and I did in this particular instance. As the patient moves into a different kind of environment, he brings back to me an account of other kinds of experiences and our whole relationship changes at that time.

Doctor Modlin: Doctor Stanton, in addition to your individual work, you function as the psychiatrist-in-chief of a sizeable hospital and must have some supervisory and administrative duties. Do you see any general criteria that one could use in arriving at the decision to terminate hospitalization?

Doctor Stanton: I think this has to be a clinical decision, and if we are in a position to do so, it should be based upon our best possible appraisal of that particular patient, including what he has been doing in his work in the hospital and what he is going to be doing outside. Certainly I should hope, as has been mentioned, that he might where indicated continue with some kind of personal relationship with the people at the hospital. My guess is that if this was frequently available, discharges could be done a good deal earlier and more sensibly. I'll carry on a bit further, if I may, and challenge the position that if a person can be outside the hospital they should be. If a patient is in fact engaged in therapeutic encounters within the hospital as a part of his hospital activity, to ignore this on the basis of what you might call—if I can load it a little bit—certain brass-band kinds of indications, is something we should not force ourselves to do. We must specifically sensitize ourselves to more important additional issues which are clinical and which bear upon each particular case. What is he doing, is he in group psychotherapy, does he belong to a certain ward group, is he profiting from this, is his wife moving toward preparing to take him back home, but if she's pushed too far, too fast, is she going to go home to mother? And there is a whole set of other kinds of issues, which ideally we should know about and which we must make a part of that judgment of when the patient is transferred from within to the outside. I think the statement, if the patient can be outside he should be, is wrong as a generalization. It is regressive as a generalization and should not be allowed to stand. There is one great justification for it, of course—it usually appears to be less expensive for the patient to be outside. And I believe that statements like patients should be outside if they can be, or they should be kept out, or they should be gotten out, are stated uncritically as assumptions from which one starts, and this is a very unhappy part of the current scene.

Doctor Gibson: One comment on that point about the economics of it. I think, perhaps happily, a lot of people are beginning to find out that it costs more to treat a lot of patients outside of a hospital than it does inside of a hospital. Day care programs where you really have a staff that works actively with the patient may be much more expensive than a standard state hospital inpatient program. I say happily, because if we can take the economic factor out of it, the judgment will be made much more on the needs of the patients and more humanitarian concerns about his welfare, rather than the economy.

Doctor Gruenberg: In the first place I should like to say that I agree with the last statement that you don't judge the worthwhileness of a program to help sick people on the basis of what is the cheapest way of doing it. Obviously there's no point in using an expensive method when an inexpensive method will do as well. But if something is costly and is of benefit to people, then one has to figure out whether society's ready to pay for it or not, rather than make decisions on the basis that something else would be cheaper even though not as good. I also have to agree with Al Stanton's statement that the notion that it's better to be out of the hospital than in the hospital whenever it's possible, under all conditions, as a generalization, is a nonsensical idea. Now, there are two contrasting views: in one the mental hospital is seen as incorribly bad, nothing but damaging, and therefore every possible means should be used to keep people out and, once in, to get them out rapidly. The other model is that the mental hospital has never been static at any point in its history, has always been changing, has developed some patterns of excessive retention and can be transformed into an acute service with specific goals for each admission and can work in close conjunction and as an intimate part of comprehensive community service. In the first model a return to the hospital is seen as a failure of the discharge, of the release. If the patient is released from the hospital and comes back again within a year or two, it is seen as a failure to set up an adequate community program. In the second model where the hospital is seen as an active and integral part of the community program, readmissions are expected and are part of the plan to release. In fact, you can only release patients properly into the community in certain states when the hospital really is highly accessible for an unpredictable need to return as well as some predictable needs to return. Now, I myself take the second point of view. To return to Doctor Stanton's remarks concerning the therapeutic activities in the hospital, this is another area of conflict. They're two streams of thought, both of them I think highly respectable and valuable, but they fight each other in practice and most people don't recognize the contradictions between them. Most of you are familiar with Max Jones's introduction of the concept of the therapeutic community, to make the whole life of the hospital part of a therapeutic experience for the patient. It is an extension of the milieu concept into something more dynamic and more structured. However, if you see the hospital as a place for acute, intermittent care of schizophrenic and other psychotic patients with specific indications at certain stages of the disorder, then one does not want to see the admission lead to a well integrated pattern of living in the hospital. If you set up a therapeutic community in a hospital, you can't possibly organize a quick rotation, revolving-door policy on the same wards and the same services in my opinion. They are in direct contradiction to each other. The object of the therapeutic community is to involve the patient in many aspects of the life in the hospital and on-the-ward activities, patient government, etc. Yet, the function of the revolving-door policy hospital is to handle the patient's problems very much in the way that a general hospital handles cardiac decompensation, or appendicitis, or something like that. The hospital is a special place you go to for a short period, for specific purposes. You only get to interact with the rest of the hospital and the other patients to the extent that it's necessary to get through those few days, or a week or two that you're there. Not that everybody's isolated from everyone else, but you don't become a part of the hospital community. You cannot operate an acute psychotic service as a therapeutic community, nor can you run a therapeutic community as a service that's organized to deal with the problems of acute decompensations in psychotics. I think these are two different kinds of services. I wanted to ask Doctor Stanton about his statement that he thinks in his setting if the hospital staff were capable of providing more frequent hours for the patients they might leave the hospital earlier. Haven't you raised the fundamental question about the way hospital staff time is allocated as between inpatient hours and outpatient hours? How do you handle that problem in your hospital?

Doctor Stanton: In the first place I think that's an extremely clear statement about the contradiction between the therapeutic community and a relatively rapidly turning over acute service. One of the things that happens if you have a school in the place as we do is that adolescents are supposed to go to school and they do. Then before long, even though the patients can continue in the school after they're discharged, you find an awful lot of discharges from the hospital planned in July and people coming into the hospital in September. So you discover that you must take a fairly close look at whether you're really doing what you think you are. On the matter of staff, I know we have attacked it in a way which exploits our fortunate position of being in a big city. As a result, we have attached to the hospital staff, on a part-time basis, more psychiatrists from the city than there are in some states. This is necessary if patients are to be brought into the hospital, started in intensive psychotherapy and then are to continue in therapy after they leave. If that weren't the case we'd soon be filled up. It seems to me entirely necessary that when patients leave the hospital there be the maximum practical continuity of care. This obviously requires certain special circumstances, but to some extent it does permit one to have his cake and eat it too, in that some acute patients can come in, start things, and then when it seems to be that their type of disorder is better handled in the community, can go out again. Certainly it also should be made as easy as possible to get back in.

Doctor Modlin: I am deluged with questions from the audience, most of them quite good ones; but we won't be able to get to all of them. I think our task here is to squeeze the best we can out of our visitors, and we'll try to proceed with that goal. We might change our focus a little bit now. Assuming that we have established some validity for some kinds of hospital practice for some kinds of patients, the question still arises how can we keep patients from becoming candidates for hospitals? One of our alumni from the Topeka psychiatric community is Dr. Harry Brickman. If I don't do him injustice by oversimplification and condensation, his general attitude is that the last thing we should do is to get a disturbed person into the medical system. We should try all other methods of help first.

Doctor Gruenberg: I think it's an awfully extreme position and I think it's irrational, literally irrational. I think like many other extreme statements that are well motivated there's a basically sound point involved. The basically sound point is that psychiatrists, like other doctors, often stick their fingers in where they're not only not being helpful but might even be more trouble than help. Also, in a city like Los Angeles (I imagine it's true of almost any city in the United States) the policeman, the courts, the teachers are all undereducated, underinformed, underequipped to use the simple pieces of knowledge that have been accumulated by psychiatrists and others as to how to relate to what they regard as disturbed or disturbing behavior. Anyone who wants to give this kind of consultation ought to master what other professions have contributed and make people recognize that you're not transmitting a psychiatric skill as such. As an argument for devoting all of his staff to such purposes I can see nothing wrong with his policy decision, but then to add on the argument that everything should be tried except medical skills in every case seems to me to be saying that there is no diagnostic process and no way of judging a situation which could be helped by psychiatric intervention. That I can't see any grounds for. Why wait till the patient's half dead before you see a surgeon? Why wait until a patient's psychotic manifestations become so severe that he tries to kill himself or somebody else before you offer him the kinds of treatment skills that we now have? I can see no justification for holding off treatment until lots of other things have been tried first. There are other real criteria for bringing in the medical profession.

Doctor Modlin: Here is a related question, which strikes me as appropriate to some other comments I've heard you make before, Doctor Gruenberg. Only one of your indications for hospitalization really requires the medical facilities that a hospital can supply. Might it not be easier, cheaper, and less associated with stigmatization to develop full-time nonhospital living institutions or situations?

Doctor Gruenberg: I think that's a very good suggestion. You'll recall that Doctor Pasamanick made the suggestion as well. I do think that this is indicated not only as a means for helping individuals who might otherwise need hospital care (e.g., temporary removal from home) but also for some of our chronic patients who are very seriously handicapped and for whom our present techniques can offer no real promise of a high level of rehabilitation. I think the question contains the suggestion that there is an area where there's a tremendous need for still more varieties of partial care and partial supervision. One of them is what I call the "noncommercial boarding house" staffed by an intelligent person who has a good working relationship with the clinical and social resources of the community and takes a kindly, but not excessively paternalistic attitude towards the boarders. It would be a place where a person could live on a commercial basis as an independent free-living citizen, but operated by an individual who sees it as a part of his social duty—as some good boarding house proprietors do on their own—to call the clinical agency that they know this person has seen before if the person appears to be getting disturbed. But trying to do this on a large scale, on a commercial basis, I've decided, is impossible in our society. I think it might be possible if some voluntary agencies would start organizing something in addition to the YMCA and the YWCA types of boarding facilities on a nonprofit basis, staffed by professional and semiprofessional personnel.

Doctor Gibson: I think perhaps still another way of accomplishing something similar to that is to use existing institutional settings that aren't hospitals. For example, a school setting is frequently an excellent place where a person can accomplish a great deal of ego growth. It may be necessary to have some kind of consultative services available to the staff of such an institution to reassure them about some of their anxieties and to assist them to intervene in more constructive ways. Perhaps even some larger businesses or industries can bring this type of consultation in, and the existing establishment can be used without creating an entirely new entity.

Doctor Gruenberg: There's an additional point that is very close to something that Doctor Stanton was saying a few minutes earlier. It seems to me we are moving into a period where we are becoming highly critical of what we've inherited in the way of the very mechanistic notions as to what various kinds of institutions and facilities can and cannot do. For example, a hospital has to be a hospital. Now Doctor Stanton's hospital has a school in it. A school can also have a hospital in it and often does; they then call it an infirmary. We very violently separate, in our administrative structures, outpatient clinics and inpatient hospital services. But this is a new phenomenon. In former times and in less "developed" parts of the world, it is not at all unusual to have an outpatient clinic in which some staff members live, and with three to six beds where people can stay overnight or for a day or two in conjunction with some situation related to their treatment without any formal hospital admission. It seems to me we're in a period now where lots of suggestions are going to come up about making all of our operations much more flexible than they have been and much less defined as inpatient or outpatient.

Doctor Will: I was speaking earlier about the individual case and suggesting that sometimes there is some relevance between such contacts and work with larger groups. The young lady about whom I spoke briefly this morning spent some time in a hospital setting, after having had the various treatments which I described, at a time when she was grossly disturbed. The decision about her moving outside the hospital was made on the basis of a number of factors. But one of them was that, interestingly enough, we felt that she was too disturbed in the hospital to stay there. Thus, we enabled her to live in an apartment in the community, which we gave her some aid in getting. This involved a learning experience which seemed to me to be very important. She felt that coming back into the hospital was a sign of her getting worse, that it was a sign of failure. We went through a long period in which we tried to indicate to her that if she came into the hospital it didn't have to be considered to be a failure. She didn't have to come in for an indefinite or prolonged period of time saying, "Well, now I'm sick and here I have to stay." We wanted her to learn that she could ask to come to the hospital because she felt there was a need for so doing. She would come in sometimes to stay for twenty-four hours and then on her own ask for her discharge and go back to her apartment in town. There were some other occasions in which I was not, as a therapist, satisfied to have her be in the hospital, nor was I comfortable enough to have her live in her apartment. On some such occasions (this was not usual nor am I advocating it as the general thing) she stayed in our home. One reason we could do this was because my wife also works with me in this sort of work. The young lady might stay with us for only a week at a time, and it was very interesting to me that on none of the occasions when she stayed with us was she in any way awkwardly psychotic. I don't think this meant that we were such wonderful people to be with at all. As a matter of fact, she was very critical of the way we ran our household. But what I'm trying to get at is that we were trying to set up an environment which had some flexibility in it and about which the patient had some options. In getting her to be able to recognize that she could exert some of these options, we felt that we were building up, if you will, a greater sense of self-esteem on her part and a recognition that she had to play an active part in what all of us were attempting to do.

Doctor Gruenberg: I remember a patient of Dr. William A. White's, at St. Elizabeths, whom I got to know long after Doctor White had died. She had recurrent psychotic episodes, but she was a fairly well-educated person. He had her trained as a laboratory technician, hired her as an employee of the hospital, assigned her an apartment in one of the women's buildings, and she lived there the rest of her life as far as I know. When she decompensated, she stayed right in her own apartment; instead of being employed, she was a patient; and the work personnel took care of her right in her own apartment. I'm only mentioning it because it's a very good illustration of the same point Doctor Will is making, that even in a mental hospital you can switch roles from employee to patient. You don't have to be all that rigid all the time.

Doctor Modlin: Doctor Will, would you care to respond to this question from the floor? It seems to me that in your present situation at Stockbridge, although you and your colleagues practice psychiatry and your people there are mostly thought of as patients, do you run a hospital? How would you characterize your institution?

Doctor Will: That's one of the most difficult questions I've ever heard. My comment is not facetious, I wish it were. In the first place, we're not licensed in the state of Massachusetts as a psychiatric hospital. When I first came, there was a great deal of anxiety amongst both staff and patients, because they felt that I might think of the institution more as a hospital and the patients more as patients. Indeed to some extent I did and do because I see no shame in that. One of the things that we wanted to get clear there was the whole question of the concept of role. Some of the inhabitants of the Center wished to call themselves students and say that our program was not a therapeutic but rather an educational one. I had no objection to this because it seems to me that learning and education are fundamental parts of any program called therapeutic. At the same time, I did not like the idea that the word "hospital," or the idea of "patient," had become so contaminated that one has to escape from these concepts and deny a part of himself by using some other terms which I considered to be euphemisms. But we always struggle within the institution, and I think maybe quite properly so, with the question of institutional identity. Of course with the people who work on the staff, we struggle in terms of our own professional and personal identities. It seems to me that this continual searching regarding who am I, what is my relation to you and the other people, and what is it that we are doing with each other, is part of the therapeutic procedure as I envisage it.

Doctor Modlin: Taking off from Doctor Will's last comment about professional identity, and within this general area of prevention, broadly conceived, there are questions having to do with the schizophrenic patient's family. Can our professional responsibility be limited to our case load? To what extent should we see as our responsibility the family, particularly the children? Should we assume the significant responsibility of giving advice to the family, or to carry it even further, intervening with the family? I wonder if any members of the panel have any comments to make about this. When we accept the patient into the hospital, just how broad a responsibility should we be accepting?

Doctor Will: I'd like to make one brief comment on this as a starter if I may, please. It seems to me when one sets himself to engage in an enterprise which he defines as therapeutic, he needs to be fairly clear as to what his responsibilities are in such a case and be ready to assume them. For example, I'd not advocate an intensive program of individual psychotherapy with someone with the expectation of considerable regression occurring and a great deal of acting out and so forth unless I, individually as a therapist, and the staff with me, were ready and able to assume the responsibilities involved. At the Center in Stockbridge, Dr. Donald Bloch now meets with families of patients at the time of their coming into the hospital. In this way, we get a broader picture of the overall family organization and the role that the patient plays in it. This seems to me a good idea in the main. My cautionary statement in regard to this is that I am not particularly amused by simply getting into a family conference and revealing various pathological and other aspects of the family relationship and then simply walking away from it. In doing that, one may reveal something which is interesting to look at, but which may also have harmful consequences. It seems to me that if you're going to start assuming some responsibility for the total family and involve them in your therapeutic contacts you must do so in a fashion that can be carried on until some possible resolution of the difficulties is reached, so that at least damage is not done. But that's a general statement.

Doctor Stanton: I think it was Thomas Main at the Castle Hospital in London who was the first person to decide that it was likely that the loss of the child by a mother in a postpartum psychosis was the reason the psychosis lasted so long. He therefore initiated the practice of bringing the newborn infant in with the mother. We have had experience at McLean with this situation, and I think that one can say that Tom Main's speculation is borne out by our experience. The question of the infant being raised by a mother who in some cases is psychotic raises a question about responsibility. When you take measures which are going to affect a great many people, you have a responsibility. The enlarging of the physician's recognition of the implications of what he and his patients do will not make his life more comfortable, because he himself and the hospital will then begin to perceive and respond to some of the very conflicts that are part of the patient's precipitating circumstances. Again, the narrowing of the concept of responsibility is impossible and the effort to do it is accompanied by, I believe, some very ataxic performances on the part of those psychiatrists who hold themselves very sharply to the position that they only have responsibility to the patient. I think patients in general should be told that this responsibility cannot be restricted to just them, and that the allegiance to the patient's benefit (which is legitimately expected of the psychiatrist) cannot be a kind of isolated total single-minded allegiance. Schizophrenia raises this question more sharply than almost any other condition, except, perhaps, the wildly acting-out patient and the adolescent, where again the problems in the family are reflected in the problems in the staff.

Doctor Gibson: While I'm in general agreement with what's just been said, I think one has to be cautious not to be overzealous in working with the families. As I watched the evolution of family therapy and the emphasis on it, there was at one point an attitude often expressed to the effect that the person who had been designated as the patient could not possibly improve or make any significant modification unless the whole family constellation and interaction changed. This sometimes was carried to the extreme that family therapy was the major therapeutic approach, and it seems to me that sometimes this is just more than we can do. Some of the family members who, while very sick in a sense in their own way, are functioning and maybe are heavily defended because of that. Sometimes I think what we have to do is almost to help them to give up the patient, and let the family problem go on if it's workable and try to separate the patient out from it. In brief, I think that we shouldn't necessarily assume that we have to make a change in the whole family group just because we see pathology there. This is not in any way relinquishing the responsibility. I mean one must take the responsibility for arriving at the judgment that this is a case where this is the best thing to do.

Doctor Gruenberg: I'd like to add to this discussion, which I think has very obviously turned out to be a provocative and terribly important one. In the first place, it's quite clear from the remarks that have already been made that everyone up here seems to think that you have to use judgment as to what extent and what kinds of responsibilities are going to be taken with respect to the family's own problems. Whether to bring them into treatment, whether to help dissect the family, these are terribly weighty judgments, and I think sometimes they're made implicitly and too casually. Obviously we have to keep making judgments of this sort; so it is a good thing for us to be more conscious about it. I'd like to point out that this problem as to who is the patient is as old as medicine itself. It is not something new that just came up in psychiatry. It's been a problem throughout the history of medicine as to whom is the doctor responsible. All the issues about when the patient is known to be a social menace, do you treat him, do you turn in your information to the police, etc., are old ones. It became a very sharp issue in the last century with the rise of bacteriology when people could be seen as a source of danger to their family and to their neighbors. If any of you haven't read Ibsen's play, *Enemy of the People,* I'd suggest you read it in the context of our current problems as to what happens when a doctor undertakes to use his knowledge for what he thinks is in the interest of the community when the community doesn't agree. I think that in the case of the schizophrenic parent—and why the schizophrenic parent is always a mother in these discussions really baffles me—we do have a responsibility for the consequences of releasing a patient in terms of what the probable effects are likely to be on the people with whom they live. It's a very serious decision to decide that a child will be better off without his sick mother than with his sick mother, if his sick mother is capable of living in the family and is not obviously a physical hazard for the child and not transparently a terrible psychological hazard. It's a terribly big decision to make, and I should like to transform the question a little bit to see if I can get some other reactions. What right do we have to keep a mother away from her children if she is not a physical hazard to them? What is our authority for doing so?

Doctor Modlin: I think that question is sufficiently uncomfortable that we might just pass it up.

Doctor Will: I agree that it is an uncomfortable question, but I'll comment. I don't know about right. At times we have exerted "rights" in terms of our current concepts of medicine, which in later times have turned out not to be the best of judgments. Our investigations may help us as time goes on to have a little clearer picture of where some behaviors are clearly pathological and at what moment the child, let us say, should not be exposed to them. I don't see how anyone could speak very clearly about schizophrenia in general and say that the child should not be with a schizophrenic mother and should be in some other kind of setting. That

I could not subscribe to. But there are some instances in which I see a very disturbed person and in which I feel that contact of that very disturbed person with a small child or someone else might be, as best I can judge it, seriously destructive even to life. There I might have to take some action. It may be an error, but I'm taking the action with the hope to spare both of them the tragedy which no amount of psychotherapy or living could ever repair. Again I might be wrong. But in general, I am more impressed by the ability of people to help each other and to get along, than I am by tearing apart social, family, and small group organizations and callously or carelessly substituting some others for them.

Doctor Modlin: I think it might be said without too much danger of controversy that the diagnosis of schizophrenia is really of little help in making such a decision. The essential problem to be decided amounts to, is this man or woman who has some degree of illness also capable of carrying out the basic minimal functions of parenthood? This may be related or unrelated to the fact that he has a schizophrenic diagnosis. So here again, the diagnostic label is not much help.

Doctor Gruenberg: Doesn't the answer to this question also depend upon who's paying you? We sort of ducked that, I think. Sometimes one's being employed by the individual patient as his doctor. Other times, a young adult is in a private hospital where the contract is really between the director of the private hospital and the parents who are paying the bill. And the person being cared for is not one of the contracting parties in a formal—in a social—sense. And in a third situation, one's working in a public hospital where the community as a whole is paying the staff to do what they can for those members of the community that the staff thinks in their professional judgment require some professional service. Doesn't the answer to the question of how much one takes in the family and other members of the community in a clinical situation depend upon for whom the doctor is working? If he is frozen in a hospital and is not free to see outpatients, is not free to ever make home visits, can't see a patient in consultation in a casual way, but must only see them if they are admitted to the hospital, is he really free in the same way as a doctor who has all these different multiple relationships and ways of working in the community?

Doctor Modlin: I think we have time for one more issue, and I'll pick out one which takes us back directly to the title of today's presentation—Hospital Treatment of Schizophrenic Patients. One observer thinks that Doctors Stanton and Will have different viewpoints of treatment of the schizophrenic patient. One, and I assume Doctor Stanton, emphasizes the social system as a whole, the other, intensive individual involvement between therapist and patient. Could you comment on the possible conflicts between these different points of view?

Doctor Stanton: In action at the hospital, the possible conflicts are infinite, intense, and deeply felt. They are limited only by the ingenuity of the people engaged in them, and these are people with a high degree of ingenuity. To a very considerable extent, obviously, there is no necessary logical conflict. There is no necessary empirical conflict. There are, as has been said, different points of view on certain things. However, I think that there are a great many conflicts in areas where we are not well able to handle them. Take for instance the matter of when to discharge. A person looking at the patient individually may find it hard to agree with someone looking socially. And neither person, when these conflicts arise, can be counted on as being right, because of his position. I believe that the psychoanalyst has historically considerably underestimated the pertinence and the dynamic importance of the immediate social circumstances and the nearly perceived future for the patient. But this is a matter of judgment and has meant in essence not really an antagonism to seeing it, but a tendency to not see it, not raise it, not be interested in it, and to tend to reduce matters to genetic and historical issues.

Doctor Will: Well, I think that's so well said that I don't hesitate to add a little something to it! The possibility of cooperation between the person very much involved in intensive individual therapy with others who deal with the more general activities of the hospital setting is frequently difficult to arrange and often covered up. It seems to me that we frequently, in my experience in working in small institutions, have a lot of our own somewhat private ideas as to what counts. It's difficult sometimes to realize ourselves that in a social system a great many things count and it's hard to evaluate just what at any one time may be more important. I don't think that the conflicts, as they were, can be exactly resolved, but one way to deal with them and I think the most useful, although a painful one, is for the participants to work with each other enough that they can be more and more frank with each other about what they think that they're doing. I think sometimes that what happens in these organizations has some resemblance with what happens in family settings. There are elements of jealousy, of competitiveness, and of a need to possess the patient or the idea. A situation where I have at times felt this very keenly is when a patient of mine finally gets along pretty well with me and then begins to find that there are other people in the organization who are more understanding than I. I may find myself

resenting this and without really being aware of it indicating to him that
he is being a little unfaithful to me and to the ideas which I have. It
seems to me that this has some relevance to a child's growing up. My own
children, for example, will come home at times and report the excellence
of other families and of other parents. And I find myself grudgingly,
because I'm a democratic person, grudgingly giving some slight credence
to their point of view, but often wishing to point out the disabilities of
the other parent or the other social system. Since this happens in the
family and seems to me to be a part of growing up, I assume it happens
in institutions. I know that when I first went to Stockbridge I was wondering whether it simply wouldn't be easier for me to focus more on the
concept of the community organization and not focus so much on the
intense individual involvement of the therapist. You can't focus on individual involvement of the therapist without paying attention to the
milieu, of course, but what I'm getting at is that this conflict, as Doctor
Stanton has very nicely described, does exist and is part of living within
an institution. I think that to try to deny the conflicts or the differences
is to try to push something out of one's awareness and to push it under
the rug in a very destructive sense. To bring it out into the open and
then to talk with each other freely about our differences may offer a
learning experience which is in itself very valuable. I hope that isn't too
euphemistic, but to me it's important.

Doctor Gibson: I think that one of the most effective ways of creating an atmosphere in which you can do this sort of thing is to insist quite
rigorously that no person becomes a complete specialist in one area. I
know at the time that I was at the Lodge everyone was doing some
individual therapy, and I certainly continue with that myself. I feel that's
the only way that I can possibly have some kind of counterbalance
against the pressures to make decisions in a certain way that are present
when you have administrative responsibilities. You can only keep your
attention very much focused on the individual need if you continue to do
individual work.

Doctor Gruenberg: I'd like to comment on this because I want to
dispute what Doctor Stanton said; I don't think I dispute what he thinks.
He very modestly said that, in his humble opinion, psychoanalysts in
their interest in one-to-one relationships had ignored, failed to pay attention to, what needed to be paid attention to in terms of the immediate
social environment and interactions with other people in the patient's
life. I don't think that's correct. I think that it is not just a matter of
his humble opinion. I think it's a demonstrated fact, but I don't know

why he picked on the analysts. I think the same thing can be said of all psychiatrists. I think we have learned so much about the hitherto unsuspected enormous consequences of slight shifts in the social climate and the social environment in the last few decades that it is not only the analysts but all psychiatrists who are guilty of this. Not only that, but I think one has to face the problem that Doctor Stanton is obviously trying to face, which is that the administrator of an institution is inevitably going to get trapped in a situation where it's very hard for him to see his decisions in the context of the consequences for the patient on the ward.

Doctor Modlin: Gentlemen of the panel, we thank you for coming to Topeka and participating in the Conference.

Section III

RESEARCH ON THE SCHIZOPHRENIC SYNDROME

15

A Review of
Current Research Directions:
Their Product and Their Promise

ROBERT CANCRO, M.D.

THE PROGRAM CALLED FOR this contribution to concern itself with research directions in the schizophrenic syndrome. Unfortunately the program was written before the paper and therefore certain problems were not immediately apparent. The very title has a certain intrinsic pretentiousness. Of what relevance is it to review directions in an area in which there are virtually no stable coordinates? It is almost as meaningless as speaking of north and south in intergalactic space. There is substantial disagreement as to what is meant by the concept, and at the very least, as much disagreement about which individuals in a given population are to be considered representative of the disorder. Diagnostic preferences as well as the basis for a particular diagnosis vary between clinicians. Severe behavior disorders associated with regressive features are routinely labeled as schizophrenic by some individuals. The unreliability of diagnosis has produced an increasingly muddled situation, which Frank (8) described recently as a "panschizophrenic nosologic chaos." It is a commonplace experience that a particular patient will be diagnosed as schizophrenic in one center and manic-depressive in another, with the only change in his status being that he changed institutions. It is not a coincidence of nature nor evidence of the intrinsic harmony in the universe that the frequency of manic-depressive psychosis has increased sharply with the advent of lithium therapy and its associated NIMH grants. Hoch (10) studied the variations in frequency of the diagnosis of schizophrenia both between and within states before the current interest in lithium. The variability could not be accounted for by shifts in population, and he was forced to conclude that the explanation must lie in differing applications of the diagnostic criteria. The irony is that he and Polatin (11) later introduced the category of pseudoneurotic schizophrenia, which only added to and compounded the diagnostic chaos.

These many and varied diagnostic habits produce patient groups labeled as schizophrenic which are not drawn from the same population. Studies performed on patients labeled as schizophrenic but assembled on the basis of differing diagnostic criteria must lead to confusing and contradictory results (16). Seymour Kety (14) pointed out ten years ago that "despite the phenomenological similarities which permitted the concept of schizophrenia as a fairly well defined symptom complex to emerge, there is little evidence that all its forms have a common etiology or pathogenesis. The likelihood that one is dealing with a number of different disorders with a common symptomatology must be recognized and included in one's experimental design." Much of the unreproducibility of the research done is the result of heterogeneity within population samples that are almost arbitrarily designated as schizophrenic. Don Jackson (12) carries this point of view even further when he argues that "the problem of diagnosis underlies the whole frustrating story of research in schizophrenia."

Clinical attempts have been made for many years to find some satisfactory way of subdividing the group of schizophrenias so that research can proceed in a more orderly fashion. Kraepelin's three-quarter-century-old subdivisions (15) are of limited use clinically. While patients are grouped according to similarities in clinical symptomatology, this only allows some very gross prognostic evaluations. His division fails to be of substantive value in research and in clinical practice. Kraepelin's classification does not increase the specificity of treatment, nor reduce the variance of the experimental results, nor particularly improve the reproducibility of the studies. The more gross classification of groups labeled as schizophrenic into paranoid and nonparanoid has recently proven to be of more value than the original subdivision.

The most fundamental problem in research in the schizophrenic syndrome remains the development of more homogeneous diagnostic categories (4). Presently the syndrome includes patients who show a range of premorbid adjustment from schizoid to normal, an onset which ranges from insidious to acute, a presenting picture which ranges incredibly, and an outcome which varies from complete deterioration to complete remission. It is nosological nonsense to have such variety within one category, even if we choose to call it a syndrome. There can be only minimally reliable statements about the nature, course, or treatment of this group of disorders until more homogeneous subgroups are identified. We are not able to predict adequately which cases are going to remit spontaneously nor to what degree. This deficit is particularly dangerous since patients may respond to a given drug but show less improvement than they would have without pharmacological treatment. If you cannot predict the likelihood or the extent of the spontaneous improvement, you cannot be sure that your specific treatment is truly beneficial. There are a number of workers who are concerned that while the tranquilizers have reduced the average duration of hospital stay, they have also reduced the extent—although not the frequency—of spontaneous improvement, i.e., the self-healing features of the acute schizophrenic episode, thereby producing more chronicity. The absence of expected outcome figures that are relevant to a particular group of patients at a given time in a given culture requires that the investigator randomly withhold the treatment under study. The many pressures on the clinician to treat with whatever modalities are available make this approach unfeasible. The simple result is that treatments are not adequately evaluated against each other.

The need to define more homogeneous subpopulations is singularly clear, but the means of doing so remain diverse (3, 6). There is work, including that done by David Rosenthal (18, 19), to suggest that patients within the broad group labeled schizophrenic vary in their degree of genetic loading. This observation promises to serve as a useful criterion variable for the identification of more homogeneous subgroups although it is best used in conjunction with other criterion variables. The division into process and reactive schizophrenia was an important attempt to alter the nosology of the schizophrenic syndrome (2, 7, 13). Historically this separation was not on the basis of prognosis alone, although in recent years the literature has read as if this were the case. The outcome is only one of the variables that contributes to the identification of a particular subgroup. This disorder is far too complex to be divided adequately and neatly into those who do and don't get better. It is obvious that a given individual may or may not recover from a disorder which is the same as or different than that from which a second person did or did not recover. To be blunt, having joined those who have recovered from an illness is not a sufficient criterion for admission to any group other than the fortunate. The attempt to divide the population into two or more groups solely on the basis of outcome has served as an increased source of variance. Outcome is neither a dichotomous nor a static variable. There are degrees of improvement and they fluctuate over time. Outcome is not predetermined in some Calvinistic, inevitable sense. There are a variety of factors that contribute to the determination or are predictive of the outcome (5). It would be more useful to identify the various internal and external factors that influence the course of the illness rather than to group duly those who have been so influenced. The practical value in identifying the contributors to outcome—in addition to any insight into the process that may be gained—is that this may permit better manipulation of those contributors and thereby produce more frequent and/or extensive improvement.

For some time the researcher in this area has utilized an administrative solution. The schizophrenic sample has been defined as those patients who have been so labeled by various treatment institutions. The researcher, much like the psychotherapist, has had to behave as if he were dealing with a real and circumscribed entity. Despite the many fundamental problems there is still some reason for hope. We have selected for inclusion several areas of research in the schizophrenic syndrome which have proven to be fruitful. The authors do not reflect an adversary system but rather modest differences in emphasis and approach. We who are attempting to do research in this field know we are too ignorant to argue. We cling to each other, not unlike motherless monkeys in the choo-choo pattern (9), and derive what warmth, support, and nourishment that we can. It has often been noted that in the treatment of patients a deep personal conviction in the value of your theoretical system is essential. In doing research the opposite is true. We who are not convinced cannot quarrel, but hope to be able to discuss, stimulate, and share.

Some colleagues have commented that the contributors to this section of the book represent the range from organic to psychological viewpoints. As with most facile observations they totally miss the point. There are differences in emphasis among the authors, with some paying greater attention to more molecular response systems and others to more molar systems. These differences in emphasis complement each other. They include approaches to data which vary from a more academic and synthetic to a more gestalt and analytic tradition. The organic-psychological dichotomy has done more harm to research in the schizophrenic syndrome than probably any other single misconception. There is still a marked tendency on the part of many psychiatrists to view a constitutional contribution as excluding psychological ones, and on the part of other psychiatrists to view a psychological contribution as excluding constitutional ones. While we all know intellectually how absurd this position is, at some deeper level many of us have a tendency to believe it. The next five chapters should not be read nor understood as supporting organic or functional biases.

The conceptual model that underlies all of this work is one in which the dynamic interaction of constitutional and environmental factors produce the psychological phenomenon under study. Theoretically we can conceptualize the contribution of constitutional and/or environmental factors by describing the amount of variance accounted for by that particular factor. This may ultimately allow us to say in a given case that constitutional factors play a more important role in determining a particular phenomenon, and environmental factors play a more important role in determining some other phenomenon. Personally, I am doubtful that this will be the case with the more interesting psychological issues; because in an effect resulting from the interaction of constitutional and environmental factors both are necessary. For example, if a biochemical, genetically-determined potential is not mobilized by the appropriate environment, for all practical purposes it does not exist for that particular case. The potential must be actualized in order to be of significance. The environmental mobilization of a constitutional potential need not be an all-or-none affair. Some environments can be more effective than others in mobilizing the potential. The identification of those actualizing or mobilizing environmental experiences is, as already mentioned, of critical importance in the treatment and prevention of the schizophrenic syndrome. If there are classes of stress and/or experience which are more likely to mobilize the genetic potential, an identification of these would be of the utmost importance (8).

Research in the schizophrenic syndrome offers us the promise of better models of mental illness in general, with a better understanding thereby of our efforts at treatment and prevention. There must be a continuous loop from research to clinical practice and back again. In a certain sense, clinical practice has the duty and responsibility to keep researchers relevant. Researchers have a reciprocal responsibility to keep clinicians precise. An example of clinical sloppiness where one term is used to cover two distinct—albeit possibly related—processes may be useful. It is a truism among clinicians that individuals with a schizophrenic reaction show characteristic alterations in their object relations. Traditionally they have spoken of premorbid withdrawal in the schizophrenic reactions, although it is more accurate to speak of a failure to develop an adequate level of involvement with objects. The same term, withdrawal, is used in acute phases of the disorder to describe the need for psychological distance in an individual whose levels of attention and awareness are fluctuating markedly, whose interpretation of sensory input is radically altered, and whose ego is at near dissolution. The use of the same term in these two situations assumes that it is the same phenomenon. It may well be the same, but the burden of proof rests on the man who says it is.

Research can help the clinician to understand better the defensive value of and the need for certain symptoms, thereby assisting in the patient's treatment. If, for example, the researcher could satisfactorily demonstrate that the so-called withdrawal of the acute schizophrenic reaction is not merely an obstacle to treatment, but simultaneously a necessary protection for a very fragile, vulnerable ego, and a self-imposed relatively successful treatment method, the clinician will recognize the necessity of respecting this defense at least for a time. It would not be the impatient respect of the eager clinician waiting until "he can take it better," but rather an accepting and humane respect based on the knowledge that the patient is undergoing a part of the healing process that only he can perform. I do not mean to imply that research has verified this hypothesis, but rather use it to illustrate how a better understanding of the processes involved in the disorder can shape and alter the treatment.

Much of the thinking stimulated by these final chapters will center on the question of what researchers should be doing. One approach I should like to suggest for consideration is the seeking out of those features which are clinically unique to the syndrome. Of the common presenting signs of the disorder, hallucination, delusion, depersonalization, estrangement, constriction of range, and diminution in intensity of affect are not unique. All of these signs and symptoms are to be found in a variety of clinical disorders. A patient with a severe apathetic depression can show an affect which is just as flat and constricted as a schizophrenic's. Perhaps the inappropriateness of the affect should be considered one of the unique features of the syndrome, but what makes the affect inappropriate is its lack of correspondence to the ideational content. One might just as accurately describe the situation by saying the ideation was inappropriate to the affect. This is an example of where our semantic designation tends to suggest that the problem is primarily affective, when in fact we do not know whether it is more in the affective or in the conceptual areas. If there is anything that is clinically unique in this syndrome it is, in this writer's opinion, the characteristic disruption of the thought processes. When we have just interviewed a Kraepelinian type of schizophrenic we are remarkably aware that awake, intoxicated, or dreaming, no one thinks and talks in quite the same way. It might be more accurate to emphasize speech rather than thought, since it is the former that makes up the material under direct observation. Yet speech and thought are so closely linked that for my purposes I shall assume that speech is a direct reflection and product of thought.

There are at least several parameters that must be considered when studying the thought disorder of the schizophrenic syndrome. Rapaport (17) and Frank (8) have insisted that the state of consciousness, the dynamics of attention cathexes, and the formal characteristics of thought must all be taken into account. If we can agree with Rapaport in his formulation, "that the cathectic conditions in schizophrenia lead to an altered state of consciousness in which the formal characteristics of thought are those illustrated by Bleuler," it could be useful to relate our various individual research efforts to this particular formulation. While it may not be possible in a particular research study to deal with several parameters of the thought disorder, even one could be useful. Some examples may help to clarify the point. When studying the process of attention, we should consider its relationship to the other parameters of the thought disorder. Are there relationships between the level and direction of attention and the presence of formal signs of thought disorder? This is a basic and unanswered question. When studying arousal or information processing, we should attempt to relate them to some parameter of the thought disorder. When studying the question of neutralization of energy in the schizophrenic syndrome, we should relate it to the characteristic disturbance of thought. If thought is an economical means of transforming energy, then disruptions in thought and energy transformations may be related. These examples illustrate how the thought disorder may, as Bleuler (1) suggested almost 50 years ago, become the keystone to an understanding of the relationships between the various processes that contribute to the syndrome. It is hoped that the chapters that follow will suggest to the reader a variety of other possible unifying vantage points or keystones that will be of assistance in this most challenging labor.

REFERENCES

1. Bleuler, E.: *Dementia Praecox or the Group of Schizophrenias.* New York: International Universities Press, 1950.
2. Bleuler, E.: *Textbook of Psychiatry.* 4th German Edition. New York: Macmillan, 1924.

3. Cancro, R. and Sugerman, A. A.: Classification and Outcome in Process-Reactive Schizophrenia. *Comprehensive Psychiatry,* 9:227-232, 1968.

4. Cancro, R.: A Classificatory Principle in Schizophrenia. *Scientific Proceedings of the 125th Annual Meeting of the American Psychiatric Association,* pp. 84-85. Washington, D.C.: American Psychiatric Association, 1969.

5. Cancro, R.: Prospective Prediction of Hospital Stay in Schizophrenia. *Archives of General Psychiatry,* 20:541-546, 1969.

6. Cancro, R.: Clinical Prediction of Outcome in Schizophrenia. *Comprehensive Psychiatry,* 10:349-354, 1969.

7. Frank, J.: Psychoanalyse und Psychiatrie. *Sammlung psychoanalytischer Aufsätze,* pp. 99-102, 1932.

8. Frank, J.: Nosological and Differential Diagnostic Considerations in Schizophrenias and Regressophrenias: Clinical Examples. *Journal of Hillside Hospital,* 17:116-135, 1968.

9. Harlow, H. F. and Harlow, M.: Learning to Love. *American Scientist,* 54:244-272, 1966.

10. Hoch, P.: The Etiology and Epidemiology of Schizophrenia. *American Journal of Public Health,* 47:1071-1076, 1957.

11. Hoch, P. and Polatin, P.: Pseudoneurotic Forms of Schizophrenia. *Psychiatric Quarterly,* 23:248-276, 1949.

12. Jackson, D.: *The Etiology of Schizophrenia.* New York: Basic Books, 1960.

13. Jaspers, K.: Kausale und "verständliche" Zusammenhänge zwischen Schicksal und Psychose bei der Dementia Praecox (Schizophrenie). *Zeitschrift für die gesamte Neurologie und Psychiatrie,* 14:158-263, 1913.

14. Kety, S.: Chemical Theories of Schizophrenia. *Science,* 129:1528-1532, 1959.

15. Kraepelin, E.: *Psychiatrie. Ein Lehrbuch für Studierende und Arzte.* 6 Aufl. Leipzig: Barth, 1899.

16. Rabin, A. I. and King, G. I.: Psychological Studies in Schizophrenia. In Bellak, L. (Ed.), *Schizophrenia: A Review of the Syndrome.* New York: Logos, 1958.

17. Rapaport, D.: *Organization and Pathology of Thought.* New York: Columbia University, 1951.

18. Rosenthal, D.: Some Factors Associated with Concordance and Discordance with Respect to Schizophrenia in Monozygotic Twins. *Journal of Nervous and Mental Disease,* 129:1-10, 1959.

19. Rosenthal, D. and Kety, S. S. (Eds.): *The Transmission of Schizophrenia.* London: Pergamon, 1968.

16

Varieties of Reality Restructuring in Schizophrenia

DONALD L. BURNHAM, M.D.

AFTER DOCTOR CANCRO ASKED ME to write about clinical research in schizophrenia, I pondered how to distinguish it from other forms of research. For me it has been closely linked to therapeutic endeavors, particularly psychotherapy and milieu therapy, in which relationships are vital and an effort is made to understand the patient as a whole person in terms of his life history, viewed as a temporally extended gestalt. This differs from approaches which take either a cross-sectional or a segmental view and attempt to focus upon parts isolated from the whole. Let me state straightaway that I believe both types of approach to be important. They are not antithetical, nor is one necessarily superior to another. Optimally they should supplement each other. We need as many angles of vision as we can find in our efforts to unravel the protean mysteries of schizophrenia.

Clinical research affords several angles of vision that are particularly relevant. One is the emphasis on the person. This is particularly relevant because schizophrenia is a disorder of the person. The person is the illness rather than the host for the illness, as in diseases that conform more readily to a medical model of illness.

Also inherent in the focus on the person is the developmental angle of vision. What factors, interacting in what way, shaped him into the person that he is today? To attempt to answer this question requires that we study, among other factors, the context in which he developed, particularly his early relationships. Clinical research is well-suited for this study, since treatment relationships provide a context that tends to mirror, if not replicate, the early relationships in which patterns of language, thought, and meaning were learned—the very patterns that are disordered in schizophrenia.

Another angle of vision in clinical research concerns the "why" of the patient's behavior, its meaning and purpose, especially its meaning and purpose for him. In other words, at what is his behavior aimed in his world, in his reality?

These are important considerations in our efforts to reach a full understanding of schizophrenia. For instance, if we set out to study hallucinations, we might want to ask what neuronal structures may be hyperirritable and what agents may be irritating them. But, we also shall want to ask what purpose the hallucinations may be serving in the patient's efforts to adapt to reality.

The topic of the patient's relation to reality has absorbed much of my recent research interest. I hope by presenting it to illustrate something of what can be learned from the angles of vision of clinical research.

It is generally agreed that a pathognomonic symptom of the schizophrenic person is his disordered relation to reality. Less agreement exists, however, as to the exact nature of this disorder. In fact, considerable conceptual confusion surrounds the topic. Part of the confusion resides in the multiple meanings of the word *reality*.

One meaning refers to the world outside the person—to the "out there." The schizophrenic person has difficulty attending to, perceiving, and adapting to this reality. He is said to have lost, withdrawn from, or broken contact with, reality.

Another meaning refers to the image, representation, or construct of reality which each person forms. Reality is not structured by a process of photographic replication. As Bleuler (3) said, "We do not comprehend the external world directly with our sense organs. We must create its image within ourselves by synthesis of and logical conclusions drawn from the material provided by our senses." Structuring of reality involves the organization of experience and the creation of meaning. From a myriad of inner and outer events each person selects those that are relevant to him and articulates them into structures of meaning that together constitute *his* version of reality. (A person's reality structure is akin to what has been variously termed his subjective world, his cognitive map of reality, his inner world, or his representational world—or simply, his world.) Confronted by the same array of outer world events, different persons will structure different meanings and different realities. In this sense, each person creates his own reality.

The realities of the majority of persons are similar enough in enough respects to constitute a shared reality. But the reality structured by the schizophrenic person differs to the extent that it is considered idiosyncratic and a handicap in his relationships with others.

At the same time, his structuring of reality is not entirely maladaptive. It also serves restitutive and adaptive functions. Freud (10, 11, 12, 13) emphasized this in several of his writings. In speaking of the remodeling and reconstruction of reality in psychosis, he wrote (11), "In regard to the genesis of delusions, a fair number of analyses have taught us that the delusion is found applied like a patch over the place where originally a rent had appeared in the ego's relation to the external world. If this precondition of a conflict with the external world is not much more noticeable to us than it now is, that is because, in the clinical picture of the psychosis, the manifestations of the pathogenic process are often overlaid by manifestations of an attempt at a cure or a reconstruction." C. Macfie Campbell (7) perhaps even more explicitly stressed the adaptive function of reality distortions when he stated, "Delusion, like fever, is to be looked on as part of nature's attempt at cure, an endeavor to neutralize some disturbing factor, to compensate for some handicap, to reconstruct a working contact with the group, which will still satisfy special needs." Study of the misperception of other persons in schizophrenia further convinced me that restructuring of reality is not just a means of escape and denial, but may also help to avert complete disorganization, particularly if distortion in one sector preserves and strengthens key object relationships in other sectors (4).

The present chapter is an effort to extend our understanding of the various forms of reality restructuring in schizophrenia. Structuring or organizing events into patterns of meaning entails placing the events in contexts or frames of reference and assigning them to various levels or regions of reality. A different meaning is created according to the context and level in which an event or item of experience is placed. For example, an event may have one meaning in the region of play, another in the region of serious interaction. A word has one meaning on the level of metaphor, another on the level of literality. Similarly, an event takes on different meanings in the regions of fantasy, perception, recollection, and dream.

Discriminative awareness of these various regions or spheres of reality arises out of the developmental process of differentiation. In the normal course of differentiation a person becomes able to assign unambiguous events to the appropriate region of reality rather easily—almost automatically and without conscious deliberation. More ambiguous events may require conscious reality-testing to determine their proper categorization.

In schizophrenia, however, these capabilities go awry, partly as a result of the faulty differentiation of the schizophrenic-vulnerable personality and partly as a result of *dedifferentiation*. In fact, much of the symptomatology of schizophrenia may be understood as a product of de-differentiation (22). The boundaries between regions become blurred and the placement of events confused. Foremost of the boundaries which are blurred in schizophrenia is the self-nonself boundary, normally a keystone in a person's structure of reality. Its blurring causes inner-outer confusion, which is at the root of many of the major symptoms of schizophrenia, to wit, hallucinations and delusions of control by external forces. Rapaport (18) advanced the idea that many forms of schizophrenic thought can be understood as disturbances of cognitive "frames of reference."

Also blurred is the distinction between events of trivial and those of salient relevance to the person. In the disruption of the normal figure-ground relationship, occurrences ordinarily relegated to the background take on urgent and ominous personal significance and are the basis for ideas of reference and many delusional beliefs.

When normal discrimination and categorization break down, inner and outer events join to form peculiar and idiosyncratic structures of meaning. To quote Werner and Kaplan (23), there is a "tendency to endow objects and states of affairs with a profound meaning, to read deep significance into the prosaic objects of everyday life. . . ." The incidental flight of a passing bird, or the shape of a twig in the gutter, may become powerful omens that the person perceives as controlling his feelings and impulses. Events normally governed by inner controls are confused with events ruled by outer forces.

Such phenomena were abundantly exemplified by a schizophrenic patient of mine for whom the interpenetration of inner and outer was extreme. He would say, "When that light went on, I could feel it in my bowels." Or he would exclaim, "I shouldn't think that thought! As soon as I had it, the sun went behind the clouds." After speaking of his mother one day, he said, "As soon as I mentioned her name, that bell rang."

As a more vivid example I recall Harry Stack Sullivan's description of a patient (21) who, as he watched a pocket billiards game, suddenly ejaculated in his trousers when a particular ball dropped into a pocket.

One final illustration of peculiar linkage of inner and outer events is the often-noted belief of many catatonic patients that movements of their bodies have world-destroying consequences (20).

The linking of micro- and macrocosmic events in such unusual combinations involves breakdown of normal discrimination between inner and outer systems of control. The person no longer feels his thoughts, affects, and actions to be under his control; he constructs explanatory delusions of influence and persecution by outside forces. Since the maintenance of a clear self-nonself boundary is partly dependent on the sense of what is and isn't subject to one's autonomous control, uncertainty of the source of control leads to further blurring of this boundary and heightening of the general inner-outer uncertainty (1).

In another variety of reality restructuring, some distinctions are retained among regions of reality, but a particular event may be shunted from one region to another, becoming part of a different structure of meaning in each region.

The shift of meaning when an event is pulled from one level of reality to another is perhaps most readily seen in some of the schizophrenic person's communication difficulties. On hearing a word uttered in one context, he is likely to draw it into the context of his inner preoccupations of the moment. For example, a therapist said to a patient, "Glen, some things that are new and frightening have to be repeated over and over again until they become familiar." The patient, much preoccupied by a wish-fear of homosexual assault, retorted in outrage, "Oh, so you want to be familiar with me! I knew all along that you had dirty motives." On another occasion this patient heard someone say "enigmatic"; his preoccupations seized upon part of the word to produce the exclamation, "Oh, you are suggesting that the doctor give me an enema!"

Phrases, as well as single words, may be captured by rampant preoccupations. In a staff-patient meeting a doctor suggested a change in hospital administrative policy and said, "We can't just talk about this idea and then let it rest; we must keep pushing it as hard as we can." Thereupon a woman patient jumped up and said, "I want a penis in my vagina—not just fingers, but a penis pushed hard."

An even more extreme instance of word-capturing occurred when mention of Santa Claus evoked from a man the comment, "Sainted Claws—hands that have never masturbated."

Not all capturing is by sexual preoccupations. A man with deep conflict about his Jewish heritage heard someone mention Yosemite Park and asked, "Is that where they are going to make the Semites live?"

Still another patient heard a nurse humming a tune. Without warning he viciously struck her. Later he explained that he had thought she was humming "Sweet Sixteen" with deliberate intent to mock him as childish.

In a somewhat similar incident, a woman patient suddenly burst into anger at a maid who was dusting furniture nearby. She shouted, "You are doing that to remind me of Dusty, and I don't want ever to think of him again!" (Dusty was a lover who had jilted her some years before.)

The following interchange contains several shifts of context. A doctor opened a ward meeting by asking, "Does anyone have something he wants to bring up?" A long-hospitalized woman, deeply grieved by her inability to function as a mother answered, "Yes I want to bring up my children." The doctor, missing the poignancy of her statement replied, "Well, they are now at ages where they are practically grown up." The patient responded, "No, they are down at the bottom and I want to bring them up." In the patient's final statement we have an indication of how a shift toward concreteness may serve as a defense against anxiety.

These examples of the shifting of perceptual events from one context to another bring to mind Bleuler's discussion (3) of delusion formation: "Because of the far-reaching split in the psychic functions, the affect becomes all-powerful in the realm of a certain complex of ideas; criticism and correction become impossible. Thus, within the split-off complexes, the affects create fantastic worlds for themselves, ignoring reality, from which they *select* only material suitable for their purposes. The latter process is facilitated in schizophrenia by the disintegration of the association-pathways. This enables the affects to connect any *selected material* with the complex which is always in a state of *functional preparedness,* and to utilize the material accordingly." (Emphasis mine.) This is similar to Eissler's description (8) of the "social animism" by which a schizophrenic person selectively interprets outer reality to fit the emotion which possesses him at the moment.

Applying Bleuler's formulation to my examples of context-shifting, we could say that in these patients affective preoccupations, or complexes, were in a "state of functional preparedness" to selectively capture elements of the perceptual field by tearing them from their original contexts. This "state of functional preparedness" would seem to be determined by the affective intensity of the complexes and by tenuous control over them. Tenuous control over painful ideas is, in turn, often a result of efforts to totally repress, or, in Bleuler's terminology, to split off, these ideas. When the repressive effort fails, the perceptual stimuli that are captured serve as the bridge for an abrupt return of the repressed.

In the examples of capturing I have presented, key perceptual elements were drawn into contexts or structures of meaning that had intense, painful personal relevance to the perceiver.

A reverse type of context-shifting also occurs frequently in schizophrenia. This involves shunting from painful to nonpainful, from personal to impersonal contexts. Here are some examples from therapist-patient interviews:

Therapist: You seem to want very much to avoid all possible pain.
Patient: I remember reading about Thomas Paine in a history course.
Therapist: You seem to have occasional flickers of hope.
Patient: I saw Bob Hope in a movie the other day. Bing Crosby was in it too.
Therapist: You seem to fear that if you developed any close friends, they would desert you.
Patient: I wonder what's for dessert at lunch today.
Therapist: I gather that you can't bear the thought of what might happen in that situation.
Patient: Yeah, California used to be called the Bear Flag Republic.
Patient: I would like to cry, but I shouldn't.
Therapist: Is that because you think it's sissy for a man to cry?
Patient: Yes, I think it's sissy for a man to cry. I think it's sissy for anybody . . . (pause) . . . Cissy's husband—he tried to do a lot for me.
Patient: (Referring to a doctor he had requested as a substitute therapist during his regular therapist's imminent vacation) Doctor Jones will be my proctor while you're away . . . Procter and Gamble; you've heard of them . . . Doctor Jones gambles on my wanting him as my proctor.

This example reveals not only the patient's pleasure and skill at word play but also his need-fear conflict concerning his doctors, which he alternately approached and avoided by shuttling between contexts. The salience of this conflict in the object relations of schizophrenic persons is explored in detail in the book *Schizophrenia and the Need-Fear Dilemma* (6).

Another patient used context-shifting to avoid a similar conflict. In an extremely sullen, aloof, suspicious manner, he customarily denied any interest in other persons and rejected all efforts to approach him. A few weeks after his transfer to a new ward, he was startled to see his previous administrative physician visiting there. With a trace of a smile he said, "Hello, doctor, haven't seen you in a long time." This rare flash of warmth was abruptly followed, however, by his muttering, "The windows in this place are dirty—can't see through them." By shunting the word "see" to another meaning structure, he obscured and retracted his unusual admission of having missed the doctor.

How are we to explain shunting and context-shifting? We could say that they are manifestations of distractibility and thought derailment. But these terms do not take us much beyond the descriptive level. Neither does a designation of shunting as the product of loosened associations.

Perhaps we are somewhat closer to an explanation if we consider that shunting and context-shifting seem to serve a purpose—the purpose of escape from painful affects and the reduction of anxiety. This, of course, is not a new idea. Bleuler (3) observed that schizophrenic patients block off "not only the painful affects but also the concomitant events." He further commented, "Emotional reasons usually determine the process of displacement inasmuch as less unpleasant ideas are frequently substituted for highly unpleasant ones."

A present-day investigator, Mednick (15, 16), has made anxiety-reduction the keystone of a learning theory explanation of schizophrenic thought disorder. He suggests that the essence of schizophrenia consists of the learning of avoidant thoughts. According to this theory, the acute phases of schizophrenia feature a spiral of anxiety and stimulus generalization. The chronic phases feature the domination of thought by anxiety-reducing, avoidant thought sequences. These are thoughts that are irrelevant and remote from the anxiety arousing them and are acquired as tangential associations in the course of the generalization process.

Many of my examples of shunting and context-shifting seem to fit Mednick's theory rather well. An exception, however, is the "Procter and Gamble" example in which the patient, albeit somewhat obliquely, introduced an anxiety-arousing topic, then shifted to an anxiety-avoiding association, but finally returned at least part way to the original painful context of meaning. Something more than anxiety-reduction must be going on, something entailing internal conflict which impels alternating approach and avoidance of the painful topics.

The capturing of events by painful structures of meaning also involves something different from anxiety avoidance. This phenomenon seems more to fit the anxiety-stimulus generalization spiral said by Mednick to feature the acute phases of schizophrenia. Certainly, increased stimulus generalization would contribute to the transformation of ordinarily neutral stimuli into anxiety arousers. In discussing the predisposition to generalization, Mednick cited three factors: 1. low threshold for anxiety arousal,

2. slow rate of recovery from anxiety arousal, and 3. high generalization reactiveness.

I should suggest that additional factors may contribute to the readiness to incorporate ordinarily neutral stimuli into anxiety-arousing structures of meaning. I referred earlier to preoccupations that so dominate consciousness as to feed on chance, tangential stimuli. A related phenomenon concerns affects and impulses held in segregation or repression from central consciousness but threatening imminently to invade and capture it. Bleuler described such a situation when he spoke of the independent activity of split-off complexes that threaten to usurp control of thought processes. Split-off complexes are the product of excessive repression and denial, prominent features of the poorly integrated, schizophrenia-vulnerable personality.

Sudden depression must be considered one of the factors that may open the door to a flood of stimulus capturing and stimulus generalization. This may occur when tenuous ego controls of consciousness are weakened, as when acute schizophrenic restructuring of reality follows a disturbing dream, general anesthesia, or drug intoxication (9, 21).

Even chance stimuli may call forth repressed complexes that are on the verge of erupting into consciousness. MacCurdy (14), in his study of precipitation of psychosis, provided examples of disorganization triggered by seemingly trivial events that took on special symbolic meaning in terms of previously repressed preoccupations. One of his cases was a man hospitalized for a physical illness who developed an acute paranoid psychosis with delusions of homosexual assault after his temperature had been taken rectally. This man's repressed homosexual wish-fear was so strong that it broke through the repressive barrier and pulled the meaning of the insertion of the thermometer from one level of reality to another.

Having discussed varieties of restructuring in which boundaries between regions of reality are blurred or events are shunted between regions, I turn now to varieties in which the element of reconstruction predominates, with the building of new contexts, ranging from fantasy reconstruction of the whole world to revision of discrete sectors of reality or of single events. These are the sorts of effort to remodel reality that prompted Freud's earlier quoted description (11) of a delusion as comparable to a "patch over the place where originally a rent had appeared in the ego's relation to the external world," and Campbell's similar description (7) of a delusion as a neutralizing, compensating reconstructive attempt at cure. Also relevant is Bleuler's statement (3) that, "Just as reality can be endowed with everything pleasant and desired, so can the unpleasant be removed from it." Equally pertinent is Silverberg's formulation (19) of the "schizoid maneuver" as the "attempt to distort mentally an unpalatable reality, external or internal, into something more acceptable."

The basic mental operation in the restructuring of reality is the replacement of an intolerable version of reality by a more tolerable one. The replacement may be global or discrete, continuing or transient, and direct or indirect.

Direct replacement is easily illustrated. Consider, for instance, a childless woman who became convinced that she was the mother of several children who had been stolen from her. Another example was a bereaved husband who believed that his wife was still alive and would soon return to him.

As illustrations of somewhat more complicated restructurings, I offer the following examples.

A young mother who felt unloved by her husband and excessively burdened by her two young children burst into uncontrolled rage one day and threw one of the children down a stairway. Thereupon she herself was plunged into panic and schizophrenic disorganization. Quickly, however, she became convinced that she and her church minister were soon to be married; a suffusion of love replaced her overwhelming rage and she partly reorganized.

A chronically schizophrenic young man sat talking with a nurse in a hospital hallway when another patient strode by wearing his Ivy League varsity letter sweater. Suddenly the first young man switched from talk about impersonal topics to interject, "Did you know that I won a tennis championship at Wimbledon?"

The immediate sequence in the second example permits us to see clearly that, by restructuring, the patient is attempting to deny a painful sense of inferiority. A more complex but similarly pathetic restructuring in the service of denial features the next example.

An elderly artist was visited in the hospital one day by two friends who were professional musicians. Almost his first words to them were, "We won't talk about music; there is entirely too much of the stuff written anyway!" Later in the visit one of the friends asked whether he had been painting recently. He answered, "I've been prevented from it by burned hands that I received rescuing a person from a fire recently." The friends did not question his story but later asked a nurse about it. She told them that a few weeks earlier there had indeed been a fire in a neighboring building, but that the artist had not been out of his room at the time.

Restructuring may shut off various disruptive affects and impulses. A hospitalized patient struggling to repress homosexual urges found himself initially attracted to two new aides who seemed pleasant and friendly. He was disturbed by his response to them, but soon was greatly relieved when he decided that actually they were hostile detectives who were only pretending to be friendly.

Frequently restructuring helps to control potentially disruptive rage. A schizophrenic man spent the first half hour of a therapy session mute, rigid, and breathing heavily. In an effort to break the barrier of silence, his German-born therapist urged him to speak, whereupon the patient retorted angrily, "How do you expect me to talk when I think of the dirty, corrupt swine who have caused two world wars?" The therapist, shaken by the patient's abrupt rage, managed to reply, "That sounds like an insult," at which the patient hastily said in a placating tone, "I know you are actually British." When the therapist decided to refute this restructuring of reality by insisting that he was German, not British, the patient violently assaulted him.

Here restructuring momentarily enabled the patient to sustain his perilously unsteady control of rage, until the therapist refused to accept the revision of reality. It should be added that this patient held a stereotyped view that everything British was all good. On other occasions he had commented that his therapist resembled Prince Philip, and at times would actually misperceive him as Philip and ask after Queen Elizabeth's health. (An intriguing sidelight in this restructuring of reality is that Philip's forebears did, of course, come from Germany and changed the family name from Battenberg to Mountbatten. Whether these historical facts played any part in determining the patient's misperception is doubtful.) This was linked with delusional fantasies that he himself was destined to marry Princess Margaret, who at the time was not yet married. His misperception of his therapist appeared to be an effort to construct an all-good image of a benevolent object.

Misperceptions of bad objects also featured this patient's versions of reality. At the time of the Suez crisis between Egypt and Britain, the patient assaulted a Negro aide whom he misperceived as Nasser. Possibly this was a post hoc justification of his action, but in any event it seemed to give him a sense of greater rational control over the organization of his experience than actually was the case. It also afforded him considerable relief from a severe need-fear dilemma (6).

Another paranoid man who attempted to control his rage by reality restructuring I shall call Mr. Johnson. He had been transferred from another hospital where he had been considered extremely dangerous and unpredictably assaultive and had been controlled by close custody and several hundred electric shock treatments. He, in turn, had made frantic and repeated efforts to escape.

At the new hospital he was allowed much more freedom of movement, partly because his sparse funds would permit only a short inpatient stay before he became an outpatient. This freedom enabled him to handle episodes of face-blackening rage by fleeing the hospital grounds for hours at a time.

One morning Mr. Johnson arrived late for a therapy appointment; profusely apologetic, he said that he had been downtown at the telephone company office. Then, bit by bit, he recounted that the previous evening he had developed a headache and had approached the ward nurse to ask for an aspirin while she was playing bridge with three patients. She replied, "Yes, of course, but would you wait until this hand is finished." Johnson sat and waited in the dayroom for nearly an hour, but the nurse did not come. Meanwhile his headache had worsened, and finally he returned to the nurse who, though finished with the bridge game, now was in the nursing office chatting casually with the patient who had been her bridge partner. On seeing this, Mr. Johnson thrust himself into the nursing office to ask again for the forgotten aspirin. The nurse snapped, *"Just a minute,* Mr. Johnson, patients are *not* allowed in the nursing station." Mr. Johnson, barely able to contain a rush of rage, suddenly thought, "What sort of a place is this?" The next morning he went to the phone company to inquire whether the place was listed as a hospital or as a hotel. (I am indebted to Dr. Robert A. Cohen for this example.)

Mr. Johnson's idea that he might be in a hotel was not yet a firm delusional belief; it was more a delusion in *statu nascendi,* a sample of the microscopic anatomy of delusion formation. It seems clear that by restructuring the situation he buttressed his precarious control of rage. At other times he had managed control only by literally escaping from the environment. This time he escaped by altering the symbol referring to the environment. This is the same symbolic maneuver employed by the patient who misperceived his German therapist as British. This and other forms of autistic manipulation of symbols, without regard for their referential validity, are hallmarks of schizophrenia.

Restructuring often involves shifts from one symbolic level to another. Bleuler (3) observed a Swiss patient who shifted from concern about serious conflict with his German-born wife to a delusional preoccupation that Switzerland was at war with Prussia.

I recall a woman whose struggle to control aggressive and sexual impulses was displaced to a ritual of alternately turning on the hot and cold water faucets dozens of times in order to draw a sink of warm water. She explained that if she did not exert great care the "hot water man," who she thought was downstairs holding the pipe, might be burned. This woman's family had first become convinced of the seriousness of her illness when they discovered her pouring water into the furnace. It is noteworthy that she displaced her struggle for control not only from one symbolic level to another but also from the inner to the outer realm of events.

A shift from one form of displacement to another is revealed in the following example. Ten or fifteen minutes before a scheduled therapy appointment, a schizophrenic patient of mine noticed me having coffee with a woman colleague in the hospital canteen. He approached me and asked, "Are we having an 'hour' today?" I answered that I would join him shortly, and he went to the waiting room to wait.

He began the ensuing interview by saying, "I hope that dentist doesn't spend so much time occupying himself with that nurse that he forgets my appointment with him—it's for next week some time." (The dental office happened to be located just across the hall from my office.)

I replied, "It sounds as though you were perhaps somewhat angered by my keeping you waiting just now." At this the patient began to squirm and grimace. Soon he said, "You remind me of Professor Culver of the University of Illinois—you look like him—only he was stockier—oh, you know him." When I answered, "No, I don't know him," the patient went into a rather disjointed monologue, "Culver of Culver City, Oklahoma . . . Culver City, California . . . Culver . . . C-U-L-V-E-R . . . I remember Professor Culver's office at the University of Illinois—there were other offices above it—you could take out the offices and have an elevator there."

Later in the interview, after intervening discussion, the patient returned to the topic of Professor Culver, saying "He was a cover-up . . . cover-to-cover man . . . covering his anger . . . getting a high blood pressure look." In this statement the patient seemed close to explaining the displacement, cover-up function of his partially misperceiving me as Professor Culver.

Taking this as a cue, I ventured to extend the discussion of anger a bit further by saying, "People can get sick by swallowing too much of their anger." The patient responded, "That's the true statement of the year; did you by any chance have someone in mind? I feel awfully sick today myself." I answered, "I do think that you do a lot of swallowing of your anger."

At this point the patient asked obsequiously whether he might leave the room to get a drink (swallow) of water. Upon returning he spoke in scattered fashion about body hair and shaving and of his father's and uncle's capabilities for wrath. An undertone of castration anxiety was readily apparent, especially when he spoke of his uncle's being in the meat-packing business.

Misperception of other persons, such as almost occurred in this example, is a common form of reality restructuring in schizophrenia. It is a variety of splitting, similar to reduplication or doubling, and revises the reality structure in a manner that permits avoidance of painful affects which the patient is unable to integrate into full consciousness, particularly the affects associated with the need-fear dilemma.

The pain of loss and separation is an example. One man misperceived hospital attendants as members of his family. Later he explained that on entering the hospital he had been seized by the terror that he would never see his family again and was relieved to "discover" that some of them were there with him.

Denial via restructuring may involve reduplication of time, place, or person. This was abundantly exemplified by a schizophrenic man who could not integrate the fact of his mother's death. Whenever this topic was approached, he would reach into his bag of symbolic reduplicative tricks, a sampling of which includes the following: "There is a U.S. and a U.S.A.; my mother is alive in one of them . . . state laws are different from federal laws . . . I am bound only by military law, not by civil law . . . there are two Washingtons, one on the east coast, the other on the west coast; one is concerned with art and beauty, the other with business . . . my mother remarried and is living in South America under another name . . . the constellations of stars have one name given them by the Greeks and another given them by the Arabs. . . . Pacific time is different from Atlantic time." His repertoire of reduplicative maneuvers was highly reminiscent of Bleuler's description (3) of double registration of events in schizophrenia.

This patient also was fascinated by all manner of homonyms, and had frequent recourse to the belief that various present persons were doubles or twins of others he had known in the past. Clues to the dynamic defensive function of such beliefs were furnished in his psychotherapy sessions with me. One day just before my vacation, I said, "I shall miss you while

I am away." He answered, "I shall miss you, too, but as soon as I'm out of this room, I'll start saying critical things about you, and thinking that I knew you somewhere else under another name." The reduplication defended against the need-fear conflict, ambivalence, and object inconstancy aroused by the impending separation. To think of me as a different person during the separation might enable him to preserve a good image of me as his doctor.

The same motive was conspicuous in another patient's intensely ambivalent relationship with me. She was unable to integrate feeling so differently toward me at different times, and once said, "They keep sending different doctors and pretending that they are the same one." One therapy session was interrupted by another patient's opening the door and entering the room. After the intruder had been persuaded to leave, my patient said, "I know now that you are really Loretta's doctor, and that you were just pretending to be my doctor."

On many other occasions this patient revealed how plagued she was by the inconstancy of her objects. She would complain, "Your voice changes and it comes from different parts of the room, sometimes near, sometimes far away. What are you doing—splitting yourself up?" Not surprisingly, this patient's ego and percept of herself were severely split, and she was extremely sensitive to inconsistencies among the persons in her immediate environment. This type of patient and some of the associated problems in therapy have been described elsewhere (5).

In the treasure of clinical observations bequeathed us by Bleuler (3) are several excellent accounts of reduplicative remodeling of reality: One woman insisted that she had two husbands, one good, the other bad; a man fantasied a double of himself; a woman wrote her husband that she was in a convalescent home *near* the Burghölzli insane asylum, when actually she was *in* the Burghölzli.

The last example brings to mind a patient of mine who angrily denied his hospital patient role by shouting, "This is *not* a hospital; it is a *hospice!*"

Wordplay of various sorts may be employed in denying and restructuring painful sectors of reality. A woman, greatly distressed by signs of aging, spoke of growing new teeth to replace those she had lost. She contended, "There are roots in there, and after all things do grow from roots." Confronted by news of her mother's death, she said, "My mother is not dead; she is just dead tired and needs a rest." A man usually denied illness and rejected the role of patient, but momentarily acknowledged that he was "mixed up"; hastily, however, he made a wordplay emendation, "Not mixed up about things, but mixed in with things."

Not all reality restructuring evades the painful. It may also be a way to reexperience painful events and perhaps to work them through more satisfactorily than when they originally occurred. For example, a young woman misperceived a Negro maid as a girlhood friend with whom she had engaged in sex play who now was being punished by her skin having turned brown and by being forced to do demeaning labor like cleaning the hospital ward bathroom. The patient was further convinced that her own skin was changing color. This restructuring, rather than evading painful guilt, brought it into focal consciousness.

The use of current perceptual elements in the construction of the misperception is similar to the word-capturing phenomenon I described earlier. Both phenomena illustrate how a powerful preoccupation can dominate the organization of individual percepts and total consciousness, especially when ego controls of consciousness are weak.

Capturing of consciousness by a previously repressed complex occurred in another young woman who, in the course of acute schizophrenic disorganization, misperceived many of the hospital staff members as persons from a particularly painful period of her adolescence. It was as if she had assembled a cast of characters with whom to work through the troubles of that era of her life. She recreated many specific episodes involving jealousy and rivalry with peers, and intense need-fear and dependency-hostility conflicts with her elders. Her restagings of earlier life episodes featured many new outcomes in which fantasy had the quality of full reality for her. Among these restructurings were glorious triumphs for her and death and humiliation for her hated rivals. It is especially significant that this was a transient phase which led not to permanent, autistic restructuring of her world but to subsequent working through of many of the same problems in shared reality. Thus, it was an important step toward recovery.

Restructuring as a means of working through brings to mind a too little known paper by Bertschinger (2), published originally in German in 1911 and translated into English in 1916, on processes of recovery in schizophrenia. He observed patients who passed through a whole series of delusional experiences which little by little brought about wish fulfillment. When the dramatic play of the wish fulfilling delusions was complete, the patients emerged as if reborn or as if from a long sleep, with regained control of the unconscious spheres of their minds, and eventual recovery.

Obviously, wish fulfillment is as important in shaping schizophrenic reality revisions as in shaping dreams. An example of positive aspirations giving rise to misperception was provided by a young man who hoped for a career as an actor or playwright. In the course of an episode of schizophrenic disorganization, he misperceived me as Maxwell Anderson. This restructuring of reality afforded him considerable temporary comfort. It had multiple determinants, including his wish that I might directly aid him to achieve his theatrical ambitions. Of course, his restructuring was in itself a dramatic production of which he was the director. Also pertinent was a wish to associate with famous persons, a wish that had been cultivated by his adoptive parents sending him away to an exclusive private school where he could associate with the sons of wealthy and socially prominent families, but where he felt he was playing a role that really didn't belong to him.

Another similarity between dreams and reality restructuring concerns the dream's preservation of sleep in the face of intruding stimuli that threaten to interrupt it. In this regard I recall a dream of my own in which I was on a ship that suddenly turned over and began to sink. I clung to the outside of the overturned hull. Just then a phone rang. Without considering it peculiar that a phone would be available, I picked it up and heard a voice say, "I just wanted to tell you that the ship is sinking." I hung up in annoyance, thinking, "I don't need anyone to tell me *that*." As the dream continued, the phone soon rang again. This time I decided to ignore it. The ringing persisted, however; finally I awoke sufficiently to realize that it was my bedside phone that was ringing.

The formation of such a dream seems remarkably similar to the reality restructuring which handles a potentially disruptive perceptual event by building it into a nonpainful meaning structure.

Schizophrenic reality restructuring also bears strong resemblance to the thinking and play of children at certain stages of their development. In discussing the symbolic play of children, Piaget (17) has employed the terms "compensating and liquidating combinations" to refer to the child's use of make-believe to remodel reality in ways that may relieve pain, neutralize fear, or transpose roles in difficult situations. As we have seen, these are some of the defensive functions of schizophrenic reality restructuring. An important difference is that rather early the normal child establishes a clear distinction between the realm of make-believe and the realm of shared reality. In the dedifferentiation of schizophrenia this distinction becomes blurred.

In commenting on the similarity of the spheres of reality of the schizo-

214   *The Schizophrenic Reactions*

phrenic patient and the child, Werner (22) wrote, "The schizophrenic world of fantasy, like the child's play reality, has the value of the real, not because things appear true to nature, but rather because strong emotions bring them to life." Werner also cited Storch's asking a patient whether he really believed he could purify the world by smearing his saliva on everything, and receiving the answer, "My heart tells me yes." I once asked a patient whether in deciding what to believe he trusted more what he saw or what he heard. He answered, "I believe what *feels* right."

REFERENCES

1. Angyal, A.: The Experience of the Body-Self in Schizophrenia. *Archives of Neurology and Psychiatry*, 35:1029-1053, 1936.
2. Bertschinger, H.: Processes of Recovery in Schizophrenics. (Translated by Charles L. Allen) *Psychoanalytic Review*, 3:176-188, 1916.
3. Bleuler, E.: *Dementia Praecox or the Group of Schizophrenias*. New York: International Universities Press, 1950.
4. Burnham, D. L.: Misperception of Other Persons in Schizophrenia. *Psychiatry*, 19:283-303, 1956.
5. Burnham, D. L.: The Special Problem Patient: Victim or Agent of Splitting? *Psychiatry*, 29:105-122, 1966.
6. Burnham, D. L., Gladstone, A. I., and Gibson, R. W.: *Schizophrenia and the Need-Fear Dilemma*. New York: International Universities Press, 1969.
7. Campbell, C. M.: *Delusion and Belief*. Cambridge: Harvard University Press, 1927.
8. Eissler, K. R.: Notes Upon the Emotionality of a Schizophrenic Patient and Its Relation to Problems of Technique. *The Psychoanalytic Study of the Child*, 8:199-251. New York: International Universities Press, 1953.
9. Federn, P.: *Ego Psychology and the Psychoses*. New York: Basic Books, 1952.
10. Freud, S.: Psycho-analytic Notes on an Autobiographical Account of a Case of Paranoia. In *The Standard Edition of the Complete Psychological Works of Sigmund Freud*, Vol. 12. London: Hogarth Press, 1958, pp. 9-82.
11. Freud, S.: Neurosis and Psychosis. In *The Standard Edition of the Complete Psychological Works of Sigmund Freud*, Vol. 19. London: Hogarth Press, 1961, pp. 149-153.
12. Freud, S.: The Loss of Reality in Neurosis and Psychosis. In *The Standard Edition of the Complete Psychological Works of Sigmund Freud*, Vol. 19. London: Hogarth Press, 1961, pp. 183-187.
13. Freud, S.: Constructions in Analysis. In *The Standard Edition of the Complete Psychological Works of Sigmund Freud*, Vol. 23. London: Hogarth Press, 1964, pp. 257-269.

14. MacCurdy, J. T.: A Psychological Feature of the Precipitating Causes in the Psychoses and Its Relation to Art. In *Studies in Abnormal Psychology*, Series V. Boston: Badger, 1915.

15. Mednick, S. A.: A Learning Theory Approach to Research in Schizophrenia. *Psychological Bulletin*, 55:316-327, 1958.

16. Mednick, S. A.: The Children of Schizophrenics: Serious Difficulties in Current Research Methodologies which Suggest the Use of the "High-Risk Group" Method. In Romano, J. (Ed.), *The Origins of Schizophrenia*. New York: Excerpta Medica Foundation, 1967.

17. Piaget, J.: *Play, Dreams and Imitation in Childhood*. New York: Norton, 1962.

18. Rapaport, D.: Cognitive Structures. In Gill, M. M. (Ed.) *The Collected Papers of David Rapaport*. New York: Basic Books, 1967.

19. Silverberg, W. V.: The Schizoid Maneuver. *Psychiatry*, 10:383-394, 1947.

20. Storch, A.: The Primitive Archaic Forms of Inner Experiences and Thought in Schizophrenia. *Nervous and Mental Disease Monographs*, No. 36, 1924.

21. Sullivan, H. S.: Cultural Stress and Adolescent Crisis. In *Schizophrenia as a Human Process*. New York: Norton, 1962.

22. Werner, H.: *Comparative Psychology of Mental Development*. New York: International Universities Press, 1957.

23. Werner, H. and Kaplan, B.: *Symbol Formation*. New York: John Wiley & Sons, 1963.

17

Perceptual Dysfunction in the Schizophrenic Syndrome

PHILIP S. HOLZMAN, Ph.D.

I SHALL DISCUSS THE WORK of a number of investigators—both clinical and experimental—in the area of perceptual functioning in the schizophrenic syndrome. Recently I surveyed a large number of published reports about perception and psychopathology in order to discern regularity in a vast and confusing literature (20). From that review, I suggested that in spite of a bewildering heterogeneity of claims and counterclaims, and in spite of obvious methodological deficiencies in practically all of the studies, two heuristic conclusions could be drawn. These conclusions represented promising areas that merit more careful study with improved methods. One conclusion focused on nondisordered but exaggerated aspects of schizophrenic patients' perception, aspects that reflected neither psychopathology nor perceptual dysfunction, but personality trends, or *cognitive styles* (13). I also concluded that the feedback stage of the perceptual act, that is, that stage of perception which involves proprioceptive and autonomic functions in response to sensory input, may indeed be disrupted and play a crucial, but as yet undetermined role in the unfolding of the schizophrenic syndrome. Since I completed that review, I have examined several newer studies, all of which have been consistent with the previous work and support the conclusions I came to in that review.

In this chapter I shall briefly discuss these findings and refer to some clinical observations that illustrate the thesis of disordered proprioceptive feedback. In this endeavor, I shall also refer to a number of clinical theorists who have come to similar conclusions, thus giving my thesis an aura of authority but depriving it of originality. Finally, I shall outline several tasks for future research that follow from the findings.

216

In my earlier paper, I viewed perception as a complex act of transferring physical stimulation into psychological information. Such stimuli may arise from within or outside of the organism. A perceptual act includes four stages, or rather aspects of a complex process: reception, registration, processing and feedback. Even at the stage of reception by sense organs, organizing processes lawfully select and shift accents of stimulus attributes. These organizing processes reflect the fact that perception, never a passive process, bears the unmistakable stamp of the perceiver's individuality. The effects of the stimuli are registered and again subjected to further reorganization and processing by other psychological factors such as affects, memory engrams of previous experiences, needs and intentions. Another stage of the perceptual act is that of feedback; it is defined in terms of the motor consequences of sensory input. The view of perception I adopted emphasizes the role of set, intention, and expectation in all acts of perceiving and at all stages of the perceptual act. We are always set to perceive something, that is, a drive- or intention-relevant object. We know whether the object sensed is the object sought by observing the motor consequences—motor reports as Freud (11) called them in 1895—of the sensory input. These reports involve autonomic and proprioceptive processes which may or may not be in awareness and which, as Sherrington (42) pointed out, involve receptors in muscles, tendons and joints as well as those in the vestibular apparatus. More recently Gellhorn (14) has argued that such proprioceptive impulses stimulate the posterior hypothalamus, and hence the sympathetic division of the autonomic nervous system, which in turn leads to changes in movements and interoceptive shifts. This stage of perceptual feedback—or more accurately feedback and feed-forward—is crucial for determining the meaning of percepts, for quickly sizing up whether the object sensed is the one sought. A number of experiments have convincingly demonstrated that curtailing or distorting feedback will distort contact with reality and will diminish autonomous control over thoughts and acts (23, 19); increasing or amplifying feedback, on the other hand, augments reality attunement and voluntary control (5, 18).

Thus, perception is a complex cogwheeling of sensory intake, registration, organization, and feedback; it implicates cognitive, conative, motivational, and motor functions at each stage.

In this chapter, I shall bypass a discussion of the term schizophrenic syndrome. Much has been written about the word schizophrenia in the first section of this volume and I shall not labor the point of the ambiguity of the term. The term refers to no simple pathological process.

Although there is no agreement about the definition of the word, there is probably consensus that we are referring to a polyvalent process representing a final common path of genic—probably polygenic, and non-Mendelian in its transmission (37)—biochemical, physiological, psychological, interpersonal and social parameters. The search for what is essence in the picture has been joined by many able people among whom are Kraepelin, Bleuler, Sullivan, Federn and Rado. At this juncture, I want only to underscore my agreement with Rado (33) and with Grinker (16) that schizophrenic pathology is not synonymous with psychosis. The latter, as Grinker has recently noted (16), is a behavioral anomaly which may appear and remit suddenly or slowly or remain chronically present. On the other hand, the many modifiers of the word schizophrenia, such as *pre, incipient, remitted, acute, undifferentiated, schizophrenic character, schizoid character, schizophreniform,* etc., attest to the empirical distinction between schizophrenia and psychosis. This distinction may later help in defining the essence of the schizophrenic syndrome by calling attention to necessary study of what has been called schizotypic people who are nevertheless not psychotic (30, 33).

I turn now to a summary of about 25 years of accumulated studies of perception-schizophrenic behavior relationships. In my earlier review, I noted that one series of experimental studies made use of typical laboratory perceptual tasks, like size- and time-estimation, the testing of various constancies and thresholds. The usual findings in these experiments have been that schizophrenic patients as a group are significantly more variable than nonschizophrenic patients. While mean differences in their scores tend to be nonsignificant, wide fluctuations within groups of schizophrenic patients is the reliable finding. This fact of high intragroup variability has lessened the chances that two experimenters independently will report similar results. Hence this literature is punctuated by claims and counterclaims.

Even within the context of high variability, the scores reported for schizophrenic patients on these tests, e.g., brightness constancy or size-estimation, are neither so extreme nor so inappropriate as to question the efficiency of general perceptual performance. For we have not established the precise role in adaptive perception of "thing mediators" like high or low brightness constancy or high or low size-estimation. Nor has repeated testing been undertaken on individual patients to discover whether variability is characteristic of individual patients, and if so whether such variability is lawful.

Although I shall not dwell on this series of studies, there are two aspects of them that I wish to bring to the readers' attention. The first is methodological and the second interpretative.

These studies, extending back three and four decades, are subject to several methodological criticisms. One of their glaring deficiencies is that many of them fail to describe the phenomenon they are investigating. Merely to call a group of people schizophrenic and not to provide the behavioral referent of that diagnosis gives insufficient information to a reader, since the term schizophrenia has been applied to a heterogeneous array of phenomena which themselves vary in temporal and intensity dimensions. Thus, the validity of the independent variable in these studies is in question. Likewise, the reliability of the diagnosis is in many of these studies unknown. "It is rare to see specified in any published report who the person is who has made the diagnostic determination, what his training and experience have been, the length of his contact with the patient, and the nature of his contact with the patient—that is, on the basis of what instruments he has reached his conclusions. Further, there is often no effort to get a second independent confirmation of the diagnostic appraisal." (20)

Recently, with the heavy use of the phenothiazines in the treatment of the schizophrenic syndrome, it has been extremely difficult to separate effects of drugs on experimental results from those of psychopathology. Withdrawing patients from medication has not diminished the complicating factors, for there are some patients who can and who cannot remain off drugs without jeopardizing their clinical state. An assessment of the clinical and personality differences between those groups of patients must be made before one arrives at general conclusions about schizophrenic pathology from drug-removed patients(22). The more recent attempts to derive a phenothiazine dosage index and to use it as a covariate, as Spohn and Thetford (43) have done, may be a helpful solution. That method remains, however, an indirect way of circumventing the contribution of drugs to the patient's performance.

A further difficulty has been the small size of patient populations tested and the use of inadequate and at times irrelevant comparison groups. The problem of comparison groups has usually been met by choosing samples of nonpsychopathological subjects, most of whom are not hospitalized, such as hospital workers or college students. The use of other nonschizophrenic but psychopathological patients is rare. Thus, in these studies it is very difficult to know the meaning of the results.

But, even if one were to ignore these methodological flaws, one may reasonably question whether these studies get at the essence of perceptual experiences in the schizophrenic syndrome. For these studies scrutinize the perception not of things and objects, but of those properties that mediate the perception of things. We generally see tables, chairs, people and books, we do not see sizes, brightnesses, hues, slants and textures. We do not know, for example, whether wide variations in the perception of thing-mediators like size, shape, brightness necessarily reflect deficient or deviant or unadaptive perception. "The use of these tasks seems geared to assessing not perception-psychopathology relationships, but the enduring cognitive-perceptual response dispositions of subjects—the style and form of reality attunement which we have called *cognitive controls*. These studies, then, highlight variations in the stable regulatory strategies of subjects, strategies that are relevant to the experience of perception but which themselves are not to be considered as the perceptual act." (20) For it is a person with an established and describable character structure and personality organization who becomes schizophrenic and perhaps psychotic; and that personality organization will show itself even in disease, in stressing circumstances and in states of disorganization. Such processes "may exaggerate or minimize a person's characteristic perceptual functioning. Conversely, the style of perceptual and cognitive functioning may determine the *nature* of the psychopathological organization—not *whether* disorganization will occur, but if it does occur, for whatever reason, the form it takes will be determined by the perceptual and cognitive strategies of the person. Thus, the subclasses of the schizophrenic syndrome themselves may reflect these stable personality dispositions." (20)

Let us turn to the clinical literature for descriptions of what perceptual dysfunction may be like in the schizophrenic syndrome. There are several vivid clinical descriptions that merit examination. Renée, a pseudonym for a girl who had plummeted into the depths of schizophrenic disorganization, wrote an autobiographical account of that experience. "One day we were jumping rope at recess. Two little girls were turning a long rope while two others jumped in from either side to meet and cross over. When it came my turn and I saw my partner jump toward me where we were to meet and cross over, I was seized with panic; I did not recognize her. Though I saw her as she was, still, it was not she. Standing at the other end of the rope, she had seemed smaller, but the nearer we approached each other, the taller she grew, the more she swelled in size.

"I cried out, 'Stop, Alice, you look like a lion; you frighten me!' At the sound of the fear in my voice which I tried to dissemble under the guise of fooling, the game came to an abrupt halt. The girls looked at me, amazed, and said, 'you're silly—Alice, a lion? You don't know what you're talking about.'

"Then the game began again. Once more my playmate became strangely transformed and, with an excited laugh, once more I cried out, 'Stop, Alice, I'm afraid of you; you're a lion!' But actually, I didn't see a lion at all; it was only an attempt to describe the enlarging image of my friend and the fact that I didn't recognize her.

"In the gymnasium I didn't understand the commands, confusing left and right. As for the sewing lesson, it was impossible to understand the technique of placing patches or the mysteries of knitting a sock heel. Varied as these subjects were, they presented similar problems, so that more and more, despite my efforts, I lost the feeling of practical things.

"In these disturbing circumstances, I sensed again the atmosphere of unreality. During class, in the quiet of the work period, I heard the street noises—a trolley passing, people talking, a horse naying, a horn sounding, each detached, immovable, separated from its source, without meaning. Around me, the other children, heads bent over their work, were robots or puppets, moved by an invisible mechanism.

"All the objects were transformed. I no longer recognized them. They suddenly took on other forms and I lost the only stability I had. I did not want to move, because if I did everything changed around me and upset me so horribly, so I remained still to hold on to a sense of permanence." (40)

Curiously, although Renée recognized Alice in spite of her disclaimer —for she did call her by her name—there was something altered in her ability to maintain size, shape and distance constancies, abilities that are necessary for stable orientation to objects. Percepts had registered, but their recognition and meaning were altered. In the intact perceptual system the changes in size of retinal images as distance between perceiver and object changes are accommodated by postural and proprioceptive adjustments that maintain object-size constancy. The anchoring of the visual world is also maintained by these same processes. Witness the strange instability of objects when we use our fingers to move our eyes; that is, when our eyes are passively moved, thus interfering with the perceptual feedback processes and hence with the constancy of objects.

Hilda Bruch (3) described a 21-year-old girl whose seclusiveness, poor scholastic achievement in college, irritability and suspiciousness led her parents to seek psychiatric hospitalization for her. Doctor Bruch described her bodily sensations as follows, "Often she felt befuddled, not knowing whether she was asleep or awake, and she would move her muscles vigorously in an effort to make herself feel awake. At times she was confused about temperature sensations, and she did not know whether she felt warm or chilly. As treatment progressed, she recognized that she had been anxious all her life, without being aware of it."

Freeman (10) remarked that, "My colleagues and I have noted that a close relationship exists between catatonic symptoms and disturbance of visual perception. Sometimes patients are aware of this connection and sometimes not. I would like to report on . . . a catatonic patient . . . a young man of 23 who spent many hours in a state of complete immobility. During psychotherapy it became apparent that any movement was associated with visual-perceptual distortion of the environment which he variously described as a flatness, a piece of stage scenery, a flat streak of color. Moving faster increased the severity of this disorder. To quote his own words, 'moving is like a motion picture. If you move, the picture in front of you changes.' By stopping all movement the patient found he could cancel the visual disturbance. He said, 'I've got to slow down to see. Stopping obviates the flatness—you only see a still picture if you don't move your head and eyes.' It was noted that sudden changes in visual perception, brought about by sudden alterations in his visual field, always led to catatonic phenomena. 'It's the sudden change that matters.' If visual perception remained constant, the patient was able to move freely. He could walk without much difficulty along a straight road with a fixed distant horizon. Freedom of mobility was only possible for this patient whenever there was a guaranteed stability of visual perception."

There is a series of experiments which, although they seem rather disparate when considered singly, implicates the proprioceptive and autonomic feedback and feedforward processes in the perceptual behavior of schizophrenic patients and is thus congruent with the clinical illustrations. These experiments, like the clinical descriptions, strongly suggest a consistent, although perhaps not invariably present deficit in the perceptual feedback function. This evidence is adduced from six areas of investigation. But here, too, we must keep in mind that methodological faults, similar to those discerned in the experiments mentioned above, characterize practically all of the experiments in this series.

The six areas of converging evidence are as follows:

1. There are reports of high states of basal psychophysiological arousal in schizophrenic subjects, particularly in EMG recordings and systolic blood pressure. Further, some investigators (26, 27, 28) report that the highest resting levels of EMG are found in the most withdrawn patients; and Funkenstein (12) reported reduction of systolic blood pressure basal

level when clinical improvement of the schizophrenic psychosis occurred. High muscle tone and other aspects of heightened basal arousal would primarily influence not the process of receptivity, but the proprioceptive response to the stimulus input, and thus the subsequent integration of the stimulus.

2. Many experimenters report that schizophrenic patients, however defined or ill-defined, show an underreaction to specific stimuli. Thus, pain thresholds are raised in psychophysiological experiments (17), a finding that is consistent with clinical reports of chronic schizophrenic patients who show no overt pain response to serious burns or even to coronary attacks. A related finding is DeVault's report (9) that when his chronic process schizophrenic subjects watched threat-connoting stimuli their heart rates decelerated, but his nonschizophrenic controls and chronic reactive schizophrenic subjects showed cardiac acceleration to the same stimuli. Since the cardiac acceleration response is coupled with a working-over of already registered percepts and it seems reasonable to assume that it facilitates control and gating of further stimulus input, DeVault's subjects seemed unable to react adaptively to the stimuli that had already registered.

3. Many performance deficits of schizophrenic patients seem to improve when the tasks are simple, when the backgrounds are underarousing, or when the stimuli are unambiguous. Thus, schizophrenic subjects when compared to normal subjects seem to show very little performance decrement in sensory isolation experiments (6). In complex situations it is as if the schizophrenic patient has too much to deal with, too much to react to, but not because he cannot handle complexity—for complex thoughts and convoluted inferences are not at all atypical—but because reaction to the input is in some way impaired and thus response is put awry.

4. A number of investigators have studied reaction time in schizophrenic subjects (41, 44). All of these investigators report similar results: schizophrenic patients are always slower than nonschizophrenic subjects, whether the stimuli are presented in the visual or auditory modality and whether a simple or complex response is called for. These results have been interpreted as reflecting an attention impairment, an interpretation that is probably correct insofar as attention dysfunction is no doubt involved. But I doubt that attention impairment can be considered the casual factor in slowed reaction times. It would seem rather that proprioceptive and autonomic adjustments to the stimulus input impede response. For the subjects *do* respond; they do perform the tasks; but they

simply respond more slowly. This slowed reaction time disappears when the stimulus is presented *tactually* as a mild electric shock (35). This finding suggests that it may be input principally from distance receptors, such as vision and audition, rather than from contact receptors, like touch, that precedes impaired feedback. The development of adaptive distance receptors with their feedback information is essential for the development of functions of anticipation, purposeful action and planning, as Goldfarb (15) has noted. Notions of space, body proportions, a sense of continuity and certainty of one's place in the outer world with respect to objects are developed through the smooth functioning of distance receptors. It would seem from the reaction time literature that proprioceptive and autonomic feedback from these distance receptors is somehow impaired in schizophrenic patients. Feedback from contact receptors seems to be intact, or at least not as obviously implicated. Explanations of these findings in terms of attention seem strained.

In this context, I include the recent study by Spohn, Thetford and Woodham (43) on attention span. In what is probably one of the most carefully done experiments to date, these investigators demonstrated that schizophrenic subjects' attention span was significantly lower than that of normal subjects, and the more time given for scanning the stimulus array, the greater the difference between the two groups. Further, the autonomic accompaniment of focused attention differed between the groups, with the schizophrenic patients *not* showing the usual and expected initial rise in heart rate and skin conductance followed by adaptation and habituation. Indeed, those few schizophrenic subjects who did show that expected pattern of autonomic response did much better in their attention span than those who did not. It is not at all unlikely that the deficit here may well have been in the integration of input, aided by autonomic and proprioceptive response, rather than in a variable or inconstant set.

There is a set of studies which demonstrates the crucial role of meaning in performance by schizophrenic patients. Rousey and Goetzinger (38), for example, using standard speech discrimination tests, reported that schizophrenic patients were significantly poorer than nonschizophrenic patients and normals in identifying words whose meanings were ambiguous. But this difference did not obtain on another discrimination test where the meaning of the words was less ambiguous. Here again there is no evidence that the schizophrenic patients were not paying attention to the input. But where there was a chance for the meaning of the stimulus to play a challenging role, response decrement appeared.

There is a recent finding that schizophrenic thought disorder appears principally when meanings of words and situations are tapped. Thus, Chapman et al. (4) report findings that schizophrenic patients show a thought disorder analogous to that of Arieti's description of paleological reasoning *only* when certain denotative meanings of words are predominant. Cohen and Camhi (7) have reported that schizophrenic and nonschizophrenic patients are equally successful in receiving unambiguous messages. But the former do quite poorly in *transmitting* simple messages. Cohen's task required subjects to guess what word a second subject has chosen. Thus, for example, the words "freedom" and "liberty" were exposed and the task for subject 1 was to choose a third word that will make subject 2 select the word "freedom." The words "speech" or "academic" will usually evoke the choice of "freedom," and indeed did so for schizophrenic and nonschizophrenic subjects equally. Associations to both words by schizophrenic and nonschizophrenic subjects were similar. But schizophrenic subjects did quite poorly when they had to *transmit* the message rather than *receive* it. Cohen concluded that schizophrenic patients possess the same meaning hierarchy of words that nonschizophrenic patients do, but they differ when they are forced actively to discover and choose the meaning of a word and then to transmit it to another person.

Willner's highly useful tests of abstraction (46, 47) show congruent results. Schizophrenic patients, Willner has discovered, can solve analogies problems and concept formation tasks if the solutions require logical categories such as "opposites" or functional relations. For example, schizophrenic patients have little or no difficulty with the problem of "white is to black as tall is to (*short*)"; or "hammer is to nail as screwdriver is to (*screw*)." But when the meaning of an item is the key to the solution rather than a logical category, schizophrenic patients show disordered analogic reasoning. These studies require us to note that acquisition of meaning and employment of consensual meaning occur along with stable and appropriate response to sensory input, a response which in this chapter has been called perceptual feedback.

5. A series of studies done at the Lafayette Clinic using the drug Sernyl (phenocyclidine hydrochloride) offers another line of evidence. This drug, administered to nonschizophrenic subjects, apparently produces the effects mentioned above. It heightens basal levels of activation, slows reaction time in the visual and auditory modalities but not in response to shock; there are subjective experiences of estrangement, accompanied by a thought disorder. Schizophrenic subjects show exacerbation of their

symptoms when administered Sernyl. Interestingly, chlorpromazine diminishes these effects. Rosenbaum et al. (35, 36) noted that Sernyl interferes with proprioceptive functions, increasing muscle tonus. It thus interferes with sensory perception at a postinput phase, most likely at the phase of proprioceptive feedback.

6. The last line of experimental studies I shall mention directly implicates diminished vestibular function in the schizophrenic syndrome. These studies include Paul Schilder's clinical observations (39) and the findings of the Worcester group (21). Schizophrenic subjects were typically less unstable following rotation than were control subjects, and they showed less nystagmus. Diminished nystagmus has been found in schizophrenic children by Colbert et al. (8), and Ornitz et al. (31) and these results have been replicated for adults several times. Leach (25), for example, tested 75 male schizophrenic patients and found that compared to normal subjects, the latency of rotation nystagmus was significantly greater, the number of nystagmic shifts significantly fewer and the rate of nystagmus per second significantly less. Pollack and Krieger (32) compared the oculomotor and postural patterns of 15 schizophrenic children with those of 7 nonschizophrenic children who were hospitalized with behavior disorders and those of normal children, most of whom were hospitalized on the pediatric service of a large general hospital. Nine of the 15 schizophrenic children showed deviant oculomotor and vestibular responses. Seven of these children showed minimal or absent postrotational nystagmus, compared with only one of the 7 nonschizophrenic behavior disordered children and one of the 8 normal children.

It is a curious thing that in normal adults nystagmus diminishes when interest in the surroundings diminishes, when attention flags (45) or when the orientation to the environment is altered (1). Further, Wendt reported that a reduction in postrotational nystagmus can be overcome by keeping the subject attentive. On the other hand, Ritvo (34) reports that when schizophrenic children close their eyes, their reduced nystagmus returns to normal levels. There thus is a highly suggestive relation between focused attention and vestibular functioning. It is not yet possible, however, to attribute a causal role to either of the variables.

Paul Schilder (39) is among those who speculated about the crucial role of the proprioceptive and particularly vestibular functioning in schizophrenic phenomena. "The vestibular nerve," he wrote, "occupies a special position among the senses. Its sensations do not form a part of our conscious knowledge of the world . . . The vestibular apparatus is not only an organ for perception [of movements and gravity], it is an organ which gives rise to very important reflexes . . . to turning and progressive movement . . . [and] which influences the muscle tone of the body . . . it is in this way a great system for orienting ourselves in the world. This system is, of course, not isolated but cooperates with the other systems of orientation, especially that of the optic perceptions. It is more closely related to a primitive motility than is vision . . .

"Whenever we perceive an object, we have already the basic knowledge about our body and about the attitude of our body. . . . The perceiving individual gets a knowledge of an object and the object as such provokes immediately attitudes in him. These attitudes make a fuller perception possible. . . . We would expect that such a sensory organ, with only half conscious impressions and leading to a motility of an instinctive and primitive type, would be very sensitive to emotions and would therefore play an important part in neuroses and psychoses. . . . Organic changes in the vestibular apparatus will be reflected in the psychic structure. They will not only influence the tone, the vegetative system, and the attitudes of the body, but they must also change our whole perceptive apparatus and even our consciousness. These general considerations make it possible that the study of the vestibular apparatus may have great importance for the understanding of psychotic and neurotic states."

Goldfarb (15) has called attention to the heightened significance of contact receptors and the diminished reliance on distance receptors in schizophrenic children. "James was typical of many autistic children. A sharp noise near his ears, for example, sharp hand-clapping, produced only eye-blinking. There was no other body or facial adjustment and no verbal indication that the sound was recognized. In one period of observation, the noises near his ears were repeated again and again for an hour without any overt adjustive response, such as avoidance by moving away, or verbal and vocal complaint and objection, or aggressive retaliation." In contrast, there is augmented reliance upon contact senses. "Paul was a child who initially removed himself entirely from the group and would sit for long periods fingering a small object. A period of residential treatment produced definite improvement in range of affectivity and social engagements. He became attached to several members of the staff. He would sit in their laps and pass his lips over their faces and exposed body parts. This act had none of the qualities of a kiss and seem to combine pressing and touching."

Visual and auditory startle stimuli thus apparently evoke diminished response in autistic children. Yet this dampened response does not necessarily reflect diminished sensitivity of these senses, since these children can, on occasion, show hyperacuteness. While such observations have been explained by postulating an attentional deficit, it would seem to me more parsimonious, in light of the findings of no impaired response to input through contact receptors, that the feedback process from these distance receptors is impaired and leads to disturbed integration of sensory input.

Kraepelin and Bleuler also were impressed by such proprioceptive involvement in schizophrenic behavior. In 1913, for example, Kraepelin (24) discussed the impairment in dementia praecox patients of what he called "active attention," that is, the required, persistent, focused response to sensory input. Kraepelin attributed the defect in active attention to a disturbance of will. Bleuler (2) attributed the defect to a disturbance of affectivity. That is, both Kraepelin and Bleuler believed that the dysfunction of active attention was a derivative of a more basic disturbance, either of volition or of affect. It may also be possible, in light of Gellhorn's speculations (14) about the complex interrelations between sensory input, hypothalamic switching, sympathetic and motor activation, that the impaired volitional and affective processes are themselves an outcome of dampened proprioceptive response to sensation, particularly from distance receptors.

Rado (33) has taken as firm a stand as Schilder's on the role of proprioception in schizophrenic phenomena. He postulated two inherited defects in people predisposed to develop schizophrenic psychoses: an integrative pleasure deficiency, and a predisposition to disordered proprioceptive response which he called "proprioceptive diathesis." The former weakens the prodding, activating and steering effects of pleasure; the latter leads to distorted awareness of one's self and to "tormenting lack of self-confidence and also, of [a] feeling that he is hopelessly different from other people."

These studies and the formulations of several clinical theorists point to the most likely site of perceptual disruption in the schizophrenic syndrome. In view of these converging lines of evidence, there are a number of tasks that need to be done to pin down more precisely the nature of the perceptual dysfunction in schizophrenia.

First, it is crucial that we develop a workable metric for establishing and describing the psychopathological phenomena we are studying. We can no longer rely simply on global diagnostic statements about schizophrenia. The issue of chronicity, too, cannot be settled by arbitrary time limits of 2 or 3 years of hospitalization. The use of certain psychological tests that permit judgment of quality and degree of thought disorganization may be one path to the solution.

Second, we need to find reliable tests of proprioceptive feedback functions, so that the experimental findings scattered through the literature can be replicated in improved experimental designs. Such designs must include sufficient numbers of psychopathological patients, both those diagnosed as falling within the schizophrenic syndrome and those with nonschizophrenic disorders, with sufficient numbers of men and women subjects. The tests should include instruments on which one expects defective performance by schizophrenic patients—such as those involving feedback functions—as well as those on which no deficit performance is expected. This would be important as a way of mapping the functioning perceptual profile and of assessing the presence of performance artifacts.

Such cross-sectional testing should ideally be supplemented by repeated testing of a smaller number of subjects. Scores obtained over several months should permit an assessment of the phasic nature of perceptual dysfunction. It is striking that although the literature is replete with studies of actively psychotic patients, there are no perceptual studies of either patients in remission or of nonhospitalized schizophrenic patients. Information about perceptual processes in patients who have recovered from the acute psychotic phase of the schizophrenic syndrome or those who have remained out of hospitals will surely add to our information about the essence of the schizophrenic syndrome as distinguished from the epiphenomena attendant upon psychotic disorganization and hospitalization. For it seems eminently in accord with clinical observation to distinguish between psychotic disorganization and schizophrenic pathology.

After an effective and discriminating battery of vulnerable and stable measures has been devised, we should then embark upon a prospective study of children with a high risk for schizophrenic pathology, following the model outlined by Mednick (29). A prospective study of high risk children is a powerful tool and should be used only when variables with a high chance for yield have been isolated.

It would seem hardly necessary to add that I am not imputing a causal role to disordered feedback and re-efferentation processes in the schizophrenic syndrome. Rather, I wish to emphasize the ubiquity of the findings of such deficits in schizophrenic patients, and, therefore, of the necessity for discovering empirically their role, whether essence or artifact, precursor or consequence, cause or effect, in the schizophrenic syndrome.

REFERENCES

1. Angyal, A. and Sherman, M. A.: Postural Reactions to Vestibular Stimulation in Schizophrenic and Normal Subjects. *American Journal of Psychiatry*, 98:857-862, 1942.
2. Bleuler, E.: *Dementia Praecox or the Group of Schizophrenias*. New York: International Universities Press, 1950.
3. Bruch, H.: Falsification of Bodily Needs and Body Concept in Schizophrenia. *Archives of General Psychiatry*, 6:18-24, 1962.
4. Chapman, L. J., Chapman, J. P. and Miller, G. A.: A Theory of Verbal Behavior in Schizophrenia. In Maher, B. (Ed.), *Progress in Experimental Personality Research*, Vol. 1. New York: Academic Press, 1964.
5. Chase, R. A., Sutton, S. and Rapin, I.: Sensory Feedback Influences on Motor Performance. *Journal of Auditory Research*, 3:212-223, 1961.
6. Cohen, B. D., Rosenbaum, G., Dobie, S. I. and Gottlieb, J. S.: Sensory Isolation: Hallucinogenic Effects of a Brief Procedure. *Journal of Nervous and Mental Disease*, 129:486-491, 1959.
7. Cohen, B. D. and Camhi, J.: Schizophrenic Performance in a Word Communication Task. *Journal of Abnormal Psychology*, 72:240-246, 1967.
8. Colbert, E. G., Koegler, R. R. and Markham, C. H.: Vestibular Dysfunction in Childhood Schizophrenia. *Archives of General Psychiatry*, 1:600-617, 1959.
9. DeVault, S. H.: Physiological Responsiveness in Reactive and Process Schizophrenia. Doctoral dissertation. Michigan State University, Ann Arbor: University Microfilms, No. 57-2232, 1957.
10. Freeman, T.: The Structure of Defense in Schizophrenia. Unpublished manuscript.
11. Freud, S.: Project for a Scientific Psychology. In *The Standard Edition of the Complete Psychological Works of Sigmund Freud*, Vol. 1. London: Hogarth Press, 1966.
12. Funkenstein, D. H., Greenblatt, M. and Solomon, H. C.: Autonomic Changes Paralleling Psychologic Changes in Mentally Ill Patients. *Journal of Nervous and Mental Disease*, 114:1-18, 1951.
13. Gardner, R. W., Holzman, P. S., Klein, G. S., Linton, H. and Spence, D. P.: Cognitive Control. *Psychological Issues*, No. 4. New York: International Universities Press, 1959.
14. Gellhorn, E.: Motion and Emotion: The Role of Proprioception in the Physiology and Pathology of the Emotions. *Psychological Review*, 71:457-472, 1964.
15. Goldfarb, W.: Receptor Preferences in Schizophrenic Children. *Archives of Neurology and Psychiatry*, 76:643-652, 1956.
16. Grinker, R. R.: An Essay on Schizophrenia and Science. *Archives of General Psychiatry*, 20:1-24, 1969.
17. Hall, K. R. L. and Stride, E.: The Varying Response to Pain in Psychiatric Disorders: Study in Abnormal Psychology. *British Journal of Medical Psychology*, 27:48-60, 1954.

18. Hardyk, C. D., Petrinovitch, L. F. and Ellsworth, D. W.: Feedback of Speech Muscle Activity during Silent Reading: Rapid Extinction. *Science*, 154:1467-1468, 16 December, 1966.
19. Holmes, C. and Holzman, P. S.: The Effect of White Noise on Disinhibition of Verbal Expression. *Perceptual and Motor Skills*, 23:1039-1042, 1966.
20. Holzman, P. S.: Perceptual Aspects of Psychopathology. In Zubin, J. (Ed.), *Neurobiological Aspects of Psychopathology*. New York: Grune and Stratton, 1969.
21. Hoskins, R. G.: *The Biology of Schizophrenia*. New York: W. W. Norton and Co., 1946.
22. Klein, E. G. and Spohn, H. E.: Further Comments on Characteristics of Untestable Chronic Schizophrenics. *Journal of Abnormal and Social Psychology*, 68:355-358, 1964.
23. Klein, G. S.: On Hearing One's Own Voice: An Aspect of Cognitive Control in Spoken Thought. In Schur, M. (Ed.), *Drives, Affects, Behavior*. New York: International Universities Press, 1965.
24. Kraepelin, E.: *Dementia Praecox and Paraphrenia*. Edinburgh: Livingstone, 1919.
25. Leach, W. W.: Nystagmus: An Integrative Neural Deficit in Schizophrenia. *Journal of Abnormal and Social Psychology*, 60:305-309, 1960.
26. Malmo, R. B. and Shagass, C.: Physiologic Studies of Reaction to Stress in Anxiety and Early Schizophrenia. *Psychosomatic Medicine*, 11:9-24, 1949.
27. Malmo, R. B. and Shagass, C.: Studies of Blood Pressure in Psychiatric Patients under Stress. *Psychosomatic Medicine*, 14:82-93, 1952.
28. Malmo, R. B., Shagass, C. and Smith, A. A.: Responsiveness in Chronic Schizophrenia. *Journal of Personality*, 19:359-375, 1951.
29. Mednick, S. A. and McNeil, T. F.: Current Methodology in Research on the Etiology of Schizophrenia: Serious Difficulties Which Suggest the Use of the High-Risk-Group Method. *Psychological Bulletin*, 70(6): Part I, 681-693, 1968.
30. Meehl, P. E.: Schizotaxia, Schizotypy, Schizophrenia. *American Psychologist*, 17:827-838, 1962.
31. Ornitz, E. M., Ritvo, E. R., Panman, L. M., Lee, Y. H., Carr, E. M. and Walter, R. D.: The Auditory Evoked Response in Normal and Autistic Children during Sleep. *Electroencephalography and Clinical Neurophysiology*, 25:221-230, 1968.
32. Pollack, M. and Krieger, H. P.: Oculomotor and Postural Patterns in Schizophrenic Children. *Archives of Neurology and Psychiatry*, 79: 720-726, 1958.
33. Rado, S.: *The Psychoanalysis of Behavior: Collected Papers of Sandor Rado*, Vol. 2, 1956-1961. New York: Grune and Stratton, 1962.
34. Ritvo, E. R. et al.: Decreased Postrotatory Nystagmus in Early Infantile Autism. *Neurology*, in press.
35. Rosenbaum, G., Cohen, B. D., Luby, E. D., Gottlieb, J. S. and Yelen, D.:

Comparison of Sernyl with Other Drugs: I. Attention, Motor Function and Proprioception. *Archives of General Psychiatry*, 1:651-656, 1959.

36. Rosenbaum, G.: Feedback Mechanisms in Schizophrenia. In Tourney, G. and Gottlieb, J. S. (Eds.), *Lafayette Clinic Studies in Schizophrenia*. Detroit, Michigan: Wayne State University Press, in press.

37. Rosenthal, D.: An Historical and Methodological Review of Genetic Studies of Schizophrenia. In Romano, J. (Ed.), *The Origins of Schizophrenia*. New York: Excerpta Medica Foundation, 1967.

38. Rousey, C. L. and Goetzinger, C. P.: Speech Discrimination in Schizophrenics and Others. Unpublished paper.

39. Schilder, P.: The Vestibular Apparatus in Neurosis and Psychosis. *Journal of Nervous and Mental Disease*, 78:1-23, 1933.

40. Sechehaye, M.: *The Autobiography of a Schizophrenic Girl*. New York: Grune and Stratton, 1951.

41. Shakow, D.: Psychological Deficit in Schizophrenia. *Behavioral Science*, 8:275-305, 1963.

42. Sherrington, C.: *The Integrative Action of the Nervous System*. New York: Scribner, 1906.

43. Spohn, H. E., Thetford, P. and Woodham, F. L.: Span of Apprehension and Arousal in Schizophrenia. *Journal of Abnormal Psychology*, in press.

44. Sutton, S. and Zubin, J.: Effect of Sequence on Reaction Time in Schizophrenia. In Welford, A. T. and Birren, J. E. (Eds.), *Behavior, Aging and the Nervous System*. Springfield: Charles C Thomas, 1965.

45. Wendt, G. R.: Vestibular Functions. In Stevens, S. S. (Ed.), *Handbook of Experimental Psychology*. New York: Wiley, 1951.

46. Willner, A. E.: An Experimental Analysis of Analogical Reasoning. *Psychological Reports*, 15:479-494, 1964.

47. Willner, A. E. and Reitz, W. E.: Association, Abstraction, and the Conceptual Organization of Recall: Implications for Clinical Tests. *Journal of Abnormal Psychology*, 71:315-327, 1966.

18

Genetic-Environmental Interactions in the Schizophrenic Syndrome

SEYMOUR S. KETY, M.D.

IT SHOULD NOT COME AS MUCH of a shock to well-read psychiatrists to suggest that the relative roles of genetic and environmental variables in schizophrenia have not been clearly elucidated. It is for this reason that schools of thought have developed to take the place of evidence. One of these has held that schizophrenia is a genetic disorder. Another teaches that schizophrenia is transmitted by the psychological interactions between a child and his parents. Other, less committed positions, including perhaps the largest number of adherents today, are that there must be some interaction between genetic and environmental variables in this disorder.

The evidence which the genetic school has used is interesting but not compelling. There is the well-known fact that schizophrenia runs in families. All of the studies which have been made seem to agree that there is a roughly 10% prevalence of schizophrenia in the immediate families of schizophrenics, i. e., in their parents, their siblings, and their children. Although this is compatible with a theory of genetic transmission, it by no means proves it, since the environmentalist school has used exactly the same information to support the idea that the schizophrenic learns his schizophrenia from his interaction with the family members. Obviously, this finding is compatible with either genetic or

---

This chapter is based on a paper by S. S. Kety, D. Rosenthal, P. H. Wender and F. Schulsinger, The Types and Prevalence of Mental Illness in the Biological and Adoptive Families of Adopted Schizophrenics. *Journal of Psychiatric Research*, 6 (Suppl.) : 345-362, 1968.

environmental transmission, and does not prove either. The child shares both a genetic endowment and an environmental interaction with his family. Other evidence which has been used to support the importance of genetic factors is the finding in a large number of studies (1, 5, 6, 7, 9, 10, 12, 18), with only one exception (20), that there is a high concordance rate for schizophrenia among monozygotic twins, and a relatively low concordance rate—about the same as for siblings—among dizygotic twins. Doctor Rosenthal and I (8, 13, 14) have separately on previous occasions pointed out certain deficits in some of the earlier twin studies. These deficits include a selective bias in the way the twins were selected originally and a possible subjective bias in the characterization of zygosity and in the diagnosis of schizophrenia in the co-twin. As we all know and as Section I of this volume has emphasized, the diagnosis of schizophrenia is a difficult and a subjective one which could easily be influenced by unconscious knowledge of its relationship to the hypothesis under examination.

For a number of these and other reasons, three of us independently arrived at the conclusion that a technique which held great promise in the disentanglement of genetic and environmental factors (17) and had not previously been used to examine the transmission of schizophrenia was the study of adopted children and their families. The adopted child, if he has been separated from his biological family early enough, has a genetic endowment from one family and an environmental interaction with another family.

When we learned that we were each interested in the same approach, we decided to pool our efforts and so David Rosenthal, Paul Wender, and I decided to undertake a number of studies in the transmission of schizophrenia, using the adoption phenomenon as a crucial device.

I should like to summarize one of these studies, the first phase of which has been completed, and to present some of the results which we have obtained. This study asks the question, "What is the prevalence and the types of mental illness in the biological families and the adoptive families of adopted children who have become schizophrenic later on in life?" After some initial attempts to carry out such a study in Maryland and in the District of Columbia, we became impressed with the difficulties involved and decided that another country might offer some advantages. With the help of Sarnoff Mednick, we began a collaboration with Fini Schulsinger in Copenhagen. Of crucial importance was the Danish registry of adopted children to which we were generously given access by the State Department of Justice with, of course, appropriate guarantees of confidentiality. We have been fortunate in the choice of Denmark for these studies because, as you will see as we go on, the types of records, the kind of cooperation and the homogeneity of the population make such studies extremely rewarding. We began with the idea that to avoid selective bias we should not start with schizophrenics and find out which of those had been adopted, but that we should start with all the adopted children in a population.

From all the adoptions in Denmark, we chose a sample which would represent those children who were now between 20 and 40 years of age so that they would be within or beyond the major risk period for schizophrenia. We excluded from the sample those children who were adopted by people biologically related to them, e.g., their maternal aunt, or maternal grandmother, so that we would have a clear separation between biological and environmental factors. For the first phase of this study we decided to limit the study to those adoptions which had been made in Copenhagen and its environs (Greater Copenhagen), which accounts for about one-quarter to one-third of the population of Denmark. It was decided that if the study turned out to be feasible in that sample we should someday extend the sample to all of Denmark.

This process of cutting down on the sample size gave us an initial sample then of about 5,500 adoptions between the age periods indicated, within Greater Copenhagen, by people not related to the biological parents. These adoption records are also remarkably complete in that they contain not only the names and identification of the adoptive parents but a considerable amount of information about their socioeconomic status. They also contain the name and address of the biological mother and of the putative biological father. Even the latter item of information is probably more reliable in Denmark than it is in most other countries since it is not enough for a mother to name a biological father; he must also acknowledge paternity and contribute to the cost of maternity care and adoption.

From the information which we gathered in the adoption records we then went to another remarkable record system in Denmark, which is the Psychiatric Register of the Institute of Human Genetics. It is a remarkably complete index of all the people in Denmark who have been diagnosed as having a nervous or mental disease by any of the psychiatric or medical facilities in that country. Our first question was how complete was that Register. We knew that one hospital, the Bispebjerg Hospital, did not cooperate with the Institute of Human Genetics and had not been reporting its patients to that Institute for reasons which are not important. Therefore, we had to include a search in the Bispebjerg Hospital records. We made a survey of all of the psychiatric hospitals in Denmark and from the patients found in their records, we then turned to the Psychiatric Register to see how many had been missed. We found that only about 5% of the psychiatric diagnoses made in these facilities had not been reported to the Institute of Human Genetics and were not included in their Psychiatric Register. By taking the names of our 5,500 adoptees and the various name changes that any adoptee might have undergone (which we got from another register I shall describe) and by checking those names against the Psychiatric Register of the Institute of Human Genetics (and the Bispedjerg Hospital), we could find all of those adoptees (about 500) who had at one time or another been diagnosed with a nervous or mental disease. The psychiatric records were obtained on these 500 cases. They were abstracted and the abstract translated into English by a Danish psychiatrist. These were sent to the four collaborators (Rosenthal, Wender, Schulsinger, and Kety) who, then, independently attempted to make a diagnosis based upon the abstract and the hospital diagnoses. The diagnosis which we forced ourselves to make at first was one of three: schizophrenia, possible schizophrenia, or not schizophrenia. We also had to define in advance what we meant by schizophrenia. We started with the assumption that there would be good agreement about the phenomenology and that the difficulty in the diagnosis was in what one was going to call schizophrenia. For the purposes of this study, we decided to call any of three clusters of phenomenology schizophrenia. The first subgroup was chronic schizophrenia, which was the typical, chronic, long-term resident of a mental hospital type of schizophrenic. Another group we called the borderline schizophrenic, and these were defined by criteria which we outlined and agreed upon. They are criteria which would be acceptable to the APA and to most American psychiatrists. Synonyms for this group would be ambulatory, schizo-affective, or pseudoneurotic schizophrenia, among others. A third group was the acute schizophrenic reaction, which again we defined mutually among ourselves according to acceptable criteria in this country. It should be pointed out, of course, that in Denmark an acute schizophrenic reaction or a borderline schizophrenia is rarely diagnosed as schizophrenia, but as a variety of other conditions. On the other hand, there was little disagreement in diagnosis of chronic schizophrenia between the Danish hospitals and ourselves. Where all four of us agreed that the individual was schizophrenic, he became an index patient. Where at least one of us had raised a question of schizophrenia, we obtained more information about that individual and had a conference. If we finally arrived at a consensus of schizophrenia he also became an index case. Thus, we included as index cases only those in whom we all agreed that schizophrenia was the best diagnosis. This gave us 33 index cases. In order to control a large number of diagnostic and population variables, and in order to maintain objectivity in the diagnosis, we then chose an equal number of control adoptees from the population who had not been diagnosed with any nervous or mental disease, and which were matched with each index case for age, sex, socioenvironmental class of the adoptive family, and the type of preadoptive history. The latter includes the lengths of time spent with the biological family, in an institution, and in a foster family. This gave us 33 controls, at which point we shuffled the index cases and the controls randomly and sent the batch of 66 back to Denmark with instructions now to find the biological and the adoptive relatives of these 66 individuals.

Now that can be done relatively easily in Denmark because of another remarkable register, the *Folkeregister* which has in it all the names and the addresses of everyone who lives in Denmark for longer than a period of a few weeks, as well as every change of address, every change of marital status, every addition to the family and every death. The *Folkeregister* can be entered with the name of an individual and his date of birth. The adoptive records also gave us the names of the biological mother and father, and the adoptive mother and father. From this information a search of the *Folkeregister* served to generate the names of the siblings and the half-siblings of these 66 adoptees on their biological and on their adoptive side. This gave us somewhat less than 500 such relatives. These 467 relatives were then assigned to another part of the staff in Denmark with instructions to search the Psychiatric Register and the Bispebjerg Hospital to find out how many of these relatives had ever been diagnosed with any nervous or mental disease. From this point on the investigators scrupulously avoided the possibility of knowing, for any relative, whether he was a biological or adoptive relative, and whether he was a relative of an index case or a control. Also, in the case of the relatives, we could no longer permit the luxury of excluding those who were not clear-cut schizophrenics, we had to make a diagnosis even if our information was incomplete. In other words, we had to find as much information as we could from the records we could tap regarding possible schizophrenic characteristics in these relatives. We set up in advance what we called a schizophrenia spectrum of disorders, with chronic schizophrenia at one extreme, then acute schizophrenic reaction, and borderline schizophrenia. Next followed three other less definite diagnoses, which we called possible chronic schizophrenia, possible acute schizophrenic reaction and possible borderline schizophrenia. These were individuals who seem to have the characteristics that we should use in making the diagnosis of definite schizophrenia, but where these characteristics are blurred or attenuated enough to keep them out of the more definitive categories. Finally, we included at the mildest end of the schizophrenia spectrum of disorders another category, which in the APA nomenclature is listed as Inadequate Personality. In attempting to make a diagnosis of schizophrenia in the index cases, we found that we had great difficulty making a clear and satisfying distinction between "inadequate personality" and mild "borderline schizophrenia," and so we developed the hypothesis that perhaps the inadequate personality was an even milder form of borderline schizophrenia. With that hypothesis in mind, we included inadequate personality in the schizophrenia spectrum of disorders.

We now used not only the Psychiatric Register but every other source of information we could get to establish whether or not a relative had ever been diagnosed with any mental illness or had ever shown behavior which might lead to a question of schizophrenia. These other registers which were made available to us were the Military Registers containing information on men rejected or discharged from military service for psychiatric reasons; the prison records where a question of psychiatric diagnosis had come up; and the Mother's Aid Organization, an agency which assists pregnant women and mothers in various ways. It may help to arrange a legal abortion if there is a history of mental illness in her family or in the family of the father. It also assists the mother with maternity and neonatal care, and has a great deal of information about the mother and some information about the father regarding behavior and possible mental illness. We thus obtained all of the information we could from each of these registers upon each of the 467 relatives relating to their behavior or possible mental illness. All of this information was abstracted, translated into English and edited to remove any cues which would permit a sophisticated observer to guess that a particular relative was a biological or adoptive relative of an index case or of a control. From these edited abstracts the four of us made independent diagnoses, either one of the schizophrenia spectrum disorders or, if we decided it was not in that group, another psychiatric diagnosis. Where we all agreed, that became the diagnosis of the relative. Where we disagreed, we attempted to get more information, and we held a conference on that individual. With the aid of the additional information, we thrashed out the diagnosis. If we could come to a consensus, that became the diagnosis. In four instances a consensus was not reached, the four raters splitting evenly between schizophrenia and not schizophrenia, and those cases were not included in the subsequent tabulation. Their inclusion, incidentally, would not have affected the results significantly. Having made a diagnosis on each relative in whom we found any report of mental deviation, we then broke the code and allocated these relatives to their respective place in Table I.

TABLE I

DISTRIBUTION OF SCHIZOPHRENIA SPECTRUM DISORDERS
AMONG BIOLOGICAL AND ADOPTIVE RELATIVES

Sample of 33 Index Cases and 33 Controls

	Biological Relatives	*Adoptive Relatives*
Index Cases	13/150	2/74
Controls	3/156	3/83
P	0.0072	N. S.

Numerators = number with schizophrenia spectrum disorders
Denominators = number of identified relatives

Among the biological relatives there were 150 who were relatives of index cases and 156 who were relatives of controls. The number of schizophrenia spectrum disorders fell out this way: thirteen among the index case relatives and three among the control relatives, a difference which is highly significant from the one-sided exact distribution. Now in the adoptive relatives there were fewer relatives, and there were two schizophrenia spectrum disorders among the index case relatives and three among the controls—obviously not a significant difference. Now it should be pointed out that although the use of the controls permits one to make a valid comparison between index case relatives and control relatives on the biological side or on the adoptive side, there are certain differences that prevent comparison between them. The biological parents, in general, tend to be younger and are of different socioeconomic class from the adoptive relatives. The biological parents have not been screened by a social agency as is usually the case for adoptive parents. There are nearly twice as many biological relatives as adoptive because of the large number of biological half-siblings. The biological parents tend to be fertile and frequently promiscuous, and each generates other children than the index case—these children usually being half-siblings of the index case. Therefore, one cannot fairly compare the prevalence of mental illness between the biological group and the adoptive group. What one can do is to test separately two hypotheses—the hypothesis that genetic factors operate in the transmission of schizophrenia and the hypothesis that certain types of environmental factors operate. On the basis of this, we feel that it is warranted to conclude that genetic factors operate to a significant extent in the transmission of schizophrenia and that we do not have data which support the operation of environmental factors. However, in the latter connection we should point out that we are really examining only one environmental factor and that is the presence of a person in the adoptive family with a mental illness. There are thousands of environmental factors which we have not examined: the personality of the family, their child-rearing practices, the diet which the individual has had, the lead in the drinking water and many perhaps undreamed of. Therefore, these data by no means rule out the operation of environmental factors. They simply indicate that at least one of these factors, namely, having a mentally ill person with a schizophrenic form of illness in the immediate environment, is not an important or significantly operating variable. Now it may have already occurred to the reader that I did not specify how early these children had been separated from their biological families, but simply that age of separation was one factor which was matched in the selection of controls. As a matter of fact, because we did not know how large our sample size was going to be, and because we wanted to make sure that we had a large enough N to be meaningful, we did not reject adoptees who had spent even a year or two with their biological families. The three cases of schizophrenia-related disorder in the controls occurred in individuals who had left their biological families at 9 months of age or later and there is at least the presumption that psychiatric illness in the biological family may have been a factor in putting the child out for adoption.

Fortunately, among these 33 index cases there were 19 who had been separated from their biological families very early, actually within the first month and in most cases within the first week of life. In most of these instances the separation occurred when the mother left the maternity hospital. Let us look at what happens when we compare the results in these 19 index cases and their controls who had also been separated very early from their biological family.

In the biological relatives, there are 93 relatives of index cases and 92 relatives of controls. Whereas no instance of schizophrenia spectrum dis-

TABLE II

SMALL OF 19 INDEX CASES AND THEIR CONTROLS SEPARATED
FROM THE BIOLOGICAL FAMILY WITHIN 1 MONTH OF BIRTH

	Biological Relatives	Adoptive Relatives
Index Cases	9/93	2/45
Controls	0/92	1/51
P	0.0018	N. S.

Numerators = number with schizophrenia spectrum disorders
Denominators = number of identified relatives

order was found among the biological relatives of controls, nine were found in those of the index cases. The results here are essentially the same as they were before. The significance is even higher, and what has happened is that the prevalence of schizophrenia-related disorders has not changed in the index case families, but the control families have had the prevalence of these disorders markedly reduced by removing a group (put up for adoption late) where mental illness in one of the parents could have been a predisposing factor in that separation. Again, the adoptive relatives show no significant difference from index to control.

Because of these observations we have decided to elaborate this study in two directions. We feel first that it is warranted now to extend this type of study to all of Denmark, and secondly, we feel we can get a richer yield of possible environmental variables as well as evidence of mental illness by a personal interview with all of these relatives. We had not previously seen any of these people, all of the work being done on the basis of records and registers. Now we are in process of obtaining intensive interviews with each of the relatives in an effort to learn as much as we can about their possible personality deviations, the presence of undiagnosed mental illness in them, their child-rearing practices, life experience, and so forth.

It is of interest to examine how the pattern in the family separates out in terms of the type of schizophrenia present in the index case. We recognized for purposes of this study, three kinds of schizophrenia— chronic schizophrenia which we called B1, acute schizophrenic reaction which we called B2, and borderline schizophrenia which we called B3.

Now let us examine the diagnoses in the biological relatives of the three types of index cases. There were 16 index patients with a diagnosis of B1 (chronic schizophrenia). In their biological relatives there were:

one with chronic schizophrenia and three with borderline schizophrenia. There were also two in the doubtful borderline class and one in the inadequate personality group. The acute schizophrenic reaction index cases (B2), of which there were seven with 30 biological relatives, showed no schizophrenia spectrum disorder in any of these relatives. This finding suggests that perhaps the acute schizophrenic reaction is not a form of schizophrenia which would support the notion that exists in Europe. On the other hand, the borderline schizophrenic index cases (B3), of whom there were 10 with 38 relatives, showed a pattern of schizophrenic spectrum disorder in their relatives which was quite similar to that in the biological relatives of the chronic schizophrenic index patients: three with borderline schizophrenia, one with possible chronic schizophrenia, one with possible borderline schizophrenia, and one inadequate personality. We believe that this finding supports the notion that borderline schizophrenia is a form of schizophrenia and is related to chronic schizophrenia. Here, at least, the Americans appear to be on safer ground than the Europeans who do not consider the borderline state as a form of schizophrenia. These findings suggest that whatever genetic factors operate in schizophrenia appear to be polygenic (2) rather than monogenic and that what is transmitted is not schizophrenia as such, but a vague personality characteristic which may move into the schizophrenia spectrum and may go all the way to chronic schizophrenia, depending upon the particular constellation of affected genes or upon their interaction with environmental factors (15). If that is the case, the transmission of intelligence with its genetic and environmental components, rather than the transmission of PKU, would seem to be the appropriate model for the transmission of schizophrenia, which lessens somewhat the likelihood that schizophrenia is the result of a simple biochemical process. It may perhaps be just as difficult to find a biochemical test for schizophrenia as it might be to find one for high intelligence.

REFERENCES

1. Gottesman, I. I. and Shields, J.: Schizophrenia in Twins: 16 Years' Consecutive Admissions to a Psychiatric Clinic. *British Journal of Psychiatry*, 112:809-818, 1966.
2. Gottesman, I. I. and Shields, J.: A Polygenic Theory of Schizophrenia. *Proceedings of the National Academy of Science USA*, 58:199-205, 1967.
3. Hermansen, L.: Schizophrenic Patients on a Psychiatric Ward in a Provincial General Hospital. A Follow-up of Schizophrenic First Ad-

missions 1956-1966. *Ugeskrift for Laeger,* 129:1445-1449, 1967 (in Danish).

4. Heston, L. L.: Psychiatric Disorders in Foster Home Reared Children of Schizophrenic Mothers. *British Journal of Psychiatry,* 112:819-825, 1966.

5. Inouye, E.: Similarity and Dissimilarity of Schizophrenia in Twins. In Cleghorn, R. A. (Ed.), *Proceedings of the Third World Congress of Psychiatry,* Vol. 1. Montreal: University of Toronto Press, 1962.

6. Kallmann, F. J.: *The Genetics of Schizophrenia.* New York: Augustin, 1938.

7. Kallmann, F. J.: The Genetic Theory of Schizophrenia: An Analysis of 691 Schizophrenic Twin Index Families. *American Journal of Psychiatry,* 103:309-322, 1946.

8. Kety, S. S.: Biochemical Theories of Schizophrenia. *Science,* 129:1528-1532, 1590-1596, 1959.

9. Kringlen, E.: Schizophrenia in Twins: An Epidemiological-clinical Study. *Psychiatry,* 29:172-184, 1966.

10. Luxenburger, H.: Vorläufiger Bericht über psychiatrische Serienuntersuchungen an Zwillingen. *Zeitschrift für die gesamte Neurologie und Psychiatrie,* 116:297-326, 1928.

11. Mednick, S. A. and Schulsinger, F.: Some Premorbid Characteristics Related to Breakdown in Children with Schizophrenic Mothers. In Rosenthal, D. and Kety, S. S., (Eds.), *Transmission of Schizophrenia.* London: Pergamon Press, 1968.

12. Rosanoff, A. J., Handy, L. M., Plesset, I. R., and Brush, S.: The Etiology of So-called Schizophrenic Psychoses with Special Reference to Their Occurrence in Twins. *American Journal of Psychiatry,* 91:247-286, 1934.

13. Rosenthal, D.: Sex Distribution and Severity of Illness Among Samples of Schizophrenic Twins. *Journal of Psychiatric Research,* 1:26-36, 1961.

14. Rosenthal, D.: Problems of Sampling and Diagnosis in the Major Twin Studies of Schizophrenia. *Journal of Psychiatric Research,* 1:116-134, 1962.

15. Rosenthal, D.: Theoretical Overview: A Suggested Conceptual Framework. In Rosenthal, D. (Ed.), *The Genain Quadruplets: A Case Study and Theoretical Analysis of Heredity and Environment in Schizophrenia.* New York: Basic Books, 1963.

16. Rosenthal, D., Wender, P., Kety, S. S., Schulsinger, F., Welner, J., and Ostergaard, L.: Schizophrenics' Offspring Reared in Adoptive Homes. In Rosenthal, D. and Kety, S. S. (Eds.), *Transmission of Schizophrenia.* London: Pergamon Press, 1968.

17. Skeels, H. M. and Dye, H. B.: A Study of the Effects of Differential Stimulation on Mentally Retarded Children. *Proceedings of the American Association for Mental Deficiency,* 63:114-136, 1939.

18. Slater, E.: *Psychotic and Neurotic Illnesses in Twins.* London: Her Majesty's Stationery Office, 1953.

19. Slater, E.: A Review of Earlier Evidence on Genetic Factors in Schizophrenia. In Rosenthal, D. and Kety, S. S. (Eds.), *Transmission of Schizophrenia*. London: Pergamon Press, 1968.
20. Tienari, P.: Psychiatric Illness in Identical Twins. *Acta Psychiatrica Scandinavica*, 39 (Suppl. 171): 1-195, 1963.
21. Wender, P., Rosenthal, D., and Kety, S. S.: A Psychiatric Assessment of the Adoptive Parents of Schizophrenics. In Rosenthal, D. and Kety, S. S. (Eds.), *Transmission of Schizophrenia*. London: Pergamon Press, 1968.

19

Genetic Research in the
Schizophrenic Syndrome

DAVID ROSENTHAL, Ph.D.

IN THE LETTER INVITING ME to write this contribution, I was asked to write about the promise that genetics holds for the understanding, prevention, and treatment of mental illness in general and schizophrenia in particular. That is better than being asked to write about man in relationship to his universe, but not much better. At any rate, I shall try to catch the spirit and intent of the request and address myself to it as best I can.

Before we can talk intelligently about the contributions of genetics to the understanding of schizophrenia, we must first assure ourselves that schizophrenia has some hereditary basis. Without presenting tables and figures or going into great detail about the hundreds of studies concerned with heredity in schizophrenia, let me summarize briefly the main evidence that indicates that schizophrenia does in fact have a genetic basis.

The first body of evidence comes from what we might call consanguinity studies. The nature of the evidence takes two forms. The first is that the incidence of schizophrenia in the immediate families of schizophrenics has repeatedly been found to be much higher than the incidence of the disorder in the general population. This is a consistent finding whether the investigator has a genetic or an environmentalist bias. In fact, investigators who emphasize the *psychological* factors in the etiology of schizophrenia report a much higher incidence of schizophrenic-type pathology in the families that they have studied than do genetic investigators who have not examined the families as intensively.

An additional form of evidence obtained in the consanguinity studies involves a consistent correlation between incidence of schizophrenia in the relatives of schizophrenics and the closeness of the blood relationship to schizophrenic index cases. Thus, the incidence of schizophrenia is higher in the siblings, children, and parents of schizophrenics than in their aunts, uncles, nephews, and nieces. The incidence of the disorder among second-degree relatives is in turn higher than the incidence in the general population, although not very much higher.

This body of evidence can be criticized on two main grounds. The first is methodological. Investigators who have carried out these studies have known the diagnosis of the index case and have primarily had a genetic rather than a psychological orientation to the etiology of schizophrenia. However, the diagnoses have usually been based on hospitalized cases among relatives, and, in the main, the hospital diagnoses corresponded with the diagnosis of schizophrenia made by the investigators. Also, investigators who have a psychological orientation to schizophrenia have reported similar or higher rates of the disorder among first-degree relatives of the probands in their studies. Thus, the general finding of a correlation between incidence of the disorder and degree of consanguinity is probably valid.

The second objection is the more serious one. Here, the argument runs that it is not the genes transmitted from parent to child that are responsible for the mental illness in the children but rather the type of rearing, the behavioral irrationality, and the chaotic climate of the familial relationships that really induce the behavioral disorder in the child. Investigators favoring this view have had no difficulty in demonstrating the chaos and irrationality that exists in these families. Thus, we have two equally valid bodies of evidence that lead investigators to two different and opposed conclusions. As long as the genetic and psychological variables coexisted in the same family, it was impossible to decide on which one was in fact the culprit factor that induced the psychopathology in the child.

The second body of evidence comes from twin studies which, up until recently, provided the most salient data favoring a genetic basis for the etiology of schizophrenia. In almost all the twin studies done to date, the concordance rate for schizophrenia in monozygotic twins has been appreciably higher than the concordance rate in dizygotic twins. Thus, in ten of eleven studies the rates are in accord with what genetic theory predicts. Although all studies encounter problems of sampling and diagnosis, there is no question but that the *direction* of differences in concordance rates between the two types of twins is valid.

The interpretation of these findings has been a matter of some controversy. One argument holds that psychological factors regarding mono-zygotic twins are very different from those regarding dizygotic twins. The higher concordance rate for monozygotic pairs might be attributable to the fact that identical twins share a unique and intense identificatory bond. If one member of the pair becomes schizophrenic, the identificatory bond is likely to lead to a similar pattern of psychotic behavior in his co-twin. Thus, the difference in concordance rates between the two types of twins could have a psychological explanation.

However, case reports of monozygotic twins reared apart provide serious difficulties for the identification argument. Sixteen cases of mono-zygotic pairs reared apart have now been reported in which at least one of the twins was diagnosed as schizophrenic. Among these pairs, ten were concordant and six discordant. The overall concordance rate is compara-ble to rates obtained for twins reared together. Although there may well have been some sampling bias which led to this concordance rate being inflated, it is clear that an identificatory bond could hardly have account-ed for the many pairs who were concordant. It is difficult to imagine how such a frequency of concordance could have occurred without some com-mon genetic basis.

The third body of evidence comes from studies in which the child generation has not been reared by the parent generation. The child may have been reared in an adoptive home, in foster homes, institutions, or in the homes of relatives. Five such studies have now been reported (9), three of them by my colleagues, including Dr. Seymour Kety, Dr. Paul Wender, and myself. Two of the five studies were carried out in Denmark, one in Iceland, one on the West Coast, and another on the East Coast of the U.S.A. All five studies are consistent in their finding of a higher inci-dence of schizophrenia or schizophrenic-spectrum disorder among the biological relatives of schizophrenic probands than among relatives who were not biologically related but with whom the subjects studied shared the rearing experience. All five studies differed in the details of their re-search design, but regardless of whether the schizophrenic index cases were the biological parents or the foster-reared or adopted children, the results point consistently in the same direction. Although one could raise questions about any one of the studies, when the five are considered to-gether they constitute such strong evidence for the genetic hypothesis that it is difficult to see how this hypothesis can now be refuted.

When one considers the combined evidence from the consanguinity studies, the twin studies, and the adoption studies, one must admit that a genetic explanation of all the data is simpler, more parsimonious, and less ad hoc than any environmentalist explanation. This does not mean that environmental factors are not important with respect to the etiology of schizophrenia, but only that they must be considered in conjunction with genetic factors.

Let us assume now that we are all agreed that the case for a hereditary contribution to the etiology of schizophrenia has been proven. How does this knowledge help us to understand the nature of the schizophrenic disturbance? What implications does such knowledge hold for the future planning of research on schizophrenic disorders? Before we can properly appreciate such implications, we ought to know at least three things relevant to the heredity contribution: 1. the mode of inheritance; 2. the genetic or biological unity of schizophrenia; and 3. the specificity of the schizophrenic genotype.

With respect to the mode of inheritance, it is not yet entirely clear whether schizophrenic disorder can be attributed to a single major gene, to a combination of two major genes, or to a number of genes with different effects, all of which may contribute in some degree or dimension to a schizophrenic denouement. Once we accept a genetic hypothesis, whatever the mode of inheritance, we must assume that some sort of metabolic digression has taken place at some time during the development of the affected individual. If the disorder is caused by a single major gene, then investigators who are searching for a specific biochemical abnormality that discriminates schizophrenics from controls may well be on the right track.

However, the genetic research is not as encouraging to such investigators as it once was thought to be. It was not too long ago that genetic investigators were debating with considerable intensity whether the gene that caused schizophrenia was dominant or recessive. The fact that no clear Mendelian distribution of schizophrenia in families could be found did not deter the debate. The theorists spoke in terms of reduced penetrance and modifying genes to account for the deviation from Mendelian distributions. Investigators calculated what the manifestation rate of schizophrenia would have to be for homozygotes and heterozygotes if the gene were recessive or dominant. Some investigators also calculated what the mutation rate for the assumed pathological gene would have to be to maintain the population incidence of the disorder at a constant level.

Single-gene theorists classified the relatives of their probands as either schizophrenic or not schizophrenic and failed to face the possibility that a continuum of schizophrenicity might exist. Of course, there were always some cases who were not clearly schizophrenic but, on the other hand, were not clearly nonschizophrenic either. Investigators would call such cases "doubtful" or "questionable" schizophrenia, and these cases could be included or excluded in the statistical analyses of familial rates, depending on the preference of the investigator or his critics. Different investigators followed different practices in this regard. Cases called schizoid were excluded from such analyses and in fact created difficulty for some investigators since they obviously did not meet the criteria for clear-cut schizophrenia and yet, clinically, looked suspiciously like they belonged with the group of schizophrenics. If they harbored the schizophrenic genotype, why were they not clinically schizophrenic; and if they did not harbor the genotype, why should they have manifested symptoms that appeared to be related to clinical schizophrenia?

If one maintained a theory of recessiveness, one might hold that the schizophrenics had the culprit gene in double dose, whereas the schizoid relatives were heterozygous carriers of the pathological gene. This, in fact, was Kallmann's position (4).

If one supported a dominance theory, then one might maintain that the gene was a partial dominant, that all of the few individuals who were homozygous for the dominant gene were bound to develop clinical schizophrenia, and that most schizophrenics by far would be heterozygous for the dominant gene. Heterozygous carriers, in turn, would manifest a low penetrance so that only a relatively small fraction of them would develop clinical schizophrenia. This, in fact, is the kind of theory that Slater (10) has supported. Although such possible genetic interpretations are desirable, they have tended to alienate nongeneticists and to discourage them from considering any genetic hypothesis in a serious way.

In the 1960's, a polygenic view of schizophrenia attained high popularity among leading investigators in the field. There were many reasons for this. For one thing, such a view was not committed to a yes-or-no conception of schizophrenia. Rather, it viewed schizophrenic disorders as ranging quantitatively along a single continuum. For this reason, the finding in schizophrenic probands' families of cases called questionable or doubtful schizophrenia, or cases called schizoid or paranoid, posed no problem. As a matter of fact, they were to be expected. Those cases who were clinically full-blown schizophrenics merely represented the end point on the continuum. The theory did not have to provide any ad hoc hypotheses such as diminished penetrance or heterozygosity to account for the subschizophrenic cases.

Another factor favoring a switch to polygenic theory was the development in the late fifties and early sixties of new methods and better understanding of quantitative genetics. It became clearer that most traits studied by far in higher order animals had a polygenic basis. Almost all behavioral traits were clearly graded and continuous and therefore polygenically influenced, if genes were relevant at all. Since schizophrenia was a behavioral disorder in the sense that it was defined in terms of specific behaviors, it seemed reasonable to believe that it, too, should have a polygenic basis.

Twin research in the sixties provided additional reasons for thinking that a polygenic view was the correct one. In several studies done during this decade, the modal concordance rate for monozygotic twins was about forty percent. The rates reported were consistently lower than the rates that had been reported in the earlier twin studies, in which the modal rate was about seventy percent. The lower the concordance rate in monozygotic twins, the lower the penetrance that one would have to attribute to a single pathological gene. When the penetrance estimate gets to be lower than fifty percent, then the theory underlying it becomes very shaky indeed.

With respect to heredity-environment considerations, a polygenic view makes it especially important to think about the environmental factors that contribute to the evocation of clinical schizophrenia. As a matter of fact, I have subsumed the polygenic viewpoint under what I call diathesis-stress theory, a term that designates both the hereditary and environmental factors as important agents in the development of schizophrenic disorders.

There is another way of looking at polygenic theory. For example, some strains of mice and rats develop convulsions when subjected to high-pitched tones. In some of the strains, the trait of convulsing is polygenically determined. Although the animals' responses to the high-pitched tones can be graded, the investigators tend to classify their animals in terms of those who develop convulsions and those who do not. Such a trait is called a threshold character. Similarly, schizophrenia might be thought of as a threshold character, a culminating reaction in a polygenically predisposed individual to a high-intensity stress.

A human model for a threshold character may be found in a disorder such as congenital pyloric stenosis. Some geneticists have maintained that this disorder is polygenically based and that the stricture of the pylorus is of a graded character which, when it reaches a certain point, gives rise to the serious clinical symptoms of the disorder. In such a condition, one tends to be concerned primarily with the structural anomaly rather than the developmental metabolic digression that gave rise to it. If the hereditary component in schizophrenia turns out to be a polygenic one, some investigators might feel more confident in finding deviations among schizophrenics in how the central nervous system is put together, or how it is "wired," rather than in finding a specific biochemical abnormality, but, of course, the latter possibility is just as tenable under polygenic theory.

A second way in which genetics may help us to understand schizophrenia has to do with what has traditionally been called the biological or genetic unity of schizophrenia. I use the term only in the sense that it asks this question: What types of clinical syndromes are genetically related to one another and rightly subsumed under the broad category of schizophrenic disorders? More specifically, do the classical subtypes of schizophrenia have a common genetic basis; are process and reactive schizophrenia two separate disorders; or, do patients who fall ill with schizophrenic-like disorders at very early or late ages really belong in a single genetic family of schizophrenias? I shall not review in detail the literature relevant to these problems which can be found elsewhere (8), but shall try to summarize briefly what I think the evidence of past studies leads us to conclude.

With respect to the classical subtypes, we find that paranoid, catatonic, and hebephrenic forms of schizophrenic illness occur repeatedly in the same families. As a matter of fact, one case has been reported in which both parents were paranoid yet they had two children who were hebephrenic (2). The Genain Quadruplets (7) had a paranoid father and grandmother but all four girls were catatonic-hebephrenic. Such findings suggest that the classical subtypes are genetically related.

However, in studies of monozygotic twins, we find a very strong association within twin pairs with respect to subtype. For example, if one monozygotic twin is catatonic, the probability is very high that his co-twin will be diagnosed catatonic as well. In the case of twins reared together, the possibility clearly exists that the common association and/or rearing induces both twins to develop the same form of illness. From the genetic point of view, the almost constant finding of a common subtype in monozygotic twins suggests genetic specificity with respect to them.

How shall we explain such findings? With respect to the twin studies, it has almost always been the case that the same investigator made the subtype diagnosis for both twins. He may have been influenced in his judgment by the identical appearance of both twins, and his judgment regarding the first twin could have influenced his diagnosis regarding the second twin. Several studies have reported that the reliability of subtype diagnosis is not very high, a fact which indicates that judgments regarding subtype can readily be influenced by extraneous factors. Some of the variation with respect to different subtypes in the same families might possibly be explained on this basis as well.

A polygenic theory of schizophrenia could readily account for the seemingly incompatible findings. One could assume, for example, that individuals characterized as catatonic or hebephrenic had more of the pathological genes than schizophrenics called simple or paranoid. The clinical picture of psychopathology, in fact, tends to be more severe in catatonics and hebephrenics than in cases with simple or paranoid forms of the illness, and the incidence of schizophrenic disorder in their families tends to be higher as well. Individuals in the same family who harbor more or less of the pathological genes might be expected to show different subtype patterns. Monozygotic twins would be expected to have the same clinical picture since they both carry the same number and type of polygenes.

Should cases that have their onset before adolescence be classified as schizophrenic? The evidence suggests that a monozygotic twin with preadolescent schizophrenia is likely to have a co-twin with preadolescent schizophrenia as well. However, about twenty percent of the sick co-twins may develop schizophrenia *after* the onset of adolescence (5). In addition, a high rate of schizophrenia among the parents of children with prepubertal schizophrenia has been reported as well. As a matter of fact, in one study, eleven percent of prepubertal schizophrenic children had both parents schizophrenic (1). Thus, these findings suggest that there may be a common genetic anlage for both the pre- and postadolescent forms of schizophrenia. With respect to polygenic theory, the fact that one group of schizophrenics has the onset of the illness so much earlier than the second group suggests that the early onset group may have more of the polygenes. Of course, it is easy to think of environmental explanations of such findings as well.

With respect to early infantile autism, the picture is less clear. One leading investigator (6) found virtually no schizophrenia among the parents of his infant probands whereas a second leading investigator (3) reported an incidence that was quite elevated: twenty-nine percent of the mothers and thirteen percent of the fathers. When the children were divided into cases called organic or nonorganic, as determined by an intensive neurological examination, the rate of schizophrenia in the parents of the nonorganic group was higher than the rate for parents of the organic group. Among the parents of the children called organic, twenty-one percent of the mothers and fifteen percent of the fathers were called schizophrenic. Among the parents of the nonorganic group forty-four percent of the mothers and eight percent of the fathers were classified as schizophrenic. It is difficult to make genetic sense of a finding in which mothers are five and one-half times more frequent than fathers with respect to schizophrenia, especially in view of the fact that the illness tends to occur in both sexes equally, and only about twice as often in mothers, as compared to fathers, generally.

Without going into the research findings, I shall add that the disorders called schizophreniform psychosis, symptomatic schizophrenia, psychogenic psychosis, atypical, peripheral or reactive schizophrenia, schizoaffective psychosis, borderline schizophrenia, schizoid personality, or paranoid state all seem to be genetically linked to schizophrenia. The studies are many, and the findings not always consistent, but the overall evidence suggests that these disorders do indeed belong in the same genetic family.

Let me add just a few lines on what I call the specificity of the schizophrenic genotype. I use this term to cover the question: Which mental disorders, if any, are genetically distinct from the schizophrenic family of disorders? For historical reasons, I have reference primarily to the disorder called manic-depressive psychosis. With regard to the family studies of both disorders that have been reported to date, the evidence mainly favors the theory that schizophrenia and manic-depressive psychosis are genetically different. By and large, schizophrenia occurs infrequently in the families of manic-depressive probands, and very little manic-depressive psychosis occurs among the families of schizophrenics. No clear-cut case has yet been reported of schizophrenia in one twin and manic-depressive psychosis in the monozygotic co-twin.

However, some overlap of the two disorders does occur. Moreover, it is relatively uncommon for schizophrenics to have children with manic-depressive psychosis, whereas manic-depressive parents tend to have schizophrenic children at a rate that is about three to five times higher than the rate of schizophrenia in the general population.

A conclusion that the two disorders are genetically distinct would be based primarily on the pronounced clustering of one illness or the other in different families. The overlap within families that has been reported might have resulted from misdiagnosis in some cases. From a genetic point of view, the spouses of one type of psychotic might sometimes have been carriers of genes implicated in the other disorder. From the environmental side, one might hold that the clinical manifestations are strongly influenced by life experiences of various kinds. Such factors could indeed blur the overall picture, but the evidence for an inherited component in each disorder, especially schizophrenia, is now fairly solid. Any conclusions that we draw with respect to the genetic distinctness of the two disorders, however, must involve some reservation. A review of the literature suggests that further and better research might well enable us to draw clear conclusions with respect to whether schizophrenia and manic-depressive psychosis are indeed two different mental illnesses.

There is some suggestion in the literature, too, that some forms of psychoneurosis and some forms of psychopathy are associated genetically with schizophrenia. Others seem not to be related to schizophrenia at all. For our purposes, however, the question should not be limited to whether or not we can draw definite conclusions about these matters at the present time, but rather whether a clearer understanding of the role of genetics in these disorders will help us to develop a better comprehension of them and perhaps a more sensible nosology as well.

Some implications of genetics for the prevention and treatment of schizophrenic disorders are readily apparent, while others may not be quite as obvious. I shall list and briefly discuss five general implications.

1. A genetic basis for a disorder suggests the possibility of identifying a specific metabolic error which causes it. The knowledge that schizophrenic disorders have a genetic basis encourages investigators to carry on not only biochemical research, but also physiological and psycho-physiological research that helps us to obtain a clearer understanding of their functional nature. In addition, such genetic knowledge provides a sound basis for genetic counseling, so that schizophrenics and close relatives of schizophrenics can be advised about the likelihood of having a schizophrenic child. Whether one accepts a genetic or psychological etiology of schizophrenia, it is clear that a high marriage rate for schizophrenics—and possibly for their siblings—will lead to an increased rate of schizophrenia in the next generation. A sound basis for counseling such individuals could prevent an increased incidence from occurring.

2. Now that we have such strong evidence that schizophrenia has a genetic component, we can give thought to identifying who the people are that carry the schizophrenic genotype. For example, my colleagues and I are carrying out a study in which we examine intensively, for two days, individuals who have a high likelihood of being gene carriers. These individuals are adults who had a biological parent that was schizophrenic, but they were not reared by their schizophrenic parent. Instead, they were given up for adoption early in life and reared by adoptive parents. Thus, in their growing-up years, they had no direct personal contact with

schizophrenia. We also have a control group of subjects, neither of whose biological parents was known to have had a psychiatric disorder, but these individuals were also reared in adoptive homes.

Through psychological tests and an intensive psychiatric interview, we hope to be able to discriminate the two groups with respect to a number of psychological and behavioral characteristics. If we can make such discriminations, we may be able to describe the basic personality characteristics stemming from the pathological genotype. Positive findings might also provide a sound basis for assuming that a similar identification of gene carriers could be made in individuals who are much younger, perhaps even in infants. Such knowledge, if it can be obtained, is bound to give us a better understanding of what these individuals are like. It could also provide a sound basis for carrying out a rational program of mental hygiene with respect to them.

3. If the effort to identify gene carriers in early life succeeds, we should be in an excellent position to study the effects of different environmental, rearing and experiential factors on the subsequent psychological development of such individuals. For example, my Israeli colleagues and I are carrying out a study in which we examine latency age children who have a schizophrenic parent. Half of these children were born and raised in a *kibbutz* and half in the typical nuclear family situation. We have reason to believe that the child who has a schizophrenic parent but who is reared in a *kibbutz* might fare better than his counterpart in the nuclear family situation. Typically, the child who has a schizophrenic father or mother may be subjected to unusual, bizarre, or confusing behavior on the part of the sick parent, the home may be broken, the sick parent may be absent for long periods of time because of hospitalization, the child may be forced to live with relatives or friends, in foster homes or in institutions, or in any combination of these.

The child reared in a *kibbutz* has a more stable environment. The sick parent is likely to have less daily contact with him and perhaps, therefore, less influence upon him. During most of the day, the child is under the care of normal caretakers and teachers. He retains a stable set of peers, no matter what happens to the parent. When the parent becomes ill, he or she may be removed to a hospital but the child suffers no serious disruption of any other part of his life. He still has the other parent with him and can visit this parent regularly during the evening as he does ordinarily every day of his life. In his growing-up years, he has normal parent surrogates with whom to identify, as compared to the child in the nuclear family situation whose daily intimate associations may include only a sick parent.

In this study, we have control children as well. One-half of the controls come from the same *kibbutz* as the index case who has a schizophrenic parent. The control child has grown up in exactly the same circumstances as the index child, but the parents of the control child do not have any known psychiatric illness. We also have a control group of children from the towns, who come from the same classrooms as the town index children. These control subjects also have normal parents. The four groups of children are studied intensively over a two-day period. They are brought to examination in pairs and the examiners do not know which one is the index case and which is the control. The children are also observed together in natural situations, often in the same social group.

Not only do we hope to be able to distinguish the children who have a schizophrenic parent from the children who do not with respect to a number of personality characteristics, but the design also permits us to tease out interaction effects between the different types of rearing and the different types of parentage. Thus, we hope to provide clear experimental evidence regarding the nature and direction of some heredity-environment interactions. As a result of this study and, hopefully, other studies carried out in the same vein, we might be able to generate a better understanding of what kinds of environmental factors have what kinds of impact upon the gene-carrying children. Such knowledge should permit us to recommend the kinds of rearing and experiential influences that should be avoided or practiced in order to reduce the possibility of subsequent schizophrenic pathology.

4. Genetic studies of schizophrenia also provide the possibility of a more *positive* outlook regarding such disorders, in that people who are gene-carriers may possess not only a special predisposition toward the development of behaviors we call pathological, but they may also possess special talents and abilities which we should deem to be highly desirable. At least two genetic studies have pointed out that first-degree relatives of schizophrenics were—more often than controls—spontaneous in their behavior, colorful, artistic, and creative. Clinicians have long noted a type of originality in the thinking of some schizophrenics, but in their psychosis the originality was often detrimental to the affected individuals themselves. On the Rorschach, such patients may produce a number of O-minus responses. However, if we are able to identify the gene-carriers early, then we may be in a strategic position to nurture these latent heightened capacities for unusually imaginative and creative thinking. Thus, we could

in the future not only help to ward off the development of negative effects, but we could foster as well the positive aspects of the gene-carriers' possible inherent potential.

5. With respect to the implications of genetic studies of schizophrenia for therapy, we can make the following points. First, there is always a possibility that genetic studies in association with biological studies of schizophrenia will lead to new medications that will have a more beneficial effect on clinical symptoms than current drugs have. Certainly, this avenue of research should not be discouraged. Second, if we are able to identify heredity-environment interactions that influence the development of gene-carriers in a positive or negative way, we might be able to generalize from such findings to techniques of treatment which would be conceptually related to the environmental factors that produced the beneficial effects and avoided the noxious ones. And third, once we recognize the fact that genetic influences are important in schizophrenia, we should try to understand how such influences exert their effect on behavior. With respect to the psychological-behavioral level, it is likely that they increase the probability of certain behaviors occurring while diminishing or precluding the occurrence of other types of behavior. One implication of this hypothesis is that therapists may often have expectations or goals for a patient which he is simply not able to meet. Such impasses may lead to increased feelings of self-derogation in the patient, resentment toward the therapist, and pangs of frustration in the therapist plus feelings of his own ineffectiveness.

Of course, given our current state of knowledge, all the implications of genetics for prevention and treatment that I have listed are highly speculative. However, ongoing research suggests that we may be on the right track and that some of these speculations may be confirmed in the next decade.

REFERENCES

1. Bender, L.: Mental Illness in Childhood and Heredity. *Eugenics Quarterly*, 10:1-11, 1963.
2. Elsässer, G.: *Die Nachkommen geisteskranker Elternpaare.* Stuttgart: Thieme, 1952.
3. Goldfarb, W.: The Subclassification of Psychotic Children: Application to a Study of Longitudinal Change. In Rosenthal, D. and Kety, S. S. (Eds.), *The Transmission of Schizophrenia.* London: Pergamon, 1968.
4. Kallmann, F. J.: The Genetic Theory of Schizophrenia. *American Journal of Psychiatry*, 103:309-322, 1946.

5. Kallmann, F. J. and Roth, B.: Genetic Aspects of Preadolescent Schizophrenia. *American Journal of Psychiatry*, 112:599-606, 1956.
6. Kanner, L.: To What Extent Is Early Infantile Autism Determined by Constitutional Inadequacies? In Hooker, D. and Hare, C. C. (Eds.), *Genetics and the Inheritance of Integrated Neurological and Psychiatric Patterns*. Baltimore: Williams and Wilkins, 1954.
7. Rosenthal, D.: *The Genain Quadruplets*. New York: Basic Books, 1963.
8. Rosenthal, D.: *Genetic Theory and Abnormal Behavior*. New York: McGraw-Hill, in press.
9. Rosenthal, D. and Kety, S. S. (Eds.): *The Transmission of Schizophrenia*. London: Pergamon, 1968.
10. Slater, E.: Clinical Aspects of Genetic Mental Disorders. In Cummings, J. N. and Kremer, M. (Eds.), *Biochemical Aspects of Neurological Disorders* (2nd series). Oxford: Blackwell, 1965.

20

Attention, Psychophysiology, and Scanning in the Schizophrenic Syndrome

HERBERT E. SPOHN, Ph.D., PAUL E. THETFORD, Ph.D., and ROBERT CANCRO, M.D.

OUR SCHIZOPHRENIC RESEARCH PROGRAM here at The Menninger Foundation has been guided by two general hypotheses, which we have sought to examine empirically through a series of related experimental studies.

One of these hypotheses is that a major locus of disorder in schizophrenia is to be found in those phases of the perceptual process subsumed under attention. In part, this hypothesis originates with Bleuler (1). While he held that perception was not disturbed in schizophrenia, he did observe that many acute schizophrenics appeared to be "enslaved by their optic impressions." The hypothesis also owes an obvious debt to the work of Shakow (8), which has pointed so consistently to the difficulties schizophrenic patients have in selecting relevant stimuli and screening out irrelevant stimuli in complex tasks calling for an organized response. In 1964 Silverman (9) advanced a model of psychological deficit in the schizophrenic syndrome in which attention dysfunction played a central role. This model has also influenced our thinking and work. Most directly related to our formulations, however, are the observations and studies of a group of British psychiatrists and psychologists—principally Chapman, McGhie, and Venables (2, 6, 10).

We share in the postulation of these investigators that in all phases of the schizophrenic reaction attentional processes in their selective and inhibiting functions are significantly and systematically altered. Sensory data do not reach awareness in schizophrenics in the same form, to the same extent, and with the same subjective intensity as they do in non-schizophrenic individuals. In some phases of the illness and in some forms of schizophrenia the attention gates are open too wide; selective functions have broken down; too much information for orderly processing is permitted to enter the information processing channels. During other phases of the illness, and in other subgroups, inhibiting functions are hyperactive, the gates are shut too tight, and only a narrow span of information enters the system. In the acute paranoid type the information seeking functions are hyperactive, and the external environment is hyperscanned for signs of threat and danger.

By way of clarification, it is useful to distinguish our conceptions from those of Doctor Holzman (3), who also implicates perceptual processes as the locus of a mediating mechanism of dysfunction in schizophrenia. Holzman takes the view that primary dysfunction is to be found in the reperception or feedback phases of the formation of percepts. We are pursuing the hypothesis that disorder may also be found in an earlier stage of the perceptual process, that is, in the scanning and intake phases of perceptual information processing.

It is logically possible to infer from attention dysfunction aspects of thought disorder in schizophrenia, which have traditionally been regarded as the primary disturbance. A condition of information overload in the early phases of psychotic breakdown might well lead to the confused, disconnected, and overinclusive cognitive performance characteristic of the acute phase of the disorder. The fragmented and impoverished thought content of the chronic process patient is consistent with a narrowed focus of attention to external information. In the paranoid schizophrenic reaction the need to keep intact a protective delusional system is consistent with hyperattention to confirming information in the external environment. It should be very clear, however, that we have not fallen into the seductive trap of claiming primacy for attention dysfunction. We think it likely that attention dysfunction is an aspect of a probably quite complex series of mediating mechanisms that give rise to the multiform symptom picture in the schizophrenic syndrome.

The second hypothesis guiding our research is that level of arousal is significantly linked to attentional processes. By arousal we mean an internal state of the organism ranging continuously from sleep to watchful alertness, which may be indexed indirectly by measurement of various peripheral physiological responses, such as skin conductance or GSR, heart rate, blood pulse volume, etc. Attentional processes, insofar as they exercise control over the amount and kind of sensory data entering the perceptual system, may be functionally related to level of arousal.

Until relatively recently it was generally assumed that arousal mechanisms were impaired in schizophrenic patients, that such patients were characteristically hypoaroused. There is now, however, a considerable body of evidence indicating that arousal mechanisms are not impaired, that in fact hyperarousal rather than hypoarousal is the more characteristic state in the schizophrenic syndrome, or at least in certain of its major subgroups. Hypoarousal has been postulated as characteristic of certain other major subgroups—the acute and reactive patients. As yet, however, no convincing evidence to this effect has been offered. We are interested in determining the nature of the functional relationship between characteristic levels of arousal and attentional disorder in the schizophrenic syndrome. Venables' hypotheses (10) exemplify the kinds of relationships that may be envisioned. He speculates that hyperarousal, which he regards as typical of chronic and process patients, is associated with a restriction of the focus of attention to external stimuli, while hypoarousal in acute and reactive patients is associated with a breakdown of selective and inhibiting functions and has the consequence of flooding the information processing system with an excess of exteroceptive information.

Our research strategy in examining these issues is basically one of a series of laboratory studies, in which we measure concomitantly various aspects of attentional processes and monitor by polygraphic recording peripheral indices of level of arousal, as well as phasic reactivity to stimulation. Rather than manipulating level of arousal experimentally, we have relied on naturally occurring ranges of variation in samples of patients and on differences between schizophrenic and nonschizophrenic subjects to test hypotheses concerning arousal and attention dysfunction relationships. The extensive measurement of peripheral indicants of arousal, such as skin conductance, heart rate, blood pulse volume, and muscle tension, that we have done and are doing over a series of experimental sessions in schizophrenic patients will also add to the clarification of the arousal status of schizophrenics in general and within various schizophrenic subgroups.

A part of this chapter will be concerned with the methods and results of the first completed experimental study in our series. In this study we measured the span of apprehension under several conditions of presentation and report, while monitoring arousal level in four channels of polygraphic recordings. Before proceeding to this, however, we shall briefly describe two other studies currently in progress, which exemplify the general approach, and shall discuss two major methodological problems that bedevil experimental research of this kind.

The use of eye movements in scanning and examining the external environment is an important aspect of attentional processes. The systematic study of eye movements in scanning gives promise of disclosing characteristic information seeking and information avoiding maneuvers. Accordingly, in a study whose data-gathering phase is almost complete, the lateral and vertical eye movements of schizophrenics, nonschizophrenic patients, and normal controls have been recorded under three conditions. First, electrodes on the surface of the skin around the eyes record the standing potential on the eyeballs, while the subject is free to explore visually the unfamiliar environment of the experimental room. This procedure is repeated in a second session when the subject has had an opportunity to familiarize himself with the setting. Head movements are simultaneously recorded.

Secondly, eye movements are recorded in a size-estimation task, in which visual scanning strategies in the solution of a structured visual problem can be systematically examined and related to objective measures of perceptual accuracy.

Finally, eye movements are being recorded during the performance of a series of mental tasks, that is, when attention is presumably directed inward to the cognitive demands of such tasks.

In this study we are also interested in a major independent variable, namely, the effect of affective value upon accuracy and scanning strategies in the size-estimation task. Accordingly, all subjects perform a color-discrimination task with pairs of disks of the same size and color, as two of three standard stimuli in the size-estimation task. One half of all subjects receive a predetermined schedule of verbal feedback upon making their discrimination judgments, in the form of "right" or "wrong." For those subjects one color series, yellow, receives 80% "wrong" judgments. The other color series, magenta, receives 80% "right" feedback. This color discrimination training is administered in the second of two experimental sessions, after baseline size-estimation scores have been obtained, and just before a second administration of the size-estimation task.

Throughout both experimental sessions, GSR, recorded from the plantar area of the right foot, and heart rate, recorded from chest leads, are continuously monitored.

We have some preliminary results from this study bearing on a hypothesis of long standing that has never been directly tested. It appears that the subgroup of schizophrenic patients who showed paranoid symptoms at time of testing manifest the highest level of visual scanning activity in the free-scanning period. That is, they shift fixation point more often than nonparanoid schizophrenics, nonschizophrenic psychiatric patients, and normal controls.

A second major study which is also now under way focuses on selective attention. In this experiment we are examining the ability of schizophrenic subjects to extract relevant and to screen out irrelevant information in two ways. First, they are required to perform a task in which they selectively report lower- and upper-case consonants from tachistoscopically presented matrices that contain both types of letters. In another task, subjects are required to report consonants from tachistoscopically presented matrices under conditions of distraction. A tape recording of an animated group conversation begins broadcasting abruptly at the start of this task and continues until its completion. Base line performance levels in this task are obtained prior to the distraction condition. A general base line for span of apprehension is obtained by the tachistoscopic presentation of dots. Arousal level during preperformance rest periods and throughout the performance period are indexed by skin conductance and heart rate measurement.

In these experimental studies of attentional disorder and arousal in schizophrenia we are confronted by two major methodological problems. One of these has been a focus of this volume, namely, the validity of the concept of schizophrenia. The other is represented by the unwanted variance that psychotropic drugs—received by most schizophrenic patients—introduce into the measurement of psychophysiological arousal levels. It is relevant to a full understanding of our approach to discuss briefly the kinds of solutions to these problems that we have worked out.

We do not assume that the schizophrenic syndrome is a homogeneous entity. We recognize that under the general diagnostic label of schizophrenia are subsumed several distinctive groups of patients differing significantly with respect to etiology, prognosis, course of illness, and symptom formation. We expected therefore that with respect to attentional dysfunction, arousal level, and their interrelationship in schizophrenia several distinctive patterns were likely to emerge. In order to be able to identify these patterns as to origin, we have built into the design of our experiments three dimensions which subclassify the schizophrenic patients whom we select as subjects. These are classifying dimensions that represent individual differences among schizophrenics, that on the basis of available empirical evidence and clinical observation are thought to reflect underlying, coherent subsyndromes. To put it in statistical terms, they are dimensions which permit us to identify sources of variance in our data. These dimensions are length of hospitalization, the presence or absence of paranoid symptoms, and a process or reactive premorbid history. We use clinical judgment reflected in ratings of current behavior and ratings based on data in the clinical folders to classify patient subjects along these dimensions.

The problem of tranquilizing medication, mostly of the phenothiazine group, being received by most schizophrenics who are subjects in our research is a very thorny one. We have ample evidence from our first experimental study that phenothiazines affect the peripheral physiological responses—such as skin conductance and heart rate, which we measure to index arousal level. Phenothiazines suppress skin conductance level, elevate heart rate, and reduce cyclic variability in heart rate. In other words, these drugs are a source of variance that masks the disorder-related conditions we are attempting to study. As will be seen, in our first experimental study we used statistical means to control drug variance. In the two subsequent studies, however, we are accepting only schizophrenic subjects who are and have been drug free for some time. We are able to do this because we have negotiated agreements with the several psychiatric hospitals in Topeka to test schizophrenic patients—new and readmissions—before drug treatment is instituted.

The remainder of the chapter will be devoted to a description of a completed experimental study in this series and a discussion of some of the results. In this study we used span of apprehension for consonants to measure span of attention. This involved the visual presentation of a series of matrices of letters for brief durations, usually less than a second. Subjects were required to report the letters seen and their positions in the presentation matrix. This entire sequence from presentation to report, of course, engages other processes besides the focus of attention. The letters must not only be seen, they must be cognized, stored in short-term memory, retrieved, and written down for report. In this final product, i.e., the number of letters reported, all these processes are reflected. We sought, by systematically varying conditions of presentation and of report, to make it possible to isolate the contribution of attention.

Skin conductance was chosen as a principal measure of arousal, because it has been shown to vary with general alertness. Moreover, significant differences in basal skin conductance level and reactivity between normals and schizophrenic patients have been reported, as well as ranges of variation within unselected samples of schizophrenic patients. Heart rate measurement was included, since Lacey's work has indicated that heart rate may be particularly sensitive to attention and anticipation. Also, there is evidence of normal-schizophrenic differences in heart rate, as well as of such differences among schizophrenic subgroups. Two other physiological responses were measured, blood pulse volume and muscle tension. The results obtained with these will not, however, be a part of this report. In summary, we chose those measures of somatic arousal which gave the greatest promise of yielding wide ranges of variation in basal level within a schizophrenic patient sample and of significant differences in central tendency between schizophrenics and normal controls.

The subjects in this study were 32 male patients with a primary diagnosis of schizophrenia, between the ages of 18 and 55 years. Sixteen men in the Topeka Fire Department, who volunteered their paid services, served as normal controls.

The patient sample was selected to include in equal numbers patients with and without the presence of paranoid symptoms, first admissions with less than 18 months of hospitalization and patients hospitalized longer than three years, and patients with a rated poor or good premorbid history of social and psychosexual adjustment. Ratings of current behavior on the IMPS (5) were the basis of the paranoid-nonparanoid classification, and ratings on the Phillips (7) premorbid history scale, based on historical data in the clinical folder, served as the criterion for the good and poor premorbid history classification. Of the 32 schizophrenic subjects, 29 were receiving varying daily dosage levels of tranquilizing medication, all of the phenothiazine group.

All subjects were seen in four, hour-long experimental sessions. The procedures and results of the fourth and last session is the principal focus of this report. In this session, as in the preceeding sessions, subjects first had a ten-minute rest period during which resting heart rate, skin conductance, and reactivity were continuously recorded on a four-channel polygraph. Then subjects were instructed in the use of a tachistoscope, a device for the brief presentation of visual material. Forty cards, each with a rectangular array of 6 consonants, were then presented at exposure durations of 50 msec., 250 msec., 750 msec., and 1.1 sec. respectively. This condition of presentation will subsequently be referred to as *varied exposure duration*.

Following this procedure an additional 40 cards, again each with a rectangular array of 6 consonants, were presented for report. Exposure duration for each of these trials was 50 msec. This condition will be referred to as *constant exposure duration*. Throughout the performance of these tachistoscopic tasks, basal skin conductance level, reactivity, and heart rate, among other physiological responses, were monitored. In addition to these procedures, the Wechsler Memory Scale and WAIS Vocabulary Subscale were administered to all subjects.

After initial testing with all of these procedures, 20 of the 32 schizophrenics were withdrawn from tranquilizing medication and placed on placebos. Of these 20, 15 lasted the minimum 3-month period required for dissipation of phenothiazine body deposits. With these drug-free patients and 9 normal subjects the above procedures were then repeated.

In analyzing the data gathered in this fashion, we found that the normal subjects had significantly higher Wechsler Memory and Vocabulary scores than the schizophrenics; moreover both Wechsler Memory and Vocabulary Scale Scores correlated positively with the span of apprehension scores we obtained. In other words, it was evident that there were significant differences in general ability between schizophrenics and normals, which might account for differences in span of apprehension. Therefore, and before any further analysis, we used statistical methods designed to equate the span of apprehension scores of the two groups in this respect.

Analyses of data thus corrected indicate that span of apprehension, when exposure duration is a constant of 50 msec., is significantly lower in schizophrenics than it is in normals. The former report fewer letters correctly in place than the normal controls. When exposure duration is varied from 50 msec. to 1.1 sec., normal subjects report a larger number of consonants with each increase in exposure time. Schizophrenic patients show a similar improvement but at a lower level and a significantly lower rate of increment. This information processing deficit was also evident in the 15 schizophrenic patients withdrawn from phenothiazine medication, which along with other evidence, indicates that the deficit was not because of drug influence. It is of interest that variability in level of performance was about the same in schizophrenics and normals. Of all the comparisons made among the schizophrenic subgroups only one proved significant. Paranoid schizophrenics, particularly in the acute phase, show a significantly *lower* span of apprehension than nonparanoid schizophrenics.

As indicated earlier, the information processing deficit observed here in schizophrenics cannot be unequivocally interpreted as due primarily to a narrowed focus of attention to external stimuli. Other processes enter into determining the letter report response where the deficit is observed. However, the failure of the schizophrenics to improve their performance substantially as read-off time was increased in varied exposure durations is consistent with an interpretation that they permit significantly less information to enter the visual information processing channel.

That paranoid schizophrenics should perform more poorly in these tasks than nonparanoids appears surprising in the light of the presumed hyperattention of such patients. It should be noted, however, that in very brief presentations of letters visual hyperscanning would tend to interfere with efficient information extraction. Since, as reported above, we find paranoids to be visual hyperscanners, it seems highly probable that this tendency lowered their span of apprehension. It is of particular interest that paranoids, whom we generally assume to be exquisitely alert to the external environment, are actually under certain circumstances less efficient in deriving informative cues than other schizophrenic subgroups.

The data obtained through measurement of arousal show a rather complex picture and one that in the schizophrenics is obviously influenced by phenothiazine. Basal skin conductance levels during rest in schizophrenics are not significantly different from normals, but in the course of performance, the normal subjects show a characteristic rise in basal level and then a gradual adaptational return to resting level. The basal level of schizophrenics in performance, by contrast, at first drops and then rises gradually back to resting levels. In heart rate schizophrenics are significantly higher, both during rest and during performance, than normal controls. That the schizophrenic psychophysiological pattern is largely because of drug influence is evident in two ways. The 15 patients who were withdrawn from medication for 3 months show upon withdrawal resting and performance basal skin conductance levels that are significantly higher than those of the repeated normals and their own prewithdrawal levels. Heart rate drops significantly but remains higher than that of normals. In other words, on withdrawal of drugs this subgroup of schizophrenics relative to normal controls can be regarded as hyperaroused.

We developed a phenothiazine dosage index which represents daily dosages of phenothiazine as milligrams per kilogram of body weight, corrected for potency differences among phenothiazines, to further assess drug influence. The pattern of correlations of this index and arousal measures from patients on drugs indicated principally that phenothiazines lower basal skin conductance and elevate heart rate. These findings made it possible, by means of regression analysis, to derive arrays of skin conductance and heart rate scores for the schizophrenic patients, which were independent of the influence of dosage level. It is these drug-free scores that were used to assess the relationships between arousal level and attention as measured in this study.

Our findings in this regard are entirely negative. Individual differences among schizophrenics and among normal controls in basal skin conductance level and in heart rate are not significantly correlated with individual differences in span scores, that is, with information processing efficiency. The same negative results are obtained in the albeit small sample of drug-withdrawn schizophrenic patients. If basal skin conductance level and heart rate level are taken as valid measures of arousal, the conclusion must be that within the limits of the range of variation, as obtained in the normal and schizophrenic samples, arousal level and attentional efficiency are not related.

These first results in our series of studies of attention-arousal relationships are not decisive for schizophrenics because even with the statistical correction, the phenothiazines compressed variability in arousal level in the patient group.

This inference is underlined by the fact that both skin conductance level and heart rate scores, reflecting autonomic reactivity, which appeared to be uninfluenced by drugs, correlated with span scores. A skin conductance level difference score, reflecting individual differences in the rate of adaptation of basal level during the performance trials, correlated positively in normals and negatively in schizophrenics with span of apprehension scores. This suggests that normals whose basal level dropped more rapidly and schizophrenics whose basal level rose more rapidly were more efficient in information processing. In heart rate a score reflecting individual differences in pre- and post-trial deceleration proved to be positively correlated with information processing efficiency. It seems reasonable to infer from these findings in both schizophrenics and normals that a variable such as autonomic flexibility is related to attentive alertness to the external environment, but that the results of the present study do not permit decisive conclusions about the relationship between basal levels and efficiency in information processing.

REFERENCES

1. Bleuler, E.: *Dementia Praecox or the Group of Schizophrenias*. New York: International Universities Press, 1950.
2. Chapman, J.: The Early Symptoms of Schizophrenia. *British Journal of Psychiatry*, 112:225-251, 1966.
3. Holzman, P. S.: Perceptual Research in the Schizophrenic Reactions. In Cancro, R. (Ed.), *The Schizophrenic Reactions: A Critique of the Concept, Hospital Treatment, and Current Research*. New York: Brunner/Mazel, Inc., 1969.

4. Lacey, J. I.: Somatic Response Patterning and Stress: Some Revisions of Activation Theory. In Appley, M. H. and Trumbull, R. (Eds.), *Psychological Stress*. New York: Appleton, 1967.

5. Lorr, M. and Klett, C. J.: *Inpatient Multidimensional Psychiatric Scale* (Manual and Centile Ranks). Washington: Authors, 1966.

6. McGhie, A., Chapman, J., and Lawson, J. S.: The Effect of Distraction on Schizophrenic Performance. (I) Perception and Immediate Memory. *British Journal of Psychiatry*, 111:383-390, 1965.

7. Phillips, L.: Case History Data and Prognosis in Schizophrenia. *Journal of Nervous and Mental Disease*, 117:515-525, 1953.

8. Shakow, D.: Psychological Deficit in Schizophrenia. *Behavioral Science*, 8:275-305, 1963.

9. Silverman, J.: The Problem of Attention in Research and Theory in Schizophrenia. *Psychological Review*, 71:352-379, 1964.

10. Venables, P. H.: Input Dysfunction in Schizophrenia. In Maher, B. A. (Ed.), *Progress in Experimental Personality Research*. New York: Academic Press, 1964.

21

Panel Discussion on Research on the Schizophrenic Syndrome

ROBERT CANCRO, M.D., DONALD L. BURNHAM, M.D.,
PHILIP S. HOLZMAN, Ph.D., SEYMOUR S. KETY, M.D.,
DAVID ROSENTHAL, Ph.D., HERBERT E. SPOHN, Ph.D.,
and PAUL E. THETFORD, Ph.D.

Doctor Cancro: There were two questions raised by Doctor Rosenthal's paper that I shall bring up in general terms for the panel to react to, and then we shall address ourselves to questions that came up from the floor. Doctor Rosenthal mentioned that the clinical picture of psychopathology tends to be more severe in catatonics and hebephrenics than in simple or paranoid forms of the illness. On the other hand, prognosis does not seem to bear the same relationship in that the hebephrenic and simple groups tend to have a worse prognosis than the catatonic or paranoid groups. I wonder how does he reconcile this difference between the presenting symptomatology and the ultimate outcome? Another issue that struck me in Doctor Rosenthal's paper was a tremendously important practical question. He spoke of what is currently considered genetic counseling, and said, "it will lead to an increase of rate of schizophrenia in the next generation. The sound basis of counseling such individuals could prevent an increase from occurring." This, of course, raises a whole host of medical, social, ethical, and moral questions; including the effect of the push in community psychiatry to get chronic schizophrenic patients out of the hospital and into community activities and social situations, in which they are more likely to meet and more likely to mate. If we see the patient's withdrawal as psychopathology and not as an adaptive effort necessary for the maintenance of the organism, we may make many "therapeutic" efforts to overcome this social withdrawal with the resulting offspring that are to be expected when social withdrawal is overcome. This seems to be a problem worthy of comment, and as Chairman I pass it on to the panel and leave it to someone else!

Doctor Rosenthal: You raised two points and one had to do with the question of symptom severity in the different subtypes. I use the term severity in the paper in a very shorthand way, because when we talk about severity it becomes a major problem in and of itself. What I am talking about is primarily clinical severity. If you have ever tried to rate a group of patients on a ward in terms of severity, for example, ask nurses who is the sickest patient on the ward, who is the next sickest, etc., and then ask aides, then ask psychiatrists, you will find the correlations are very high. You don't have to specify what your criteria are for sickness. How does severity of illness bear on the prognosis? Well, I really don't know. The prognosis for all of them is pretty poor, and when you have different studies that have been done over a period of time, the results have not been consistent. Again, in all these studies we have the problem of who made the diagnosis. That's a kind of nebulous area, and I really can't give you a definite answer.

The second question had to do with the moral implications. It doesn't matter if the parents are schizophrenic because of genetic or other reasons, we know that there is an elevated incidence of schizophrenia in the offspring of such parents. Studies by Erlenmeyer-Kimling and her colleagues at the New York Psychiatric Institute show that when they compare the fertility of schizophrenics in the 1930s as against schizophrenics in the 1950s fertility has increased, although it is still lower for the schizophrenic as compared to the normal population. Nevertheless, there is a clear indication of increased fertility, and the more children they have the more schizophrenics they are going to produce. The implications are sociopsychiatric in nature, and I don't feel competent to discuss them.

Doctor Cancro: Let me reformulate the question slightly and then torment the rest of my colleagues with it. We recognize that the probability of the change in fertility between 1930 and 1950 being a result of an improvement in the egg or in the sperm is essentially zero, and therefore we have to assume that the fertility rate does not reflect some change in the genetic, biological potential but rather differences in social experiences. In the 1930s we were more likely to lock such patients up in the hospital and essentially to forget about them, or at least forget about them during their reproductive years. In the 1950s there was a dramatic change with the advent of phenothiazines. In the 1960s there is enormous pressure to keep patients out of the hospital and in a variety of social situations. The probability is very high that fertility in schizophrenics will continue to show the same trend and soon will approximate or equal the fertility of the population at large. The question then becomes rather loaded, in terms of the conflict between responsible genetic counseling on the one hand and our rather humanistic desire to encourage people who suffer from this syndrome to lead as "normal a life as possible."

Doctor Kety: Fools step in where angels fear to tread. I'd rather not consider the question of whether the State has the obligation or the right to impose restrictions on the freedom of individuals to become parents. But there is a matter of the right of each of us to as much information as we can have. Certainly there are no moral restrictions that I can think of to acquiring and promulgating factual information. If the medical profession can define the risk of certain types of disorders as a result of a union of two particular people, the least that we can do is to make that information available to the people involved, whether or not the State is interested in this. In fact, this is not only a question that applies to schizophrenia, but to many areas of medicine where genetic factors are more clearly known to operate, e.g., the recessive mutant disorders where heterozygotes may be quite normal clinically, and the problem arises only from the mating of two such individuals. I am sure that in the years to come more and more simple biochemical tests will be developed for determining heterozygosity for a number of genes that are involved in such disorders. That information should be made known to the individual and perhaps would be of interest to prospective mates as well. Now one could even think, since we are computer dating nowadays, how we could be computer mating in a few more decades. Although it certainly sounds unaesthetic and hard-boiled, nevertheless if you force yourself, you can see a certain amount of rationality to it. We choose our mates on the basis of certain obvious characteristics, and we make these deliberate choices on the basis of our own tastes. There is no reason at all why we shouldn't take into consideration the genes in our prospective mates. One could look at the gene profile of a potential mate just as one looks at his or her other profile, before one decides whether this is to be the one and only. Aside from that kind of speculative fantasy this kind of information is very valuable in questions of intervention in pregnancy or early treatment of mutant disorders. This information can aid the parents to arrive at their greatest exercise of enlightened freedom.

Doctor Cancro: I sincerely hope Doctor Kety does not intend to automate the entire mating procedure. Although I concede the genetic profile in many ways might be more reliable and less subject to deception than the anatomical profile, I still think his whole argument turns on the word "informed." If the patient is chronically psychotic, what meaning does "informed" have in that particular case?

Doctor Kety: Simply that it's better than "uninformed."

Doctor Burnham: One thing is clear and that is the information that we can provide as of now is not at the point that we can envision for the future. Doctor Rosenthal raised in his paper the old question of the relationship between genius and insanity, especially when you've got this schizophreniform continuum. I should certainly hate to think we conceivably might rule out the possibility of mutants who were going to be the extraordinarily creative scientific or artistic geniuses. We might lose a Strindberg or a Fechner, who went through a schizophreniform episode and emerged with an extraordinary burst of creativity in a new direction. We'd also want to look at this on such a profile, if we could.

Doctor Thetford: Interestingly enough, a Russian researcher has been working with some word-association and word-conception tests which are almost tests of creativity in that the patient has to think of unusual uses for objects such as a tin can. In his studies he noted that the schizophrenic was much more original in this kind of test than his normal controls.

Doctor Cancro: We have a question for Doctor Burnham. Given the studies of dreaming using REM technology, is it still possible to maintain Freud's view that the function of dreams is to preserve sleep? Secondly, is it necessary to your thesis that at least part of the restructuring behavior of schizophrenics serves to control stimulus input or intensity to utilize the psychoanalytic theory of dreams?

Doctor Burnham: The preservation of sleep is not the only purpose of dreaming. One of the things that the REM studies have shown is that dreaming serves other vital psychic functions. In response to the second part I'd say no, it is not necessary.

Doctor Holzman: There is a vast empiric literature that's been increasing by large proportions since the Aserinsky and Kleitman study in the early 1950s. The finding that rapid eye movement sleep and low voltage fast EEG waves coincide with the reports of dreams does not, in my view, contradict the psychoanalytic views of dreaming. Even in that experimental literature there are almost as many interpretations of the purpose of REM sleep as there are studies—a hyperbole that makes the point that the correlation is not an explanation. For example, Berger proposes that the purpose of dreaming is to maintain binocular convergence. There are many other theories ranging from the neurophysiological to the highly psychological. Indeed, we are now finding that the experience of dreaming is not to be identified with REM-stage 1 sleep. If I were asked what I thought was the main aspect of Freud's dream theory, I'd say all Freud meant was that the content of dreams is not without meaning, not without significance. They are not somatic, and they do not occur by chance. I don't think the neurophysiological studies of dreaming really touch on those issues at all.

Doctor Cancro: Just to expand one point that Doctor Holzman made, it is essential to understand that there is no inherent contradiction just because there is some efficiency. Dreaming serves a variety of functions which can be conceptualized in neurophysiological terms, in psychological terms, or a variety of other terms. These do not necessarily contradict each other. The argument gets back to the unfortunate dichotomy between organic and psychological. If dreaming serves a physiological function then it can't serve a psychological function. Eating is a very clear instance of a biological need which has many psychological overlays. I think it is very important to emphasize that independent of the strength of the evidence that a particular phenomenon serves a certain function, it can serve a variety of other functions as well.

This question is directed to the panel at large, but I suspect the author intended it more for Doctors Kety and Rosenthal. Some researchers are interested in the effects of maternal anxiety on the fetus and find high relationships between anxious mothers and anxious infants. How might this be relevant to the genetic transmission research?

Doctor Rosenthal: I don't know of any good studies that have taken into account anxiety in the parent and anxiety in the child. Anxiety is a pretty slippery term. It depends on how you want to measure it, e.g., subjective anxiety or various psychophysiological indices. With respect to what bearing this kind of phenomenon might have on the genetic transmission of disorders like schizophrenia, the easiest way to get around that problem is to deal with fathers instead of mothers. You obtain a cohort of schizophrenic fathers, and then you obtain a cohort of schizophrenic mothers, and you look at your dependent variable (the incidence of schizophrenic disorders) in the two sets of children that arise from the two groups of parents. We are looking at this kind of phenomenon in our Denmark study. Other people who have done studies in this area report little difference between the rate of schizophrenia in the offspring of schizophrenic fathers as against schizophrenic mothers.

Doctor Kety: There was another question which I think came from Doctor Gruenberg and which relates to the question Doctor Rosenthal just answered. I'd like to read his question and then comment upon both. The high frequency of schizophrenic spectrum cases in natural relatives of your index cases could be due to gene selection, but couldn't the finding be due to familial concentrations of risk of exposure to damaging physical agents acting in early life, e.g., malnutrition, viruses, and toxins? Of course 19 of our index cases did not share any of the environment of their biological parents, having spent, with few exceptions, less than a week with the mother on a maternity ward. But, Doctor Gruenberg could have asked the question even more pointedly by saying that we had not eliminated intrauterine environment in our studies. Ideally, of course, the separation from the biological family should have occurred at the time of fertilization of the egg. That is a little difficult to do, and so we were satisfied to have the separation occur within the first month of life. But interestingly enough there are some data in our study which I think rule out the intrauterine and early environmental influences that Doctor Gruenberg was referring to. And that is the fact that of those 13 affected biological relatives with schizophrenic spectrum disorders, a substantial number were half-siblings and about 5 were paternal half-siblings. Now the paternal half-siblings don't share the intrauterine environment. The only thing they share is a portion of the genetic pool with the index case. It's still possible that in these cases the father could have inoculated the eggs with a virus of some kind, but I think the prevalence in paternal half-siblings makes it unlikely that environmental factors operating even in the course of the early life experience of the fetus were the important factors.

Doctor Cancro: I have a question here for Doctors Spohn and Thetford. You mention that phenothiazine drugs apparently cause changes in heart rate and skin conductance. You also mentioned that subjects who were taken off drugs showed some lowering of heart rate. This finding could be because of activity increases secondary to experimental manipulation and any number of other things. Critical to your finding would be the repeated measurement of the patients who were not taken off drugs. Was this measurement taken?

Doctor Thetford: No, we did not repeat another sample of patients who were still on drugs. We repeated the measurement on the sample of 15 who had remained off drugs for three months, and then we randomly selected our normal controls and repeated the same kind of tests with them. This is where we found that the heart rate decreased significantly in the patients after three months off drugs, but still remained significantly higher than that of the normal control group. Another point is that we depended upon our phenothiazine dosage index to tell us about the effect of the amount of drugs upon the heart rate. The highly significant correlation between the new index score and the heart rate gave us evidence that the phenothiazines were having an effect. Ideally it would have been best to repeat a sample of the patients who were still on drugs, but we did not do that.

Doctor Cancro: I should like to add one or two minor points to what Paul Thetford has already said. In general, one has to raise the question of the most economical explanation possible for what you observe. Now, it was very clear that when these patients were taken off drugs, as far as we could see nothing else had been changed in their State Hospital environment. Those of you who are familiar with State Hospitals know that it is difficult to find a more constant environment, and there was this consistent pattern in those patients who were taken off drugs. In addition, in running some of our normal pilot cases, we accidentally came across some who were taking phenothiazine drugs, and we were able to make this "diagnosis" of drug ingestion on the basis of the tracing. The tracing showed the characteristic high, relatively unvariable heart rate. So while this is kind of anecdotal, we do see it as supporting evidence. We also felt that the explanation offered was the most parsimonious.

We have a rather long question here directed to Doctor Kety. In view of the difficulty of making a conclusive diagnosis of schizophrenia, even by detailed personal interviews supplemented by psychological testing, the reliability of making such a diagnosis on the basis of translated records should be considered highly suspect. Only one of 150 biological relatives of his dubiously established index group could be diagnosed as chronic schizophrenia (the others being either borderline, doubtful borderline, or inadequate personality) which is a true incidence of only .67% or considerably less than in the general population. How can any conclusions concerning a genetic etiology be supported? In view of the questionable validity of the present conclusions and the doubtful significance even if such conclusions were certain, would not continuing such an obviously expensive project be a misuse of time, effort, and financial resources which could be channeled into more worthwhile pursuits?

Doctor Kety: Of course this is a perfectly appropriate question; it's one that we as scientists ask ourselves all the time, because even more important than the expenditure of public funds is the expenditure of one's short life-span on a particular thesis. So we have entertained this question at all points, but have come up with just the opposite conclusion. I think the questioner is operating upon a simple fallacy. A measurement which is difficult to make in a properly designed study that avoids subjective bias only makes significant findings more difficult to come by, but does not affect the significance of the findings. I'd turn the question around and say, isn't it interesting that in spite of the fact that it's so difficult to make the diagnosis of schizophrenia, the results come out with such a high degree of statistical significance? This suggests to me that there must be some validity to the criteria which we used for schizophrenia, to the hypothesis we were testing, and that there must be some validity to the concept of schizophrenia. If we took each of our four individual, independent evaluations of the diagnoses in the families, we would have come up with exactly the same conclusion. The preponderance of illnesses in our arbitrarily preconceived spectrum of disorders was significantly higher in the biological families of the index cases, and that was the only population in which the incidence was other than random.

Doctor Holzman: I think that questioner asked the sixty-four-thousand-dollar question. That question could be asked of all of the studies that were reported or alluded to by the members of the panel. That is, how do you know that you are dealing with what you say you are dealing with? Further, how do you know that what you think you are dealing with exists? Although we don't have an answer to it that will satisfy everybody, there is no reason to throw up our hands and say we can't do anything about it. Psychiatrists and others who have worked in state hospitals, in private psychiatric hospitals, or in general medical hospitals know that there is such an entity as the schizophrenic syndrome, although there is vast disagreement about whether or not it is unitary. There is some kind of consensus that we are really dealing with a recognizable disorder. The issue is how do you measure it? I remember a statement that Paul Meehl made about this. He wrote that if a patient says the

FBI is tapping his telephone, or he feels extremely anxious, or he thinks that his wife has been unfaithful to him, and so on, it is not possible from these introspective reports to make the diagnosis of schizophrenia. For there is not sufficient evidence. These experiences are not exclusive in schizophrenia. If the patient says, however, "I am growing my father's hair," there is a kind of alarming specificity about such a statement that makes you say, "probably schizophrenia." So I think that the task really is to come up with some kind of measure that will address itself to the quality of the thought disorder, the intensity of the thought disorder, and the phasic variations of the thought disorder. If we can get agreement on these we may be able to answer the question that was addressed to the panel.

Doctor Kety: A brief afterthought. Someone once said in reply to the controversy about whether Homer had really written the *Iliad* that it wasn't Homer but was someone else with the same name. I really think that one can finesse the question of whether schizophrenia exists. I find it very compelling that independent observers looking at a variety of individuals can come up with agreement that certain people differ from the rest and that they differ according to certain characteristics. If it happens also that one wants to call those characteristics schizophrenia, that is a useful appellation until one has a more specific and less phenomenological cluster of manifestations and symptoms, and a better term for them. It is difficult to deny that qualified observers of assorted populations can still agree that there is such a cluster.

Doctor Cancro: I should like to follow up on this question by complicating it one step further. Following along the line of reasoning that one can't step into the same river twice, perhaps not even once, it is not only a question of arriving at some sort of agreement as to a description of a syndrome and which members of the population belong to this class. Anyone who has had any clinical experience with people designated schizophrenic knows that they are no more constant than the rest of us and very likely even less constant. So when we do research, especially of a psychophysiological and psychological nature, we have several problems to consider. If you are talking about attention in schizophrenia, you are not dealing with a static factor. You are dealing with something which fluctuates in all of us. If we had a continuous barometer of level of attention, we should see that it goes through broad sweeps. The schizophrenic seems to show even greater clinical variability in issues of this sort. We also have the problem of differences which are a function of the phase of the illness. Is it an acute schizophrenia? Is it more of a chronic schizophrenia? Is he at this point acutely delusional, hallucinated, confused, and near-disoriented, or is he relatively clear with a circumscribed area of delusional thinking. You have variation in the patient as a function of diagnostic subcategory, phase of the illness, moment-to-moment fluctuations, and at this stage of our knowledge, we can only look for trends, until such time as we can arrive at tightly homogeneous populations.

Doctor Holzman: I just want to add one thing to that. There may be a distinct advantage in investigating a phenomenon that has very little specificity, that is rather vaguely defined, that we find very hard to articulate, because if you prematurely pin down your definitions, you may rule out of consideration the very phenomenon that you are trying to measure. Said another way, if you try to define it prematurely and say what it is and what it is not, you may simply lose the correlations between that concept and real data. I do not regard this kind of vagueness as really hampering our work. I think that in a way it is a mixed blessing. I'd want to continue, as a scientist, to make use of the null hypothesis but not the "nihilistic hypothesis."

Doctor Burnham: Well, I think this subtype issue is an important part of the diagnostic problem and several people have touched on the fact that once a particular subtype, not always a particular subtype. This does get involved with phase of illness, and I think one has to look at the long-term course. One of the great merits of Bleuler's work was that he lived in a relatively small and stable Swiss village. Some of the patients that eventually came into the Burghölzli he had known as schoolmates and chums, and not only that but when they left the hospital he saw them on the street as fellow villagers. He had a sense of the natural history and the phases of the disorder. There have been various people who have formulated that, for instance, a catatonic may go on to become either a paranoid or a hebephrenic. I have also seen patients who have been diagnosed manic-depressive at one time of their life and then subsequently diagnosed as schizophrenic. So even that isn't such a sharp difference.

Doctor Cancro: This question is addressed to Doctors Spohn and Thetford. In your study was attention given to how the subjects construed the experimental situation?

Doctor Spohn: We didn't give any formal attention to this. We didn't make any attempt to interview or to elicit from our subjects through other ways what their attitudes and orientations were to the experimental situation. I think it is probably fair to say that taking the patient group as a whole, their construction of the meaning of that situation was more heterogeneous than that of our Topeka Fire Department normal controls who, for the most part, were interested in doing well and demonstrating their acuity and ability in the situation, particularly in light of the fact that they knew they were a comparison group for mental patients. This raises the inevitable question in research of this kind—where a measure of efficiency in performance is a dependent variable—as to whether or not the motivation of the patient group was a factor in producing the kinds of results that were obtained. It is not beyond the realm of possibility, in fact it is a rather worrisome probability, that the information-processing deficit we uncovered was primarily because of a lower level of interest in adequate performance in that situation on the part of the patients. This is an issue that can't be dismissed lightly and indeed deserves a replicative follow-up. I might add we found a fair number of the patients, particularly those of a chronic status, with a relatively stable adjustment to the hospital situation with no active ongoing treatment program, were delighted to serve as subjects in this experiment. It got them off a relatively uninteresting ward and involved in something that apparently did offer some interest to them. Some of them keep asking us periodically, "Doctor, when am I going to get my next treatment?" So for some of them we do have information about how they construed the experimental experience. What bearing this had on their performance we can guess at, but we don't know for sure.

Let me take this opportunity to respond to a question that Doctor Cancro raised about the implications of our findings with patients who were found to be manifesting paranoid symptomatology at the time that we saw them. Our finding is one of lowered—significantly lowered—information-processing efficiency in this particular group, which runs counter to what has been a hypothesis for a long time, namely, that paranoid schizophrenics are hyperattentive to the external environment. Our finding also runs counter to findings in some experimental studies of superior perceptual efficiency on the part of paranoid types. In studies of size-estimation, of size-constancy, etc., it has been found that in these kinds of structured perceptual tasks, paranoids seem to perform at a level even above that of normal controls. The important point, as I think Doctor Cancro has already implied, is that the task we asked of the paranoid patients is one in which the visual hyperscanning (which does appear to be a characteristic propensity of such patients) could not aid them in the solution. If anything, the exposure durations—the periods of time during which the material was available for reception—were so short that a blink or a darting eye movement would have led them to miss the material entirely. This is apparently what happened to the paranoid patients. In a study that is now in progress, where we are examining eye-movement patterns on the part of schizophrenic and nonschizophrenic patients, we find that in an exploratory free-scanning situation paranoid schizophrenics are hyperscanners, i.e., they move their eyes a good deal more than anybody else. We find also, and rather unexpectedly, that they have the highest blink rate. Now in a free-scanning exploratory situation both rapid-scanning movements and blinking lead to loss of information. It is of considerable interest that in a nonfocused kind of situation, as far as the use of the eyes on the part of paranoid schizophrenics is concerned, they are much less efficient. One is almost led to suspect that these are avoidance measures, rather than maneuvers designed to bring in more information.

Doctor Burnham: Just one point. This does get into the meaning of the whole experimental session and also gets into the question of what is especially relevant to the paranoid. One might presume that the paranoid patient might be hypervigilant toward certain things but not toward others. He would be very alert to certain kinds of things because they resonated with something that was preoccupying him, and I can even conceive of experiments where he'd think you were trying to get something on him. In these he might perform extremely well. But if he felt reasonably comfortable, his vigilance might be somewhere else rather than on the task you're presenting to him.

Doctor Cancro: Let me address the next question to Doctor Kety, since he has shown a willingness to tread where angels won't, and let's see if anyone else on the panel will join him on his foray. Do you foresee any major breakthrough in biochemical studies of schizophrenia in the next five to ten years?

Doctor Kety: Ten years ago I had occasion to review the biochemical studies in schizophrenia. After giving it a great deal of consideration, I could not honestly say that there was an area of biochemistry which I could advise a young man to go into with the expectation that following that up would lead to a greater understanding of schizophrenia. I don't believe I see at the present time an area any more clearly highlighted as being directly related to etiology in schizophrenia, at least in biochemical terms. Doctor Rosenthal pointed out that the genetic factors which appear to operate in schizophrenia, although again not exclusively, must operate at a biochemical level at some point but they could very easily be determining the networks of the brain, the interconnections of the brain, and through them personality characteristics, response to environmental stress, etc. And if that should be the case, then a simple biochemical approach is hardly likely to elucidate the biological aspects of the difficulty.

Doctor Cancro: Would anyone care to comment on any clinical breakthroughs that can be foreseen in the next decade or two?

Doctor Thetford: Quite recently I finished reading a book by Philip May, called the *Treatment of Schizophrenia: A Comparison of Five Treatment Methods.* I think it is a classic and elegant study of treatment. The sophistication of those researchers was very impressive. May even had a chapter on cost accounting, which is going to please state officials all over the country when they read about the cost of different kinds of treatments. The major conclusion from Philip May's study is that the phenothiazines are extremely effective. They were as effective as phenothiazines plus psychotherapy. There were no differences between these two groups. Now I really have a strong impression that this study is so well done that people are going to be able to generalize from it to other states and to other populations of patients. I also think that it gives us a good strong hint as to approaching the problem of schizophrenia through the back door. Why do the phenothiazines work? If we can figure out in the next few years what the phenothiazines are doing to a person's autonomic nervous system, to his psychological and especially cognitive processes, then maybe this way we can get hints about multiple biochemical factors, or physiological factors, or causative factors in the schizophrenic syndrome.

Doctor Spohn: Not only do I agree entirely with Doctor Thetford that this is a productive research strategy, but I'd like to add that it may be the only strategy that is left to experimental research in this area because of the enormous difficulty in finding patients who are free of medication. Those who are drug-free represent selected individuals with special characteristics of their own. There are experimental risks involved in withdrawing patients for periods of time from medication, that have to do simply with selection and the problem of the uncertainty about the length of time required for complete dissipation of the phenothiazine and other psychotropic drug body deposits. It may be necessary as well as heuristically desirable to get under way studies that address themselves in detail to the nature, at every level, of drug action in schizophrenia.

Doctor Holzman: The Philip May study does raise the question of what kind of research methods promise potential breakthroughs. I'm not sure that the method adopted in this study is the one that promises the greatest advance in solving the mystery of schizophrenia. Rather, I'd look to a method that reflects a stroke of genius on the part of Sarnoff Mednick, the use of high risk or vulnerable children as subjects, that is, the children of schizophrenic parents, but particularly of schizophrenic mothers. It is a most powerful tool, because we have become very well aware of all of the methodological difficulties involved in trying to study schizophrenia in already schizophrenic patients. All of the results that we have been talking about have been on studies of hospitalized schizophrenic patients. There have been very few studies of patients in remission—and those studies have been mainly follow-up studies. They have not been process studies of the same kind as we were talking about in the Spohn-Thetford-Cancro study or in the studies I reported on this morning. These are extremely difficult to do. In other words, we really don't know what is characteristic of the schizophrenic patient. I think the only way to really get at this is to do a thorough study of high risk children, a significant number of whom will develop schizophrenic psychoses at some time in their lives.

Doctor Kety: There is another study which fully corroborates the Philip May study, and that was a collaborative study in which a number of institutions participated. It was reported by Cole and his collaborators. The phenothiazines were clearly of great efficacy in the treatment of acute schizophrenic reactions. And I would certainly agree that a knowledge of how these drugs work in schizophrenia would be extremely useful. At the present time I don't see a clear biochemical hypothesis, as I do in the case of many of the drugs which are effective in the treatment of affective psychoses. The fact that a drug works doesn't necessarily imply a simple, biochemical etiology. A drug may work, not necessarily by antagonizing or blocking a single enzyme defect, but by acting upon systems of neurons in a way to compensate for deficits elsewhere. Nevertheless, I'd heartily agree that it would be most worthwhile to continue efforts to find a mechanism of action in the phenothiazine drugs.

Doctor Cancro: Please comment on the association between concordance rate and severity, and the differences in concordance rates in monozygotic twins as a function of the sex of the pair. Can there be a sex-linked polygenic model?

Doctor Rosenthal: There's no good evidence to think that schizophrenia involves any kind of sex linkage. At one time a couple of investigators tried to check this out with the known data, and they gave up on the entire hypothesis. Since then all the data would go counter to thinking in terms of any kind of sex linkage. Now with respect to concordance in the two sexes, when I reviewed the literature in the past I found that concordance rates were higher for female monozygotic twins as compared to male monozygotic twins. The same thing held true for female and male dizygotic twins. There seemed to be a higher concordance for sex in first-degree family relatives. Now this review was based on older studies, most of which were done in Europe and done at a different time. My own conclusions about these findings has a kind of familial-psychological orientation, because I think girls at that time were more confined to the home, more restricted in the activities that they could engage in, more inhibited with respect to various kinds of patterns of living. Males were permitted to roam freely, to separate from a family more, to become more detached. And it may be that the concordance rates that we found reflected this difference in living pattern between the two sexes. Now with the great revolution and emancipation of women, it would be nice to have studies that had enough twins so that you could make comparisons between the two sexes. The studies that have been done recently—one in England and one in Norway—had moderate-sized samples. And in these two studies there was not much indication of a difference in concordance rates between male and female monozygotic twins. Now this serves to support my former hypothesis or bias, if you will, but I doubt that we'll find these kinds of differences in the future. With respect to severity, one of the main points I've raised in the past was that if you begin with the cohort of twins where the twins are severely ill, you will get a higher concordance rate with respect to schizophrenia than in a study that begins with schizophrenics who were not as severely ill. The studies that have been done since I proposed this hypothesis have all pretty much corroborated this notion. Doctors Pollin and Stabenau have been fortunate in obtaining a roster of all twins who had been in military service. Now schizophrenics who are able to get into military service have gone past a certain kind of screen and therefore are not a random sample which would include very severely ill schizophrenics. They came up with a concordance rate in these veteran twins of approximately 15%, which is quite low and quite a contrast to the 86% Kallman reported. And so this, too, I take as corroborative evidence for the notion that I raised in the past that you can influence the concordance rate according to how you select your index cases in the twin studies.

Dr. Cancro: Doctor Rosenthal will have to leave us in about fifteen minutes in order to make a flight; so I'm going to give him some consecutive questions from the audience. First, isn't there a contradiction between Doctor Kety's report that acute patients were not hereditarily linked and Doctor Rosenthal's statement that they were?

Doctor Rosenthal: The answer is yes.

Doctor Cancro: We still have fourteen minutes to go.

Doctor Rosenthal: Let me just add a little bit to that. If you look at the literature and start with hard-core schizophrenics, and ask what is the incidence of acute schizophrenic reactions (which in Europe they might call schizophreniform psychoses) among their families, you would find an elevated incidence of such disorders. Why didn't we find that? Well, I have a sneaking suspicion that one of our problems was that in cases that we called B2 or acute schizophrenic reaction, we were dealing with a group where the clinical conditions involved things like postpartum psychosis or acute psychotic reactions in senile people. We didn't know what to do with them, and the best diagnosis seemed to be a B2. Now it may be that this kind of psychotic reaction really does not belong in what we typically call reactive schizophrenia in this country. In another study that we're doing—the adoptee study—we deal with the offspring of a biological schizophrenic parent that is reared adoptively. If the biological schizophrenic parent was given a B2 diagnosis (and we weren't concerned here with postpartum or any of the other possibly confounding types of biological disorders), we are finding that we do get an elevated incidence of what we call schizophrenic spectrum disorder among such offspring. This would be more consistent with the old European findings. Now these are just conjectures and we can't say anything definite about it at this time.

Doctor Kety: I want to contradict Doctor Rosenthal slightly and to amplify some of the comments that he made. The highly questionable acute schizophrenic reactions were those in which we had a divided opinion. I remember specifically one in which two of us called it a post-partum psychosis and two called it an acute schizophrenic reaction, and because we didn't arrive at a consensus that case was not included in the tally. Another one was an amphetamine psychosis in which there was a divided opinion. I think that the apparent contradiction can prob-ably be explained by the fact that the acute schizophrenic reactions in the study which I reported were those in which no other schizophrenia diagnosis was entertainable. In other words, if a patient came into a hos-pital with what looked like an acute schizophrenic reaction at one time, but then came back repeatedly with other schizophrenic reactions either acute or of a more chronic nature, that individual would not have been called an acute schizophrenic reaction by us but would have been called a borderline or a more chronic kind of schizophrenia. In that particular study we had a long-time scale over which to examine the diagnostic categories into which the patient fell, so we'd have excluded the early schizophrenias because they would eventually have become one of the other types. Now if one is looking at a single instance without that history, it may very well be that what we are today calling acute schizophrenic reaction in America and what we may call acute schizophrenic reaction in other phases of the study are those who are eventually going to become chronic schizophrenics and in the adoption study would actually have been called chronic schizophrenics.

Doctor Rosenthal: Let me just say one sentence here, and that is, when we look at the parents whom we've called acute schizophrenic reactions they also were primarily one-time admissions, and that's why we call them B2; but we didn't have any of this confounding of some other possible organic disorder.

Doctor Cancro: If you identify gene carriers early in life, aren't you risking the problem of the self-fulfilling prophecy that Doctor Menninger warns us of? Informing a person that he has a high risk for schizophrenia might be stressful enough to serve as a precipitating or, at least, a pre-disposing factor in itself.

Doctor Rosenthal: I certainly wouldn't tell the children that they have a high risk for schizophrenia; I don't see that there's any need to do this. If we really learn enough from studies like Sarnoff Mednick's or the one I'm conducting in Israel about the environmental variables that either encourage the development of a schizophrenic process or tend to discourage such development, then there's no reason why these things that we learn couldn't be transposed to special kinds of schools and the potentials of these children assured so that they will find expression in a nonpsychotic way. This is a goal I have and a goal I plan to stick with, at least for a while.

Doctor Cancro: We have a question for Doctor Holzman. Could you clarify what you mean by feedback in a situation of visual observation with no precise motor or exocrine response expected? Is the orienting response eye movement or visual data feedback or what?

Doctor Holzman: I'm not sure I fully understand the question, but I'll try to clarify what I mean by perceptual feedback and hope that suffices. If you are looking for a particular person in a crowd and the room is tightly packed and you suddenly see him, you know that you have seen him partly through a postural response to the sensory input. Now this postural response is proprioceptive; it's autonomic. There may be other factors involved in it, too. It's this kind of response that reports to us that we've seen what it is that we are looking for. Now it's more than feedback, because we are responding to that kind of a motor report which then feeds forward so we know what to do. If we put our hands on a hot stove and we feel the burn, we remove them. The action is appropriate to what has happened. Now this is what I mean by feedback. Now you can attenuate feedback, you can cut it off. For example, in a study that Clyde Rousey and I did, we prevented people from hearing their own voices as they spoke. Now what happens when you do this is that people begin to express more of their impulses, more drive-relevant material, more drive-relevant content than they do when they can hear themselves. If you increase feedback as Chase has done, that is to say if you amplify, for example, finger tremor and you present this to the person so the person can see his finger tremor, you bring this under increasing control and the finger tremor decreases. We don't go around looking at our muscle potentials, but we do have reports of muscle potential, posture, and gravity cues, etc., from a number of different bodily processes, and this is essentially what I mean that perception is not simply a matter of sensory intake through the sense organs.

Doctor Cancro: Thank you. I feared that if one person was unclear, there might be more than one who had not understood what you meant by feedback. To try to summarize today's efforts in a few sentences would be beyond me, but I think the panel was able to bring up a number of areas of research which hopefully will encourage the audience to leave with a little more confusion, a little more doubt, more questions, fewer answers, and a generally higher level of uncertainty. As we said on the first day, if the Conference has been successful in making you confused, then we have achieved our scientific goal.

Index